PADDY FINUCANE

PADDY FINUCANE

FIGHTER ACE

Doug Stokes

Crécy Publishing Limited

First published in 1983 by William Kimber & Co. Ltd.

Crécy Books Ltd edition published 1992

First paperback edition Crécy Publishing 2015

ISBN 9780859 791809

Printed in Malta by Melita Press

Crécy Publishing Limited
1a Ringway Trading Estate, Shadowmoss Road, Manchester M22 5LH
www.crecy.co.uk

Contents

Acknowledgements

I am particularly grateful to the following for their assistance: Wg Cdr Alan Aikman DFC RCAF, Mrs Sylvia Austin, Gp Cpt Sir Douglas Bader CBE DSO DFC, Lord Balfour of Inchrye PC MC, Sqn Ldr David Baker, Fr Peter Blake, Air Chief Marshal Sir Harry Broadhurst GCB KBE DSO DFC AFC, Air Commodore Peter Brothers CBE DSO DFC, Mr David Bungey, Gp Capt Laurence Burgess DFC, Robert Carson, Sqn Ldr Max Charlesworth DFC, Flt Lt Keith Chisholm MC RAAF, Jack Clements, Flt Lt Raife Cowan RAAF, Mrs Jean Crang, Air Vice-Marshal William Crawford-Compton CB CBE DSO DFC, Alex Davis, Frank Decmar, Air Commodore Alan Deere DSO OBE DFC, Sqn Ldr John Dennehey DFC, General Avi Michel Donnet DFC, Wg Cdr Alan Douglas DFC, Sqn Ldr Boleslaw Drobinski DFC, Air Commodore Roy Dutton CBE DSO DFC, Gp Capt Ian Easton, Flt Lt Jack Elphick RAAF, Andy Finucane, Kevin Finucane, Raymond Finucane, Trevor Field, Sqn Ldr John Fifield DFC AFC, Herbert Firth, General Adolf Galland, Gp Capt Tom Gleave CBE, Wg Cdr Alastair Goldie, Sqn Ldr Dave Glaser DFC, Air Vice-Marshal Stanley Grant CB DFC, Mrs Trixie Gregory, Air Vice-Marshal John Hallings-Pott DSO AFC, Dr Harry Hands, Sqn Ldr Charlton Haw DFC DFM, Gp Capt Laurence Holland CBE, Mrs Claire Kelsall, Sqn Ldr Dick Kilner DFC, Gp Captjohn Kent DFC AFC, Wg Cdr Robert Ker-Ramsey mbe, Air Vice-Marshal George Lott CB CBE DSO DFC, Wg Cdr Bill Loud DSO DFC, Bill Lathey, Flt Lt Dick Lewis, Mrs Ada Locke, Sqn Ldr James Lacey DFM, Gp Capt Bud Malloy RCAF, Lt Col John McLaren, Flt Lt Fred McCann RAAF, Roland Morris, Flt Lt Sidney Moston, Wg Cdr Bob Morrow DFC QC RCAF, Flt Lt Alfred Munns, Sqn Ldrjohn Niven DFC, Sqn Ldr Frank Neubert, Flt Lt Jay O'Byrne RAAF, Wg Cdr Gordon Olive DFC, Charles Ott, George Outch, Wg Cdr Geoffrey Page DSO DFC, Wg Cdr George Potter OBE, Wg Cdr Leon Prevot DFC, Air Commodore Tom Prickman CB CBE, Maurice Pownall, Joe Parker, Air Vice-Marshal John Pope CB CBE, Geoffrey Quill OBE AFC, Wg Cdr Ralph Sampson OBE DFC, Wg Cdr Sammy Saunders DFC, Flt Lt Les Scorer DFC, Gp Capt Duncan Smith DSO DFC, Air Commodore Arthur Strudwick CB DFC, Wg Cdr Harold Sweet, Sqn Ldr Ron Stillwell DFC DFM, Flt Lt Len Thorne, Sqn Ldr Dickie Turley-George DFC, Sister Ethel Turner SRN, Flt Lt Denys Lane Walters, Flt Lt Ken Waud DFC, Gp Capt Edward Wells DSO DFC, Flt Lt Clive Wawn RAAF, Alan Wilson, Sqn Ldr Ron Wigg, Hubert Wood.

Documents consulted are on the Air references at the Public Record Office, Kew, and I am also indebted to the Imperial War Museum for assistance and the National Library of Ireland for a copy of the document Genealogy of the O'Finucan of County Clare; Clare County Library, Ennis; the Air Historical Branch, Ministry of Defence, and the RAF Association Journal Air Mail. Books and documents consulted were Years of Command by MRAF Lord Douglas of Kirtleside (Collins), Battle Over Britain by Francis K Mason (McWhirter Twins), Dowding's despatch on the Battle of Britain (HMSO), and the Defence of the United Kingdom by Basil Collier (HMSO).

Foreword to the 2015 Edition

Following my uncle Brendan Eamonn Fergus Finucane's death on the 15th of July 1942 there appeared in the same year published in New York a small book entitled "Paddy" Finucane: A Memoir by James Reynolds. It would be an understatement to say that the book contained many inaccuracies. My grandfather Andy was very much angered by its publication both because he was utterly opposed to anyone profiting from my uncle's death and because the contents were in his view mainly untrue. It took another 40 years before my family were prepared to allow any publication about my uncle Brendan. The reason that they agreed to the publication of Doug Stokes's biography was because Doug was so clearly devoted to the memory of my uncle and because of the enormous research that he had put into writing the book. Doug kindly left copies of all his research material to my family. Our family are now all very glad that he persevered, as his work still remains a comprehensively researched and well written account of my uncle's all too short and extraordinary life, which has stood the test of time. We are all also very grateful to Crécy for now responding to the increasing demand for second hand copies of the book, by republishing it in the 75th anniversary year of the Battle of Britain.

Following my uncle's death my grandfather Andy, father Ray and my uncle Kevin all spent time looking out into the Channel hoping that somehow his body would be washed ashore. In the 1960s my father Ray and uncle Kevin went in a light aircraft and laid a wreath on the sea at a point where it was believed that his Spitfire had sunk. There are of course roads, flats, hospital wings named after him, and as a young man I was often told by people whom I met that my name was a famous one. It still happens now. I chose my uncle's second name Eamonn as my confirmation name when I was 13. For my father Ray, who served throughout the war in both Bomber Command (more than 30 missions), and Fighter Command, finally holding the rank of Acting Squadron Leader, and for all of our family, including our cousins the Physick family, with whom we are now once again in contact, his name and achievements have been an abiding presence, and I am glad to say that this has continued with our children.

But there were others too who revered and promoted his memory, some of whom I did not meet, and others alone, not knowing of the others, who have now met each other, whom I must thank for their part in keeping the flame of his memory alive. In Ireland there was the famous journalist Madeleine O'Rourke, sadly deceased at too early an age, who wrote of him as part of her long and successful efforts to promote the history of aviation in Ireland. But as well as Madeleine there was the tireless work of Maurice Byrne in Dublin, who for a prolonged period continued almost alone to promote my uncle's name and memory, not only in Ireland but in England too, and who had arranged for a rose to be named after him and planted at Baldonnel Aerodrome, the heart of Irish aviation, and where as a teenager my uncle had first gone up in an aeroplane. On the 1st of December 2012 I was invited by Maurice to speak at the ceremony of the installation of a small memorial to my uncle at his, and my father's, and Maurice's old school, the famous O'Connell Schools in Dublin. I was honoured to be invited as it was a significant occasion and attended by a number of prominent alumni of the Schools. More importantly the ceremony and my speech were reported in the Irish Times and the Irish Independent, particularly in relation to my comments that my speech was not just about my uncle but all the Irishmen who had fought and died in the two World Wars, and how Ireland needed to acknowledge their sacrifice. The ceremony was also attended by Gerry Hanlon whose work on the aircraft flown by my uncle is an invaluable record for which he has my family's thanks.

There were others too, unknown to Maurice, in both Ireland and England who treasured the memory of my uncle, such as John Donovan in London, whose mother Georgina 'Iris' Lang had as a young teenager cycled from Walthamstow to Hornchurch during the war in the hope of seeing my uncle, and John's knowledge of my uncle's life rivalled that of Maurice. I am glad to say that they have now met and share frequent correspondence about him. I am very grateful to John for all the enormous assistance he has given in promoting my uncle's memory and in assisting in the projects now underway to continue to promote it. But there was also Carroll O'Donoghue from Kinsale who is undertaking the greatest quest of all, which could never have been undertaken by my grandfather, father and uncle, or my family, and which the whole family supports, which is to find the location of his Spitfire. To him, we are all, family and supporters of my uncle's memory, very grateful. Finally there is Gerry Johnston who is making a film in Ireland about my uncle and who has worked tirelessly to research it so that it accurately reflects his life and the role of Irishmen who were in the RAF in the Second World War. This project will involve the Mk Vb Spitfire, the type that my uncle was flying on the date of his death, and the same type as that used by the Battle of Britain Memorial Flight at RAF Coningsby in Lincolnshire. We are in contact with them, the spiritual home of the memories of the Battle of Britain, and are immensely grateful to them for all their assistance. Very recently too the Players of the St Margaret's Community Hall in Twickenham put on a play about famous local people which involved a part that dealt with the life of my uncle and his family during the Second World War.

The whole of our family, Finucanes and Physicks, are delighted at the republication of this book, now with many more photographs kindly provide from the archive compiled by my aunt Clare, and hope that it will give many more people the chance to become acquainted with the courageous and extraordinary life of my uncle.

Brendan Finucane QC
April 2015

Author's note

Fighter Command C-in-C Sholto Douglas had two widely differing views of Wing Commander Paddy Finucane DSO DFC, one contemporary, the second retrospective, and both wrong: 'The beau ideal of the fighter boy' (letter to the family) and 'a rather wild Irishman' (memoirs). Sholto Douglas did go on to add that he 'was making a name for himself as one of our outstanding fighter pilots of that time'; but more apt is the comment of a pilot who flew with him on the fighter-escort sweeps over Northern France and knew him as a freelancing fighter CO, Max Charlesworth: 'Paddy was a daring squadron commander at a time when they were scarce and it produced exciting results.'

Finucane, with his complete lack of pretence, would have dismissed all three descriptions (the first two with some vehemence) but they have to be taken into account and they conditioned my thinking on the construction of this book and how I shaped the text to provide an informative narrative, separating the man from the myth. Failure to do so simply perpetuates a legend, valueless historically and no tribute to the man himself.

The quest started at the former Kenley fighter airfield a few miles south of London in East Surrey; then research at the Public Record Office into hundreds of combat reports, the operational records of fifteen squadrons, airfields, 11 (Fighter) Group, HQ Fighter Command, and files on the Air Fighting Development Unit, air intelligence summaries, circus operations, Operation Fuller, enemy casualties, policy, tactics, operational orders, organisation of fighter wings and air fighting committee papers. These were my main references; in all I consulted 131.

Interviews followed with more than a hundred aircrew. Many were traced with the ready co-operation of the Battle of Britain Fighter Association (Group Captain Tom Gleave and Flight Lieutenant Howard Duart often put me in direct touch over the phone) and Ministry of Defence AR8(b) (RAF) who took a bit longer; pilots in Canada and Australia were contacted via Royal Canadian Air Force, Department of Veterans Affairs, Ontario, and Royal Australian Air Force, NSW Division Air Force Association, Sydney. Thanks to the generosity of two Glasgow newspaper editors, the *Daily Record* and *Evening Times,* and the editor of *The Daily Telegraph* who all published appeals from me in 1978 I located the groundcrews who serviced Finucane's aircraft.

The *Daily Record* published my letter, beginning: 'From January to June 1942 No 602 (City of Glasgow) Squadron, Royal Auxiliary Air Force, was led by one of its most famous commanding officers Squadron Leader Brendan 'Paddy' Finucane DSO DFC.' It brought an immediate response. My letter in *The Daily Telegraph* elicited 137 replies within days.

An important decision on the line the book would follow was to tackle the controversy over a few of Finucane's claims by showing with extensive quotation from Fighter Command documents (notably Operational Instructions 93 and 4/1942 and Intelligence Instruction 5/1942)[1] and a combat summary that all but four of them complied with the rules of air combat as laid down by the RAF for the guidance of its fighter pilots. Where they did not he had good reason, his

[1] See Appendices B and C.

A publicity photo of Paddy Finucane whilst with 452 Squadron.

experience, to claim them as destroyed. Criticism over the number of aircraft he shot down probably had less to do with the number of his victories than the speed with which he acquired them, but he also got on the wrong side of a senior officer at Kenley who set about making life difficult.

I decided to deal with the difference between RAF claims on the sweeps and German losses based on the Luftwaffe Quartermaster General's returns by detailing the losses and claims for one day, 13 March 1942 (a Friday), and then leaving it at that. Finucane dismissed an Fw 190 with cannon and machine guns and saw it crash, confirmed by one of his NCO pilots, and then got another, shared, which he saw go in near a railway embankment. The Luftwaffe admitted to no losses. Total Fighter Command claims were ten destroyed. There is some interesting and high level correspondence between the Fighter chief, Sholto Douglas, and the Chief of the Air Staff, Portal, relating to this.[2]

My thanks are particularly due to the Finucane family, especially to Mr Raymond Finucane, for access to family papers and photographs, and for their invaluable recollections of Brendan Finucane. I would also like to thank Wing Commander Ralph Sampson OBE DFC, Squadron Leader John Niven DFC, Squadron Leader Max Charlesworth DFC, Squadron Leader James 'Ginger' Lacey DFM, Wing Commander Al 'Butch' Aikman DFC RCAF and Flight Lieutenant Fred McCann RAAF for their assistance in reconstructing events at squadron level; and to Air Chief Marshal Sir Harry Broadhurst GCB KBE DSO DFC AFC and General Adolf Galland, former chief of Luftwaffe fighters, for promptly and courteously answering my queries to put these events into wider perspective.

Most of Finucane's wartime letters which would have helped are missing, lent and never returned to the family.

A full list of contributors will be found on p 211, but I would like to mention especially here Joy Steffen and the *Daily Express* syndication director, Peter Knight, for their invaluable guidance at a critical stage in the preparation of the manuscript. Without them this book would never have got its wheels off the runway.

[2] See Chapter 11.

INTRODUCTION

The Fighting Irishman

Despite being frequently quoted in the press as saying he liked working with figures and would be returning to accountancy after the war, Brendan Finucane would have been unlikely to have done so. Pre-war a trainee accountant in Dublin and London, the thought of returning to such a life after a highly successful career in the Royal Air Force was abhorrent to him. He could never have settled down to it again. The Gaelic restlessness in his nature, which was as much a part of his personality and character as determination and confidence in his flying skill, would have prevented him from ever sitting behind a desk again for a living.

What he would certainly have done, and he was frequently quoted as saying it, was emigrate to Australia to join his great friend and fellow fighter pilot Keith 'Bluey' Truscott. Bluey had no more thought of settling into an office than he had. Both became aces with the first Australian fighter squadron formed in the UK. It was a friendship based on personal esteem and the knowledge that your life depended often on the man flying with you. Neither Bluey nor Paddy had been let down by the other on the fighter-escort sweeps they flew together over Northern France from Kenley. It was a relationship forged in danger and cemented by personal regard.

They would certainly have gone into a business partnership of some sort – possibly air charter flying, which would have appealed to the restlessness in Paddy's nature, and the constant call for action in Bluey's make-up. Australia was the wide-open land with plenty of flying space that attracted him, as well as the people like Truscott who lived there.

Raymond Finucane, who also became a fighter pilot on Spitfires but too late to join his elder brother in Fighter Command, recalls that during the infrequent times when their brief spells away from air operations coincided on leave in wartime black-out London and Richmond, Brendan spoke feelingly about going to Australia with Bluey. Truscott himself confirmed this, and said once they'd got the war over and finished with Spitfires they could settle down to something more constructive than killing.

Ray Finucane finished the war as a flight lieutenant and went into business life. The youngest brother, Kevin Finucane, became a captain in the Royal Artillery; then he also settled back into civilian life. Brendan, the eldest of the three brothers, became a wing commander at the age of twenty-one and flew his slightly damaged Spitfire into the English Channel with the war still three years to run. Bluey went back to Australia to command a squadron and flew into the sea in a practice attack exercise. Both men went straight down, trapped in the cockpit of their aircraft.

It was restlessness that drove Finucane on to become the highest decorated and top-scoring pilot operational in Fighter Command, in 1942. On a fighter squadron this character trait found expression in a compulsive flair for air combat. It had formulated his ambition in the first place to be a fighter pilot as a teenager in pre war Dublin, and sustained him during the trouble he had in learning to fly in the peacetime air force. His first two years in the RAF were a time of setbacks and adversity.

He had all the qualities of a successful fighter pilot, superb eyesight, a fast reaction, a well-developed tactical sense, flying skill, and the indefinable flair for leadership which in his case was highly individualistic. It came to the fore when he was a flight commander with the Australians at Kenley in 452 Squadron. This was the period in 1941 and 1942 when Fighter Command, having won the Battle of Britain, was on the offensive on the sweeps over Northern France. They were the command's maximum effort at this time and were codenamed circus operations. Atypical circus formation consisted of around 220 Spitfires – eighteen squadrons drawn from six fighter wings – escorting a dozen medium bombers briefed to attack German-occupied manufacturing and industrial power station targets within range of the Spitfire's limited petrol endurance.

For Finucane 1941, not 1940, was the summer of the high scores. In ten weeks (3 August to 13 October 1941) he shot down seventeen German aircraft in fighter-versus-fighter combat over Northern France and shared in the destruction of two others. This earned three of his four decorations (Bar to the DFC, 22 August; second Bar, 15 September; DSO, 11 October) within a span of fifty-one days. For seven of those fifty-one days he was at home on leave at 26 Castlegate, Richmond, Surrey, with his family and girlfriend Jean Woolford (she lived next door but one and later became his fiancée) so they were actually earned in forty-four days. This could be – almost certainly is – a record for the award of combat flying decorations for day-fighters.

Paddy & Jean, photographed just after their engagement, 1942.

He had the characteristics of all the most successful fighter pilots, the ability and determination to get in close for a kill and make quick decisions, but was surprised to find in November 1941 that he was the highest scoring pilot in 11 (Fighter) Group. The unexpected was constantly happening.

The most unexpected event of this time was the press comparison with Douglas Bader which made Finucane a reluctant national hero. Sir Douglas pointed out to me in a letter the misleading value of such publicity and added that he had never met the young Irish flight lieutenant who was the subject of it 'but who was obviously a jolly good young fighter pilot'. Sir Douglas was at the time of the comparison in German captivity.

On the morning of 5 September 1941 Finucane picked up the newspaper at breakfast in the officers' mess at Kenley and read the opening sentence written by the distinguished war correspondent Alexander Berry Austin: 'Wing Commander Douglas Bader, famous legless fighter pilot, has a successor.' Austin named him in the second paragraph as the successor. This appeared under the heading 'RAF Gets New No 1 Fighter Pilot'.

Sandy Austin had been Air Chief Marshal Dowding's chief press officer during the Battle of Britain and had just published a book, *Fighter Command,* making clear his admiration for Bader. Austin had seen clearly that a popular air war hero of the same legendary status was needed and wrote according to his conscience without, as he saw it, compromising his integrity. From then on the publicity was relentless.

An Irishman flying with Australians was a unique and well defined pattern, instantly recognisable, as news to cheer up the civilian population and impress the United States. Britain was still fighting alone in the air war over Europe against Nazi Germany and needed all the good publicity she could get.

Finucane was promoted to squadron leader to command the Scottish Auxiliary 602 Squadron, also in the Kenley Wing, on 26 January 1942, and to wing commander on 21 June (the fact that he was the youngest in that rank was checked at the time by Fighter Command HQ) to command the Hornchurch Wing, Essex.

Paddy Finucane in his office with two of his victims' emblems behind – left is KG 26 and right LG 1.

Paddy Finucane in thoughtful mood.

RAF records differ in totalling the number of aircraft he destroyed; 32 and 29 are the two figures given. Allowing for the fact that two aircraft he rightly claimed as destroyed were wrongly downgraded to probably destroyed in the spring of 1942 (there was much bickering on the Kenley Wing at this time) and on another occasion he allowed one of his NCO pilots to move in and finish off an Fw 190 he had shot up, the true figure is 32, probably higher. He also probably destroyed another six and damaged a further eight.

Paddy Finucane was one of a generation of young Irishmen active with the Allied cause in the 1939-1945 conflict. The wartime *Daily Express* put the number at 150,000 and said: 'Eire may be neutral but the Irish are the most belligerent neutrals you ever saw.'

The centuries-long tradition of the Irish fighting the British is equalled by a similarly long history of Irishmen fighting for the British. For more than two hundred years the British Army has had famous Irish regiments who fought with distinction in all theatres of war, including the colonial wars. The division of opinion in Ireland still exists to this day between those who believe that fighting for the British is the action of a renegade and those for whom it was, and is, a family tradition. There are still thousands of families in the Republic of Ireland who think of this tradition as the inheritance of a proud past.

Brendan is one of this interesting number in that his father Andy Finucane, himself the son of a British infantryman, fought against the Black and Tans but saw no reason to oppose his eldest son's wish to apply for a short service commission in the Royal Air Force in 1938 when the family was living in England, and actively encouraged him to do so. It has been said that Brendan was not political (the subject was never discussed between father and son). But he was not politically naive and felt keenly the threat to democracy by Nazi Germany far outweighed any prejudice he may have inherited from his Republican forebears. His reason for joining the RAF though, as with thousands of other fit, alert air-minded young men of sound education, was simply a love of flying.

This was changed by the destruction of Southampton city centre in one weekend during the winter of 1940 blitz which he saw while visiting friends and relatives in Swaythling. Mr Finucane, in his neat accountant's handwriting, pencilled a note in a book margin: 'Brendan Finucane was a fighter pilot. He was out to destroy'.

Still the fighting Irishman himself Mr Finucane had applied to join the RAF as a teleprinter operator in 1939, any bitterness he once felt against the British long since gone, until his wife put a stop to that idea. He was then aged forty-four.

The name Finucane (pronounced Finoocan) is derived from the Gaelic O'Fionnmhachain or Fionnmhacain, which means 'fair little son', and is the clan name of the O'Finucan of County Clare, one of the oldest clans in Ireland founded in the third century AD and forming part of the nobility of North and South Munster. Although closely associated with south-west Ireland they had moved to other parts of the country by the nineteenth century, some going abroad, and there is a record of later Finucanes in the United States at Spokane, Washington.

The strong Anglo-military connection among the nineteenth- century Irish clansmen is confirmed by records of the O'Finucan which show it had professional fighting men on the British side: Captain James Finucane, 97th Foot; Lieutenant William Finucane, 58th Foot; Donatus Finucane, Quartermaster 17th Foot; George Finucane, Ensign 14th Foot; Frederick Finucane, Ensign 88th Foot; Lieutenant Andrew Finucane, 10th Light Dragoons, are among those named. These earlier fighting Finucanes are directly traceable to Brendan's branch of the family.

One of eight Irish fighter pilots in the Battle of Britain, Brendan was officially disowned by Eamon De Valera's wartime Eire government. Censorship dismissed his death briefly in the Dublin papers which quoted 'Paddy' but did not mention he was Dublin-born Catholic Irish. De Valera's paper the Irish Press gave him twelve lines.

The hidden irony in this, for those who care to speculate on imponderables, is that Andy Finucane had known De Valera personally long before he became the Republic's first prime minister and was with him during the 1916 Easter Rebellion against the British.

Winston Churchill found the right words:

> 'I well know the grievous injury which Southern Irish neutrality and the denial of the Southern Irish ports inflicted upon us in the recent war but I always adhered to the policy that nothing, save British existence and survival, should lead us to regain those ports by force of arms because we had already given them up. In the end we got through without this step. I rejoice that no new blood was shed between the British and Irish peoples. I shall never forget – none of us can ever forget – the superb gallantry of the scores of thousands of Southern Irishmen who fought as volunteers in the British Army and of the famous Victoria Crosses which eight of them gained by their outstanding valour. If ever I feel a bitter feeling rising in me in my heart about the Irish the hands of heroes like Finucane seem to stretch out to soothe it away.' (Parliamentary Debates – House of Commons (Hansard) 28 October 1948, columns 247-250).

The continuing tragedy of Ireland, especially what is happening there today, ensures Dublin does nothing to commemorate Brendan. That was left to the British. A memorial requiem mass at Westminster Cathedral was attended by 2,500 people and a national fund based in Richmond reached £8,000 (around £100,000 in today's money) within a year. Half was for a memorial wing at Richmond Royal Hospital and in 1964 a new outpatients' extension was opened in Finucane's name.

The reason for the delay was that the National Health Service absorbed the hospital's share of the fund donated by a grateful nation and Mrs Florence Finucane, a fighter like her famous son, assisted by his brother Ray Finucane, fought spiritedly to get it back again and restored to its original purpose.

Her battle over and life's problems solved she died in 1963 in a nursing home after a stroke, but Mr Andy Finucane and his other two sons, Ray and Kevin, were there with mixed feelings as a commemorative wall plaque and portrait were unveiled in the outpatients department waiting room:

'Paddy' Finucane
Wing Commander Brendan Finucane DSO DFC
Hero of the Battle of Britain 1940
The memorial fund inaugurated in 1942 by Councillor E A Collings JP,
then Mayor of Richmond, in tribute to 'Paddy' Finucane, killed in action
aged 21 years, formed a major contribution to the cost of the out patient's
extension opened on 16 May 1964

The rest of the money went to the RAF Benevolent Fund where the annual income from it is still helping needy RAF men and their dependents in the 1980s.

1

The Beginning

Brendan's ambition to be a fighter pilot started when he was on holiday in England with his younger brother Raymond and watched aircraft flying in and out of the Spitfire's test flying airfield at Eastleigh, Southampton.

In July 1936 the holiday period was getting into full swing and people seemed happy and content, making the most of the hot weather. In Southampton the shops were packed, and war with Germany was still three years away.

The boys were staying with their aunt Eileen Physick in Harefield Road, Swaythling, a Southampton suburb. She was Andy Finucane's youngest sister, a small firecracker of a woman with her hair done up in a severe bun, strict Catholic Irish like her brother (and like him with a hot temper). But she also had his generosity and warmly welcomed the two teenage brothers over from Ireland each year to spend their annual holidays with her and her family.

Attracted by the continuous sound of aero engines over the suburbs, Bren and Ray soon went off on their own to investigate. Eastleigh was within easy walking distance of Swaythling and Mrs Physick packed them a sandwich lunch knowing they would not be back until teatime and then filling her house with excited chatter about what they'd seen at the airfield when they did get back.

They had a clear view across the airfield from the grassy verge in Stoneham Lane which formed one side of the perimeter boundary and were highly receptive to what was going on around the hangars and landing area. Eastleigh was a civilian airfield but there was often a number of visiting RAF biplanes, mostly Harts and Furies, which they watched with the greatest interest.

A hundred miles to the north RAF Fighter Command was being formed in that same month of July 1936 and the prototype Spitfire, to be flown in its developed form by some of Fighter Command's most accomplished WW2 fighter pilots, was at Eastleigh on its early development trials.

This part of Hampshire was Spitfire country. The prototype was designed and built at the nearby Supermarine Aviation works, Woolston, by Southampton Water, and it would have been a remarkable pointer to young Brendan's future career if they had seen it. But this cannot be definitely established. Ray's recollection of the time is blurred; he was only fourteen then, seventeen months younger than Bren who was sixteen, but he recalls they were both keenly air-minded as youths and their growing interest in aviation began with the Eastleigh visits going back to 1932.

At the end of the holiday in August they caught the train from Southampton to London and Holyhead and then the ferry to Dun Laoghaire taking them back home to Sandymount, Dublin. Bren was bored with the prospect of his office job as an invoice clerk in a printing and stationery firm in Wellington Road, Sandymount, checking ledgers, invoices, order books and entering debit and credit columns of figures. The visits to Eastleigh had opened up a bold and exciting prospect. The air force was now the only one of three dominant influences in his life – the Catholic faith, sport and flying – that held out any sort of hope for a satisfying future.

At O'Connell school he had been a sports-mad young Irish rugby skipper, excelling at boxing and most other sports, and had felt the first stirrings of leadership on the rugby pitch at Clontarf, Dublin, before following his father into accountancy. At the time it seemed the obvious thing to do. But temperamentally he was unsuited for office work and it was a mistake. He determined to be a fighter pilot.

The threads were already drawing in during that summer of 1936. At the controls of the Spitfire prototype at Eastleigh and revelling in its high performance was a slightly-built former RAF pilot, now test flying for Supermarine Aviation, named Jeffrey Quill. A few miles away at Hamble, Dave Glaser, the fair-haired teenage son of a publican was watching aircraft and pilots of the newly-formed RAF Volunteer Reserve through the gap in an airfield hedge.

Quill, Glaser and Finucane were to fly with the same fighter squadron in August 1940 when, with the intolerance of youth towards experience, it was a matter of chagrin that Quill could land a Spitfire some fifty to a hundred yards shorter than anyone else!

Brendan Eamonn Finucane was born on 16 October 1920 at 13 Rathmines Road, Dublin, and was to come within the sound of gunfire for the first time at the early age of around twelve months when he and his mother were caught in the crossfire of a street battle between the IRA and the Black and Tans outside their home. She crawled with him along the garden path to seek defiant but doubtful protection behind his pram. She was heavy with her second child and said with disarming candour: 'I nearly had him there and then.' It was a favourite story told with relish in later years to thrill her growing family.

Although she made light of it to entertain the children the incident at such an early age was prophetic enough to justify a belief in the fates.

Mrs Finucane was English, formerly Florence Louise Robinson, of Osborn Road, Leicester. She was a handsome young woman of twenty-four with a mass of luxuriant brown hair and vital eyes that went with a determined and independent – some would have said wilful – character. It is doubtful that she thought deeply about the Catholic faith and on arriving in Dublin refused to curtsey to the visiting parish priest with a firmness unsurprising to anyone who knew her.

She was musical, however, and went around the house singing music hall songs, soon adding a piano to the front room furniture, and went to mass on Sundays so that she could sing in the choir. From her mother, who had crossed Canada in a covered wagon, she inherited an adventurous streak, and accepted the possibility of being shot at accidentally by the British or the IRA, or both, as one of the hazards of living in Dublin at this time.

Mr Finucane had been involved in the Irish rebellion against the British but at about this time had ceased to have anything to do with it. Thomas Andrew Finucane had known De Valera from his schooldays when he was taught maths at college by the then unknown rebel leader. In 1916, however, he was with him in the battle fought out in the Dublin suburbs at Ballsbridge and was then on the run for a time.

He is interesting for the biographer in that his father, Charles Finucane, had been a rifleman in the King's Own Scottish Borderers and that at roughly the same age as he was fighting for the British in India and on the North-West Frontier he himself was fighting against them in Dublin. This was to turn full circle with his eldest son, Brendan, in the Royal Air Force.

Mr Finucane was going to be a priest but changed his mind about this and his mother helped him to escape over the seminary wall.

Andy and Florence Finucane were married at Leicester in October 1919 and went to live in Drumcondra, Dublin, where Mr Finucane was a bank cashier. The job was not all that well paid and the family never seemed to have much money, but they managed to get by. They moved south to the Rathmines district for the birth of their first son, Brendan, a year later. This was at the time of the tail end of the rebellion but after the British left in 1921 the Irish continued to fight it out among themselves.

Shortly after the Rathmines shoot-out Mrs Finucane gave birth to her second son, Raymond Patrick. The continuing unrest in Dublin had no effect on the brothers and they grew up as normal healthy youngsters, mischievous and with a keen sense of fun although fighting among themselves occasionally.

It was a strict Catholic home. Mr Finucane was teetotal, attended 6 am mass each day and said grace at every meal. Bren and Ray served as altar boys and accepted the Catholic faith although their mother exerted some influence in the opposite direction with her more liberal views.

According to his father, Bren was a young scrapper from an early age and often came home from primary school bearing the marks of combat from rugby or fighting with other boys. This was, however, nothing more serious than to warrant a mild ticking off. Mr Finucane wanted his sons to grow up self-reliant and able to take care of themselves.

Bren's early education was at two Rathmines primary schools, Marlborough Street and Synge Street, when the family moved to Grove Road, Rathmines, until the age of twelve, in 1932.

At about this time Mr Finucane took the brothers to an air display at Baldonnell and they had a ten-minute flight. Bren glowed with youthful enthusiasm and excitement and said he wanted to be a pilot. But it was early days yet and he hadn't quite got the flying bug. The year 1932, however, seems to be the year of the awakening of his interest in aviation because this was the first year of their summer holidays at Swaythling and the visits to Eastleigh airfield.

In August 1933 the family moved to New Grange Road, Cabra, at the same time as Bren started at Christian Brothers O'Connell School, in North Richmond Street. This was a distinguished Dublin RC school with a strong blend of discipline, religious and formal education and a fine sporting tradition. The school rugby pitch was at Clontarf and one of the teachers who were watching the practices there at the time, Brother O'Driscoll, was able to recall to me more than forty years later: 'Young Finucane was a very determined rugby player with all the qualities of leadership.' Within eighteen months he was captain of the First XV, an attacking player at centre three-quarter.

Bren's final year there, 1936, was a sporting triumph. He led the First XV in the Leinster schools cup competition at Donnybrook, won a medal for boxing at the sports day in Croke Park, crewed in the junior fours and club pairs championships with the Neptune rowing club and was a prize-winning swimmer. When he left at the end of the summer term he had credit passes for the school certificate in three subjects, maths, geography and history and was reasonable in most other subjects.

It was for the sport, however, that he was most remembered and he himself seems later to have taken this view. Years later he told an American journalist[3] that the headmaster had an army boxing tide and, believing in his favourite sport as a character builder, every morning at eight-thirty had the boys turned out under a large shed in the schoolyard and told to whack each other, although Bren probably said this to amuse rather than instruct.

In July 1936, having first fixed himself up with the office job, he went with Ray over to England and Swaythling for their usual six weeks' holiday with the Physicks in Harefield Road and, with quickening interest, to the airfield at Eastleigh.

One of his childhood companions of those days was Ada McKinnon who lived in Harefield road and joined in the games with the boys:

'The two brothers were quite different in some ways. Bren was quieter and Ray a roaring Irish youngster easily egged on to a fight with the lads of the district. The older brother was always able to sort out any squabbles so that we didn't all end up fighting among ourselves. The leadership which was later to be so important to "his boys" was very apparent in those early days at Swaythling. The children of the area happily fell in with any suggestions he made for organising the day including cricket, football and races in the surrounding countryside.

'Two crippled children were always included in these jaunts. The two Irish boys pushed them for miles and if caught out in the rain it was Bren who came home soaked with the crippled boys as dry as he could keep them. His religion was an important influence but like his exploits later in the RAF never spoken of. He was not happy in accountancy and once in the RAF I never really thought he was able to fit into service life, but when he joined the Australians he seemed happier. He did not drink much and the sort of humour generally found in the mess I doubt very much that he shared. When Southampton suffered in the 1940 air raids he always found time to come over from Tangmere airfield in the evenings to see how things were with all of us.'

Bren and Ray were back home by the end of August. The family was now living at 16 Farney Park, Sandymount. It was their third change of address and was to be the last one in Dublin.

Mr Finucane was now a company director and went to England to open a London office and changes were on the way. In November 1936 the family uprooted from Ireland to live in England at 26 Castlegate, Richmond, in the London suburbs. It was a big move because there were now more and younger children in the family, Kevin, and two sisters Monica and Claire.

The house in Castlegate was the best home they'd had, a bit small, but in a quiet tree-lined road of young saplings. It was detached, mock-Tudor, and with a flagstone path to the front door. Mrs Finucane put up chintz curtains and ministered to her family with firmness and affection. She still refused to curtsey to the priest, who was now Father O'Byrne at St Winefride's, Kew Gardens, just up the road.

Bren went to an office job in Regent Street, in London's West End. He was

[3] A.J. Liebling, The New Yorker.

bored and restless, hating every minute of it. There was a strong element of the rebel in his nature from his father. They had not been getting on too well lately. They were too alike in some respects, but Bren had his mother's practical nature and it is unlikely that he would have accepted his father's high idealism in his fight against the British. He knew of his father's Republican past but had never asked him about it, nor were questions invited.

He wondered how his father would react to the news that his eldest son wanted to join one of the British fighting services. The decision to ask him had to be taken soon but the situation became complicated because Mr Finucane's new job had not worked out. It couldn't have happened at a worse time with a new mortgage on the house and a growing family. He did not want to add to his parents' worries at this stage.

On the wider front Europe was moving inevitably towards war as the last peacetime years of the thirties drew to a close. The RAF was expanding rapidly and belatedly although the new eight-gun monoplane Fighters were not yet in service, but when they were, more men would be needed to fly them. The Royal Air Force was offering short service commissions (SSC) to selected applicants. The SSC scheme filled the junior posts on the squadrons and ensured four years flying followed by six on the reserve. Bren decided to apply. Thousands of other air-minded youths had the same idea of flying and getting paid for doing it and within three years every one of them was going to be needed.

Bren eventually spoke to his father about it in November 1937. Mr Finucane was short, dark, square-jawed and a man of strong convictions. But for him the past was over and done with, his own early skirmishes were nothing compared to the fight Britain was soon going to be in. He understood his eldest son probably more than Bren realised at the time.

Sywell where Paddy Finucane undertook pilot training before the war.

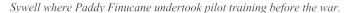

The difference between them at the same age was that he had a cause to fight for, but he saw in Bren's obvious determination to be a Fighter pilot a clear sense of direction that he himself had lacked in his own youth. He gave his approval. Both parents agreed to cash insurance policies, although they needed the money themselves, to give him a good start.

At the minimum age in April 1938 Bren dropped in his application to Air Ministry, Kingsway, at Richmond post office on his way to work. In June 1938 at about the same time as the first Spitfires entered service with 19 Squadron at RAF Duxford he had his Air Ministry interviews. Qualifications: keenness to fly, school certificate, good sporting record.

The eagerly awaited letter arrived two months later ordering him to report to 6 Elementary and Reserve Flying Training School, Sywell, Northants.

As he was leaving the house with his father on 28 August 1938 on the First stage to Sywell he may have had a premonition of the difficulties he was to experience in learning to fly because he said: 'Well, Dad, if I don't get through the course I'll not come back home again.'

2

Wings

Finucane's letters home show his early difficulties – mainly landing trouble – with the wind-in-the-wires DH82 Tiger Moth open cockpit biplane flying taught at Sywell, and he narrowly missed flying into the airfield boundary hedge in a series of mishaps on the first training flights:

> September 7: I was about five feet off the ground and about twenty or thirty feet from the hedge when a voice coming through the earphones asked me quite politely what was I going to do about the hedge in front of me. What a shock. I thought I was about a quarter of a mile from it. I pushed the throttle wide open and pulled the nose up sharply and the wheels ran along the top of the hedge. That afternoon I could not do anything right. Everything seemed to go wrong all at once. My next landing bumped all over the place and I nearly tipped the machine on its nose. The instructor cursed, said I had an off day and suggested I give up that night's studying.

Again, on 11 September:

> The last few days have been very unlucky. Yesterday morning (pay day) I was coming in to land and just as my wheels touched the ground bang went a tyre. Up I shot into the air with a terrific jerk and was barely able to land again. The instructor[4] said 'Jolly good landing'. We tried to taxy the machine back to the hangar before we noticed anything wrong. I looked over the side of the machine and saw the right wingtip resting on the ground. The instructor got out of the plane and had a look at the undercarriage. Quite suddenly he said, 'Christ almighty!' I looked up to see him gesticulating at me. His hand was pointed to the tyre and undercarriage. Another bump and

Acting Pilot Officer Finucane, Sywell.
Again, no pilot's wings.

[4] Roland Morris was his first instructor.

Unidentified cartoon from flying training at Sywell.

there would have been no more Brendan or Mr Morris.

There was just a small piece of wood holding the undercarriage to the plane. I got out of the machine with legs like rubber. Mr Morris said, 'You are not the next best thing, you're the original!' When I arrived at the hangars the CFI[5] was there. He looked at me and did not say a word. I made a beeline for the mess and had a good cup of coffee. I needed it. At the mess all the fellows started to rag me: 'Can't fly an aeroplane yet. What Irishman can, etc!'

The youthful enthusiasm for flying hid his concern and growing realisation that it was not going to be as easy as he thought. Typically, none of this was allowed to show although his early flying was a catalogue of bouncy landings, as he found he lacked the smooth touch on throttle, rudder, elevator and ailerons to hold together a good landing. With new-found friends on the course he quickly acquired the 'Paddy' which was to follow him throughout his air force career, although the name was never used by relatives or close personal friends.

Sywell was a large grass airfield with modern hangars and bungalows for the pupil pilots. There were thirty on the course and they had to complete about fifty hours' flying in two months, and pass written examinations in administration, armament, engines, theory of flight, Morse, parachutes, navigation and airmanship. 6 Elementary and Reserve Flying Training School was a civilian flying school, run

---

[5] The Chief Flying Instructor, Ian Mackenzie.

by Brooklands Aviation under contract to the Air Ministry, to give initial training to aircrew entrants for the RAF.

Roland Morris, aged twenty-six, with 2,000 flying hours mostly on instructing, told me: 'Paddy was having a lot of trouble. He was saying to himself, "This is what I've been told to do and this is what the aircraft is going to do" and tried to force the aircraft onto the ground instead of coaxing it. He was a strong character, fearless in the air despite the blunders and hamfisted flying and always came up smiling. He was completely self-assured and wanted to go solo before he was ready. It was the instructor's job to see that he didn't.'

Finucane's first solo was on 21 September after 14-05 hours' dual instruction, some four to five hours behind the rest, and he 'did a bit of fooling on take-off and nearly stalled the machine,' as he put it, 'but did the circuit and landed quite decently. The instructor then got back into the plane and we went off to do some spins above Kettering, a great sensation.'

This was the week of the Munich crisis ending on 28 September with the 'peace for our time' statement which held off war with Germany for a year. At Sywell Finucane and the other pupils wheeled the Tiger Moths, smart in their red, silver and black colour scheme of Brooklands Aviation, out of the grey hangars and onto the grass to start the day's flying at 8 -30 am and continuing throughout the day until 4pm. For them war seemed a long way off but few RAF chiefs doubted that it was coming.

Finucane was finding the Tiger Moth much easier to fly now with less effort and found time to relax more in the evenings. There was a good social life in the mess

Paddy Finucane's flying licence granted 30 September 1938; a year later, Paddy Finucane would be flying operationally with 65 Squadron after war was declared.

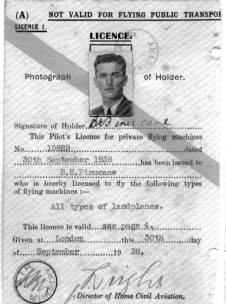
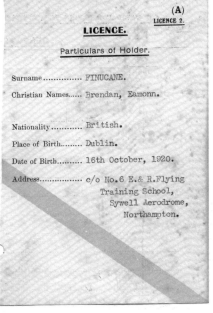

Paddy Finucane (2nd from right) with his Wings together with medical and chaplaincy officers.

and sometimes they went into Northampton. Studying for the exams was a headache and just as he rolled into bed late at night someone would come in for a chat or the sound of a Morse key in the next room tapping out messages drove away sleep. High spirits relieved the tension. Returning from a Saturday night in Northampton, they found gas fires turned off at the mains, and flying kit and clothes hidden or tied to the electric light flex. The culprits, other pupils, were hauled out of bed with free fights all over the place and it was taken as an enjoyable joke.

Finucane was not the star pupil his later flying ability would suggest; at the end of the course on 28 October he was assessed as 'average'. Only two months ago he had got out at Northampton station and asked the ticket collector for directions to the airfield, met someone else on the same mission, and over a cup of tea in a nearby cafe full of zeal and ardour decided they couldn't wait to get their hands on the aircraft! Now he was a pilot, but a long way yet from being an RAF pilot.

The next stage of flying training was at 8 Flying Training School, Montrose, a coastal airfield in the eastern highlands where he joined 10 Course in B Flight of the intermediate training squadron on 12 November 1938 after ten hours of fast travelling from King's Cross on the Flying Scotsman as 41276 Acting Pilot Officer B.E. Finucane, one of forty-five pupils who had to complete a hundred hours flying in the next eight months. The cracking RAF discipline had them at the flight lines by 7-45 am to report to the flight commanders outside the hangars where the training aircraft were lined up in a taxi rank warmed up by mechanics. If not on the flying detail they were on colour hoisting parade with the station pipeband. Many of the instructors were Central Flying School or Cranwell-trained.

Finucane's instructor from 16 to 24 November was Flight Lieutenant Laurence Burgess who recalls the landing drill imparted through the Gosport speaking tube to the helmeted pupil:

'Well, here we are at a thousand feet across wind and nicely placed to judge our final turn in. We throttle back fully … ease the control column slightly forward as our speed falls off and we hold the aircraft at the correct glide angle like this, and our speed is now right at 75mph. We wind back on the tail wheel to keep this glide angle steady, and wind in the radiator. Note how the aircraft is drifting away from the airfield as we glide across wind. We keep a good lookout for other aircraft in the circuit, and now that we are at seven hundred feet we turn in towards the airfield with a gentle gliding turn.

'We come out of the turn at four hundred feet, our speed still at 75mph, well placed for the final glide-in; check that we are dead into wind, reduce the speed slightly to 70mph, a quick touch of the trimming wheel, and here we are about to cross the boundary hedge at two hundred feet on a nice steady glide. We keep her like this down to fifty feet, and now very gently check the glide by a slight backward movement of the control column – hold it there for a moment – back a little bit more – our speed is dropping off – we are now only ten feet from the ground – back a bit more – you can feel the aircraft sinking – bring the control column back – further back – now right back and we can touch down nicely. Keep her straight with rudder and a touch of brake – hold the control column right back in your stomach until we come to a stop – there we are. Open up the engine slightly to keep a good idling speed and before moving off look behind you to see if any other aircraft are coming in to land alongside.

'All is clear, so we open up firmly, swing her across wind to see that all is clear ahead, having another look for incoming aircraft, and taxy back for another circuit. Right, you have her.'

But Finucane hadn't. The trouble was B Flight's Hawker Harts. Alastair Goldie, a fellow pupil, recalls:

'These magnificent, exciting flying machines were the last of the open cockpit advanced trainers. They were wonderful! Powerful (they were still with some frontline squadrons) they could do everything; aerobatics, navigation, front and rear gunnery and bombing. The Hart coped with magnificent aplomb with all these roles; she was a beauty. Those were our salad days in the RAF of the thirties, an epic period. We had been instructed to arrive at elementary flying school in sports jacket and flannels at lunchtime on Monday. Two lectures on airmanship and a parachute fitting in the afternoon and you started flying on the Tuesday morning. Wonderful when you think of the months it now takes before they get to grips with what they joined the Service for.'

The engine-off full glide approach technique gave Finucane trouble and the Hart was twice the weight and performance of the Tiger Moth. Bad weather hit the area early in

A very young Paddy Finucane in Mess Kit. Lack of pilot's wings would indicate he was still undergoing pilot training.

December; blizzards swept in from the North Sea, piling great drifts inland but not settling deep enough on the airfield to stop flying. He was already ten days behind the rest of the course with a wrenched thumb from a spirited guest night party in the officers' mess when the station commander, senior staff and instructors got out of the way and left the pupils to it providing they didn't smash up too much of the furniture! He resumed flying on 2 December with a new instructor, Flight Sergeant John 'Doughy' Baker, who, chatting over a drink in the sergeants' mess, remarked:

'The ground was never quite where Paddy expected it to be.'

In the air he struggled to hold the Hart in a good landing pattern, taking off and landing with snow flaring back in the slipstream, and in the evening with other young trainee officers went to the Scottish country dances in the area. The station commander, Group Captain Champion de Crespigny, encouraged them to accept invitations from titled Scottish landowners, and Finucane enjoyed the social life. On camp over Christmas without the fare to get home (he was sending cheques to repay his parents) he saw in the New Year in the town square where pipers played at midnight and the 'populace went absolutely crazy'. Finucane trained hard to get in the station boxing team and in February 1939 was in the RAF in Scotland team against Scottish Universities at the Drill Hall, St Andrews, where he KO'd a fellow 10 Course pupil named Bright in the novice welterweight bout. Matched with the Montrose town champ he wrote home that he was developing a powerful right hand and with one good punch the fight would be in the bag; result unknown.

On 1 March 1939 he was close to being dropped from flying training after the CFI's test with the Chief Flying Instructor, Squadron Leader Dickie Legg. His flying was 'below average' and he went home to Castlegate on half-term leave where a letter confirmed his position was under review. The letter weighed heavily and he walked the streets of Richmond discussing it with Ray. Legg wrote semi-officially to Flying Officer Bob Ker-Ramsey, the commander of D Flight in the advanced training squadron, that he was sending Finucane to him for an opinion but to note the slow progress and that 'the only reason I have not dismissed him from the course is that he is utterly determined to succeed'. D Flight was the 'fighter flight' which flew the Hawker Fury, a sturdy, strutted biplane fighter of sleek and elegant design, and Finucane flew one for the first time on 21 March.

The Fury was the catalyst and the next three months passed quickly as Finucane, delighting in the response of this sharp-nosed little fighter, began to fly with more precision, justifying the faith of Legg and Ker-Ramsey who decided he should get his chance. The accent was now on fighter training and tactics and Finucane revelled in aerobatics and practice attacks on target drogues. On 20 May 10 Course went to Evanton, Ross-shire, the armament practice camp, returning on 18 June. There are no records extant of 10 Course gunnery results but Ker-Ramsey told me: 'Paddy would have closed the distance until he couldn't miss and I was never surprised at his later success.'

On 23 June he was an 'average' pilot but with low marks: 2010 (from a maximum 3400), 59 per cent; pilot ability 400 (750), officer qualities 450 (750) and in the written exams 837 (1300) intermediate and 323 (600) advanced. Re-examined in navigation, meteorology, engines and armament he got 77 per cent, 54 per cent, 50 per cent and 65 per cent.

Finucane considered the only thing worth flying was a fighter plane and his posting to the pilotless aircraft section which flew radio controlled Queen Bee target aircraft at the technical airfield Henlow, Bedfordshire, on 26 June was a disappointment. Things were still not going as well as he hoped. He was actually 'grounded' awaiting the results of courts of inquiry into two Queen Bee crashes when the Second World War was declared on 3 September 1939. On 10 July the control column had jammed on take-off, and on 22 July on a ferry flight to Gosport he had forced-landed in bad weather in a field at Marlow in Buckinghamshire, and crashed into an orchard taking off again, escaping from the wreckage and scarred apple trees with a cut thumb. The RAF mobilised on 24 August and Germany attacked Poland a week later. On 2 September the RAF's advanced air striking force, which included two fighter squadrons, went to France and the next day Britain for the second time was at war with Germany. Finucane wrote home:

Glad to hear Ray is going to join the air force. Things are in a bit of a flat spin around the camp because of the war scare. I am sitting in the flight office waiting for orders to come through, time hangs heavily …

and later '… Life is getting livelier and if it keeps up I hope to be in France very soon.'

He returned to flying on 16 September after the crash inquiries announced the second one was due to inexperience; but he was as far away as ever from a fighter squadron, as he was now transferred to the practice and parachute test flight at Henlow where he was to spend a frustrating time giving passenger flights in two-seater Magisters to station ground staff and engineering course officers.

The technical men at Henlow had an important role in the RAF and newly posted junior officers were expected to be rarely seen and never heard. Squadron Leader John Pope was studying in the card room to pass his staff college exams and

Miles Magister, one of the RAF's primary trainers.

engineering finals when Finucane and a few others burst in noisily. He gave them an imperial rocket but privately sympathised. Young, and straight from flying training, they wanted something better.

With an unimpressive flying record Finucane got through the harsh winter of 1939-40 with the practice flight — doing some trips as second pilot in the parachute-testing Vickers Virginias – and in the spring of 1940 began putting in monthly applications with two Henlow friends, Dickie Turley-George, a crony from 10 Course days at Montrose, and Roy Lane, for postings to a fighter squadron until they were told to stop wasting administrative time. Turley- George and Lane staged a protest beat-up of the officers' mess at rooftop height followed by a tarmac landing (strictly forbidden) and were grounded for a fortnight.

On 10 May 1940 Finucane was flying a Magister, with Henlow medical officer Frank Neubert as passenger, over the quiet Bedfordshire countryside – Turley-George formating close by – as German Panzers supported by the Luftwaffe ended the phoney war with the blitzkrieg through the Low Countries in the prelude to Dunkirk and the fall of France. Finucane now felt that nothing could stop him getting onto a fighter squadron and in the evening, meeting Turley-George, Lane, Neubert and an engineering officer, Harold Sweet, in the crowded Henlow mess for a drink, said it could only be a question of time now. Sweet, older and soberly reflective, soothed him: 'Your time will come.'

The French collapse was swift. The German High Command dealt with the 'impregnable' Maginot Line by going around it instead of over it and on 4 June the evacuation of the British Army from the beaches at Dunkirk was complete. The Luftwaffe moved Messerschmitt 109Es into French airfields on the Channel coast in the Pas de Calais area, with the bomber fleets massed further inland, and began probing Britain's air defences with attacks on Channel convoys and coastal towns. On 18 June Winston Churchill broadcast his 'finest hour' speech: 'What General Weygand called the Battle of France is over. I expect that the Battle of Britain is about to begin.'

For Pilot Officer Finucane, aged nineteen, nearly two years of setback and adversity were suddenly over on 27 June 1940 when he was posted to 7 Operational Training Unit, Hawarden, near Chester, for a two-week conversion course on Spitfires before joining a fighter squadron.

The Spitfire was everything he hoped for; he eased back the stick on the final approach, but misjudged the height and the wheels floated above the grass refusing to settle as he rapidly ran out of airfield to land on. He was too high and too fast. Turley-George, having the same trouble, got down first, followed by Finucane who landed heavily and raised spurts of dust from the wheels as he applied the brakes, stopping with the spinner a few feet from the boundary hedge and smiling with relief at Dickie who grinned back, surprised that anyone could have landed further forward than he had.

Mechanics replacing oxygen bottles on a Spitfire.

They began taxying downwind to take off again when one of the instructors waved them back: 'The CO wants to see you two.' Wing Commander John Hallings-Pott had seen it all from the window. Experience as a pre-war instructor had taught him that the most effective cure for careless flying was to put a pilot on his mettle.

He eyed them thoughtfully from his desk and began to say pointedly that there was a need to avoid stupid accidents like landing with the wheels up and – emphasising – overshooting. Spitfires were in short supply. The Germans were already doing enough damage to our limited supply of aircraft without any help from them. 'Going around again' if not entirely satisfied with the approach and landing was a sign that a pilot knew what he was doing. It was nothing to be ashamed of and no one minded how many attempts at landing a pilot made provided he got the aircraft down in one piece so that it could continue to be used. Firmly, but not unreasonably, he made it clear that a repeat performance would not be tolerated. Bluntly he told them that if they were so keen to get their feet back on the ground that they dare not risk another circuit they would not be much use on a squadron.

Aware that he had nearly made a hash of it – there was an echo in Hallings-Pott's lecture on overshooting of what his instructors at Sywell and Montrose had said (except that he was more polite about it) – Finucane was doubly cautious and there were no more incidents.

Seven OTU was one of three training units set up in June 1940 to replace the fighter losses in France. It was crammed under canvas in one of the dispersal sites of 21 Maintenance Unit and had two hangars and a small brick-built site manager's office which was Hallings-Pott's office and bedroom, the air/ground R/T control room and site telephone exchange. The adjutant had a caravan and the flight offices, sergeants' and officers' messes were in marquees with aircrew accommodation in small tents. Finucane's course of about twenty pupils was only the second to be trained; the first course was all Fleet Air Arm volunteers who opted to fly with Fighter Command. They had cockpit drill on a Spitfire jacked up on trestles in a hangar and then briefed on the controls before their first flight. Hallings-Pott recalls: 'We had some original Spitfire Is and the undercarriage lever had to be pumped up and down. As the pump handle was on the right side of the cockpit it meant changing hands and flying left handed shortly after take-off and coming in to land, sometimes leading to fairly "interesting" manoeuvres at low altitude, especially if a pilot forgot to use his throttle lever lock and the engine lost power.' The instructors were operationally experienced pilots.

Finucane flew his first Spitfire on 3 July 1940 and in the next nine days made twenty-six Spitfire flights: handling, formation, practice attacks, R/T search, formation attacks and aerobatics. Only once, on 11 July, was he given air firing practice, thumbing for the first time the firing button on the control column and feeling the juddering impact of ·303 shells leaving the eight wing-mounted Browning machine guns at a muzzle velocity of 2,440 feet per second. He quickly learnt to respect the Spitfire's sensitive force and aft control and the much higher landing speed.

His flying logbook records that at 7 OTU he flew 2 hours 40 minutes on the Miles Master, 2 hours 25 minutes on the Fairey Battle, 15 minutes on the Hurricane and 22 hours 20 minutes on the Spitfire. It was an uncertain preparation for testing in battle but he landed on 12 July with a jubilant thumbs up to the groundcrew, and a posting to 65 Squadron at Hornchurch, Essex.

In the evening he went with Turley-George (posted to 54 Squadron, Rochford) and Lane (43 Squadron, Tangmere) into Chester for a drink and they caught the evening train, blacked-out against air raids, for London where Dickie stayed on for the weekend, Roy went home to Portsmouth, and Brendan to Richmond to see the family. When he and Ray had a moment alone to together he told him what a bloody marvellous aeroplane the Spitfire was! He was not due on the squadron until Monday, 15 July, but news was coming in over the wireless of Channel dogfights off the south coast, deciding him not to stay the whole weekend, and he left two days early the next morning Saturday, 13 July, for Hornchurch, eager to get into the fight.

3

Fighter Pilot

At Saturday lunchtime, 13 July, Finucane teamed up with another newcomer, Dave Glaser, for a drink in the Hornchurch mess. Dave's parents, Bill and Dolly Glaser, owned The Bugle pub at Hamble, Southampton, near Swaythling, and they got on well together from the start. Unlike Brendan, who had full parental approval, Dave overcame opposition to an RAF career with the compromise of joining the RAF Volunteer Reserve and learning to fly at weekends. He came straight from flying training at 3 FTS, Kidlington, and had yet to fly a Spitfire but an 'above average' assessment as pilot helped and he was able to scrounge ten hours on any spare Spitfire at Hornchurch he could get his hands on before flying into action with one. Far from considering this a disadvantage, Glaser was elated at posting straight to a fighter squadron without wasting time at an OTU! Finucane, with the advantage of the 7 OTU training, was able to fill him in a bit on the Spitfire, and they looked enviously on 65 Squadron's veterans.

The squadron ace was Flight Sergeant Bill 'Gunner' Franklin DFM who since 22 May had shot down ten enemy aircraft and shared another two destroyed. Twice he shot down two Me 109s on one sortie. In July, after chasing a 109 across the Channel to Calais, he ran into another seven, engaged five of them, and shot one down. Short, stocky with untidy thinning hair, Franklin was the scruffiest man on the squadron and the most successful. He was twenty-eight, a former aircraft apprentice from Poplar,

Pilots of 65 Squadron at Hornchurch, July 1940. Left to right: Plt Off Bill Franklin (+ 12 Dec 40), Sgt Harry Orchard (+ 5 Feb 41), Flt Lt Wilf Maitland-Walker, Fg Off John Nicholas, Flt Lt Gordon Olive, Squadron Ldr Henry Sawyer (+ 2 Aug 40), Fg Off Tom Smart (+ 12 Apr 43), Fg Off Ron Wigg, Plt Off Ken Hart (+ 28 Dec 44), Paddy Finucane, Fg Off Laurence Pyman (+ 16 Aug 40), Sgt Dick Kilner. Spitfire YT-D/P6799 joined 65 Squadron on 14 July 1940 only to be destroyed in a crash on 2 Aug 40 when Squadron Ldr Henry Sawyer stalled on take off at Hornchurch, killing its pilot.

who remustered to aircrew as a sergeant pilot and got a Bar to the DFM in August. After the blitz on London's East End he hated the Germans and the war became personal. Franklin was in B Flight which was commanded by Flight Lieutenant Sammy Saunders, aged twenty-six, tall, fair-haired and austere, usually sporting a blue polka dot scarf, a no- nonsense flyer who was known to race up to an erring pilot before the propeller had stopped spinning with a warning of 'Don't do that again!'

A welcoming familiar face on 65 Squadron was Ron Wigg, a New Zealander, who had been on 10 Course at Montrose where he and Brendan had watched the arrival of a flight of Gauntlets. They saw the pilots, fitted out in white flying overalls with the squadron crest, climbing out of their aircraft except for the last one who overshot, turning upside down after running into the fence. The pilot returned in a truck, leading the two pupils to conclude that fighter pilots were not supermen after all! Wigg got them introduced to the squadron and Glaser went off to join him in A Flight.

Fg Off Ron Wigg and Plt Off Wladislaw Szulkowski wearing the one piece suit to keep them warm at altitude and in winter, Tangmere Jan 41. Wigg would survive the war whilst Szulkowski would be posted to 315 Squadron in Jan 41 only to be killed 27 Mar 41.

Finucane went to B Flight, joining Franklin and Saunders, and the men he was to fly with in green section, Tommy Smart, the section leader and Ken Hart. Anxious to get into the air, Finucane hung about the dispersal doing a few practice trips until 24 July when 65 Squadron was moved to the satellite airfield at Rochford, Southend, where the daily routine now began with a flight across the Thames Estuary at first light to operate from the forward airfield Manston, inland from Ramsgate on the Kent coast.

July 1940 had seen 65 Squadron in some hard fighting as British and German pilots clashed head-on to gain air mastery over the Channel and the Dover Straits preparatory to invasion. If their experience was anything to go by the pilots of 11 Group which covered London and the south-east were in for an even harder time as the month progressed.

Finucane became operational on 25 July, and was at Manston on early morning readiness with B Flight when he was scrambled at 8·45am with a section on his first operational sortie. He was flying Spitfire N3128 with the squadron and individual code letters YT-W which had flown with the squadron since April and had seen better days, but it gave no trouble on the way down from Rochford. But recalled from the scramble after ten minutes it developed a glycol leak. Finucane's cockpit filled with choking white vapour from the escaping coolant liquid condensing on the hot engine – and at the same time his R/T went dead. Unable to do much about it, he hit a natural hollow in the airfield surface damaging the undercarriage, and crash-landed with the wheels up on a dead engine.

It was a creditable landing under difficult circumstances but he had to stand by with nothing to fly as the squadron went off later in the morning intercepting a raid off Dover. Franklin, dicing at sea level, shook a Me 109 off his tail and straight into the Channel, enabling him to claim it as destroyed without firing a shot.

Finucane got another Spitfire on 1 August. It was a brand-new one this time, serial R6818, and was taken on charge by 65 Squadron from 8 MU on 26 July. On 12 August the Luftwaffe changed tactics with an all-out attempt to smash Fighter Command's airfields on the ground and its fighters in the air with co-ordinated attacks on radar stations and south coast airfields. This was the prelude to the German's Eagle Day of 13 August which was meant to force Fighter Command into a decisive air battle and clear the way for invasion. Manston was right in the front line.

At 11am on 12 August 65 Squadron was scrambled, Finucane flying as Green 3. At 11·30am, at 26,000 feet over the Channel and about ten miles out from North Foreland, the squadron broke up into sections to pounce on twenty to thirty Me 109s 2,000 feet below. Turning towards one which was attacking Ken Hart, Finucane then had to take violent evasive action as he was attacked and lost a lot of height; climbing back to 20,000 feet he saw the main battle now some distance away, the sky shot with smoke trails and the debris of wrecked and burning aircraft.

The climb back to height had placed him in the ideal attacking position above and behind a formation of twelve Me 109s. He got the tail-ender with a burst from 250 yards down to 50 yards, seeing it pour grey smoke and dive towards the Channel; he landed back at Manston at IT45 am where the kill was confirmed by Sergeant Orchard who saw it continue straight down into the Channel.

Scramble-posed for the cameras, Paddy Finucane is far left; 65 Squadron, early 1941.

There was scarcely time for congratulations and analysis of his first combat before 65 Squadron was scrambled again, and this time they were caught on the ground taking off through the bomb bursts as twin-engine Me 110s and slim pencil-shaped Dornier 17s hit Manston in a low-level bombing and strafing attack which was on top of them almost before they realised it.

Saunders had been refused permission by the Hornchurch controller to move the squadron to the SE corner of Manston after the wind had veered and was blowing strongly from the west, leaving them in an impossible down-wind take-off position. He was outside discussing it with the A Flight commander, Gordon Olive, when the phone inside the dispersal hut sent them racing to their Spitfires. They were still taxying when everyone heard the R/T warning crackling in their earphones of a raid approaching the airfield. Saunders looked back to see yellow section, led by Jeffrey Quill, the former Supermarine test pilot at Eastleigh and now with the squadron for experience, moving into position. He did the fastest take-off of his career: 'I saw clouds of smoke and chalk dust as the first bombs fell and opened the throttle wide and pulled the emergency boost. Quill reckons he beat me to it by a split second.'

Quill recalled: 'We turned into wind and were ready to roll. With the cockpit canopies open the blast of engine noise and the R/T crackle through our helmets drowned everything else and the first I knew was when I looked back and saw a hangar go up in clouds of flame and smoke. From the line of bomb bursts it looked as if the next lot would land among the squadron. To my intense surprise I was airborne.'

Dick Kilner, aged twenty-four, a B Flight sergeant, sat fuming in his cockpit waiting for an empty oxygen bottle to be changed while Finucane and the others started up their aircraft and moved out. Then the groundcrews around him disappeared as if by magic and he looked up to see the flash of wings overhead and bomb bursts straddling the airfield as he dived headlong into the dugout to join the groundcrews. He had been due to fly as Saunders' wingman.

The only other one not to get airborne was Ken Hart in Finucane's section; his propeller had been stopped by the blast of a near miss as high explosive fell among the squadron. Finucane saw Hart's aircraft fall back as it lost flying speed, and then he lost sight of the section leader Tommy Smart in the smoke; he emerged at the other side of it, gained height slowly and looked back to see the glow of fire through the pall.

Coming out of cloud at 4,000 feet the other side of Margate, Finucane saw Quill on his right firing at a Me 109E 350 yards ahead, chased it himself into cloud, and lost it; then he saw it again ahead of him as he broke into the clear at 3,000 feet, and got in a short burst of fire before the German pilot again sought cloud cover. Again Finucane went in after him. The streams of cloud vapour cleared from his windscreen a few miles off the coast, Margate on his left; the Me 109 was still ahead but now at 1,000 feet as he got within range for a long burst which drew smoke as the 109 dived suddenly. It was only 200 feet above the water when Finucane had to break away sharply upwards to avoid a 109 moving in towards him, but the manoeuvre enabled him to get in a short burst from 200 yards at another 109 steep turning under the cloud base; he saw strikes and claimed it as damaged, and the first as probably destroyed.

Despite the pounding, Manston was still operational the next day, 13 August, and Finucane scrambled with B Flight at 4pm – still flying R6818 – he sent down a Me 109 in flames from 300 yards to 7 5 yards at 19,000 feet over the Channel off Dover, and got in a snap shot at another one climbing ahead of him which half rolled spinning away into cloud emitting grey smoke after a burst of fire from his guns at 200 yards.

Life on 65 Squadron was not without its humorous side and Finucane's unwillingness to admit defeat in anything enlivened things for his fellow pilots as Laurence Holland, who became commanding officer on 14 August, recalls:

'Facilities at Rochford were limited. The aircraft were lined up into wind and we did our periods of readiness in the clubhouse, leaving parked outside a 15cwt tender and a motorcycle.

'Our rest room had one telephone which served both for operational and other calls and whoever was nearest to it took any messages. An operational message got the thumbs-up signal and any other message such as the mess wanting to know how many for lunch got the thumbs-down. If it was thumbs-up, the rest of us piled into the 15cwt, raced across to dispersal, took off and climbed upwards spiralling over the airfield. The 'telephonist' took the message, rushed out, climbed on to the motorcycle, hurtled over to his aircraft and followed us upwards giving us the news as he climbed, and so to battle.

'Now to the day when Paddy was parked by the phone which duly rang and thumbs-up it was. As usual the rush took place and away we went, and as we climbed we watched the circus turn take place. Paddy on the motorcycle, followed by Paddy knocking the thing over, getting up, getting it up and so on. What we never did see was Paddy on the motorbike belting across to his aircraft. Naturally I called Hornchurch control and got the operational orders and we went on our way to attend to matters in hand.

'When we returned and asked what had, or rather had not happened, we found a very chastened Paddy having to confess that he had never learned to ride a motorbike or drive a car. And so a new rule had to be made that Paddy was not to sit next to the telephone.'

Holland was still a learner himself, as he recalls:

> 'I only fought my way out of Air Ministry late in June 1940, did a conversion course on Hurricanes at Sutton Bridge and went as supernumerary to 501 Squadron at Gravesend waiting for a squadron to materialise. When I was posted to command 65 Squadron on 14 August I had never flown a Spitfire.'

August 1940 is recalled by Ron Wigg:

> 'We shared duties at Manston with the other two Hornchurch squadrons, 54 and 74, each squadron taking a different period of the day. I can still remember clearly the dusk trips back to Rochford from Manston. We flew just above sea level across the Thames estuary. Most evenings were fine and the sea calm with masts, funnels and superstructure of sunken ships showing above the surface. Thoughts of a beer and a good night's sleep made it a pleasant trip.'

Finucane's progress as a fighter pilot was already being endorsed when the squadron on 28 August was sent to Turnhouse, near Edinburgh, to rest and replace losses. On 3 September he was promoted to flying officer and on 9 September a confidential squadron report said:

> I have great hopes of this officer. He is keen and intelligent and shows likelihood of becoming a very efficient leader. Is being trained as a leader and is learning quickly.

Later in the month he visited Henlow to see old friends. Charlie Ott, senior NCO on the practice and parachute test flight, glanced up from working in the hangar to see the familiar figure striding over. Ott noted that in the intervening three months Finucane looked a lot older, an impression verified when he told Ott he didn't like the killing and felt like a walking graveyard. There was a friendly welcome also from Frank Neubert who had to get special permission for him to have lunch in the Henlow mess because he was wearing a non-regulation roll-neck pullover.

Back at Turnhouse he flew a practice tail-chase dogfight with one of the squadron's Polish pilots, Boleslaw 'Ski' Drobinski, which developed into a head-on duel. Drobinski, aged twenty-one, had escaped through Yugoslavia, Italy and France to fly with the RAF and had done two years' advanced flying at the Polish Air Force Officers School, the equivalent of the RAF's Cranwell. He was no novice and commented: 'I don't think Paddy was prepared for my tactic of flying straight at him.'

Maybe it was the release from tension at Turnhouse or just that he had heard from some of A Flight's pilots about Ski's dogfighting prowess that prompted Finucane to suggest some practice. Whatever it was Ski was happy to oblige when the self-assured young flying officer, whose briar pipe seemed to be a permanent fixture, came over from B Flight, and twenty minutes later they were at 10,000 feet and turning on reciprocal courses to head back at a closing speed of 700mph.

Twice Ski forced Brendan to break away and easily got behind him in a tight turning circle. The third time Ski realised he did not intend to give way and the two Spitfires passed within a wingspan and continued circling with neither able to get the advantage: 'It was one hell of a dogfight. We came down to about 1,500 feet and Paddy being in charge had to stop the fight. We were not allowed to do any dogfighting below 5,000 feet and certainly not below 3,000 feet. When we landed my tunic and shirt were soaked with perspiration. My legs were shaking and I was very thirsty. Paddy came over, patted me on the back and said: "Ski, that was a good fight, but I'll bet you that next time I shall get you twice." Luckily, perhaps, there was not a second chance for us to meet again in a dogfight.'

The squadron moved to RAF Leuchars, Fifeshire, on 8 November and on 29 November were posted back to 11 Group in the south, to RAF Tangmere, near

Pilots of 65 Squadron, Paddy Finucane is third from right; to his left are Fg Off Ron Wigg and Sgt Harry Orchard. This Spitfire, serial P7856, was delivered to 65 Squadron in February 1941 whilst at RAF Tangmere; on 5 February 1941, Orchard was shot down and killed over France. 2nd from left is Sgt Peter Mitchell.

Chichester, on the edge of the South Downs in West Sussex. The onset of winter curtailed flying operations for the day fighter squadrons and at night Fighter Command could do nothing much as cities suffered in the 1940-1941 night blitz, although airborne interception radar was to lead to specialist night fighting squadrons with their own aces.

Some of 65 Squadron's officers were billeted out and Finucane shared a room with Dave Glaser at Rushman House, Oving, a few miles through country lanes from the airfield. The day after arriving, 30 November, they were having an early evening drink with Glaser's parents, Bill and Dolly, in the pleasant old oak- beamed and flagstone floor bar of The Bugle at Hamble, overlooking the harbour — the arrangement was that Finucane would go on to see the Physicks at Swaythling only a few miles away—when the first raid started at Southampton at 6·30pm.

They could hear the desynchronised throb of He lll engines over the Isle of Wight as the first target-marking aircraft headed for Southampton to light up the city centre with pathfinder flares.

From the garage behind the pub they got out the battered red Wolseley Hornet two-seater, which, minus its hood and windscreen, had cost Mr Glaser £7 10s after being 'rolled' by a previous owner, and headed for Tangmere where they found that fog had grounded the southern fighter airfields as Southampton was heavily blitzed for two nights in succession.

Cratered roads and rubble blocked the way through the city centre; the ordeal of the people of Southampton was evident from their dazed and shocked expressions. The Hornet afforded no weather protection. Muffled against the chill night air in flying gear, fur-lined leather flying boots, heavy Irvin sheepskin jackets and thick scarves they threaded their way out through the suburbs seeing further evidence of the bombing before stopping at the corner of Harefield Road, Swaythling. Dave arranged to go back to The Bugle and pick up Brendan at 9·30pm for a drink at the pub, then return to Tangmere. Having ascertained that the Physicks were unharmed, Brendan then went across the road to see Ada McKinnon. She and her mother had taken in two blitzed families and eighteen people were crowded into the small council house.

Glaser turned up on time in the Hornet, parked it in Harefield Road and went in for the introductions, then back to The Bugle and on to Rushman House at around midnight for a few hours' sleep. The valiant red Hornet became a familiar sight in Harefield Road during the winter evenings as it got them quickly from Tangmere to The Bugle to Swaythling and back again.

High explosive and the incendiaries which started fires as an aiming point were accurate and most of Southampton High Street was now wrecked and damaged property, including the shops Finucane knew from the pre-war holidays. South Hants Hospital and Southampton telephone exchange were set alight and all lines inside and outside the city were cut; the only communication was by despatch rider. Shortage of water and fire fighting equipment added to the chaos. Many homes were without gas, electricity and water.

Finucane left Drobinski in no doubt of his feelings when the Polish pilot came over to Rushman House one evening before going on to the Tangmere satellite airfield at Westhampnett where 302 (Polish) Squadron was based with a good bar in

Fg Off Brendan Eamonn Fergus 'Paddy' Finucane seen here with 65 Squadron, RAF Tangmere, February 1941.

their mess at Farrington House. After asking about Ski's family and the German and Russian invasion of Poland, Finucane continued with his shaving while Ski sat on the edge of his bed discussing the war. 'It was the longest shave I can ever remember,' recalls Drobinski. 'We talked for about an hour and a half. Speaking slowly to ensure I understood Paddy said: "Listen, Ski, when this war is over we must make sure there will not be another one. It is a terrible way to settle anything. Until it is won we must shoot every bloody Jerry from the sky."' Later that evening at Farrington House the drinks somehow tasted better.'

The New Year 1941 started well. The Luftwaffe was coming over only occasionally in daylight now and 65 Squadron spent a lot of time patrolling the Sussex coast. Finucane, leading a section most of the time, caught one of the lone raiders, a Me 110, while patrolling Selsey Bill at 9 50 am on 4 January at 7,000 feet. Visibility was good as the German pilot saw the three Spitfires and Finucane went over and down to head him off as he made for France. It took four attacks to send him down in a running fight for fifteen miles across the Channel. Finucane broke hard downwards and under the Me 110, half rolled over the top of it, still firing, and finished it with two astern attacks and flame flared from an engine as it nosed down into the Channel.

Paddy about to climb into Spitfire YT-X of 65 Squadron, winter 1940-41.

After lunch on 19 January he led Sergeant Orchard on a two-man patrol starting at 17,000 feet off St Catherine's Point, IOW, and going down to 120 feet and then fifty feet in another sea-level chase after a Ju 88 which they left, short of fuel, as a smoking wreck within five miles of Cherbourg. Both its engines were well alight but the German pilot was a skilful and experienced flyer whose tactics included low level skidding turns and flying into the sun where the glare blotted out Finucane's reflector gunsight image on the windscreen. The rear gunner was accurate, getting in some hits on Finucane's Spitfire as he pressed his attacks in close, and back at Tangmere he had to make a belly landing with the hydraulic system operating the undercarriage damaged.

Sgt Peter Mitchell far left, Sgt Harold Orchard, ?, Paddy Finucane, Fg Off George Wigg, ?

There had been some changes on the squadron. Saunders became CO while they were at Turnhouse; Franklin, newly commissioned as a pilot officer, was killed soon after arriving at Tangmere when his score was fourteen enemy aircraft destroyed, and Tommy Smart was awarded a DFC with six destroyed and now commanded B Flight with Finucane as his deputy.

For Brendan this was measurable progress as a fighter pilot and he was well satisfied with the way life was going, looking ahead to getting into the scrap and impatient on the ground as usual. His next chance to score was on 5 February when 65 Squadron flew with the other two Tangmere squadrons, 610 and 302, on an early sweep to St Omer. The squadron was split up in patches of haze at the rendezvous over Rye and Finucane only had his wingman with him at 1pm when they were ten miles inland over the French coast and he cut in on the inside of the turn of one of

65's Hut-Paddy Finucane adds finishing touches.

Pilots from 65 Squadron play cards in the dispersal-Paddy Finucane is 2nd left, to his left is Sgt Harold Orchard who would be killed in action 5 February 1941.Far right is Fg Off Tom Smart who would be awarded the DFC days after this photo was taken. He would be killed in action over Malta 12 Apr 43.

three Me 109s curving in to attack from behind. Firing a short burst from 250 yards he scored hits which slowed down the 109 and he closed in for the kill, seeing the 109 go down dragging a gash of black smoke across the snow- covered French countryside and exploding in a wood.

On 26 February 65 Squadron was posted from 11 Group to Kirton-in-Lindsey, Lincolnshire, a quieter sector in 12 Group; Robert Carson arrived as a sergeant straight from flying training:

Tangmere Jan 1941. Paddy Finucane is far left and Plt Off Wladislaw Szulkowski is sitting on the wing far right.

Paddy Finucane 3rd from left, to his left is Plt Off Wladislaw Szulkowski.

'Paddy was a flying officer and deputy commander of B Flight when I joined 65 Squadron as a very new pilot. In the short time that I was acquainted with him it was impossible not to be affected and impressed by the man. Largely he was of the type that the pre-war RAF was so successful in selecting as pilots; confident, balanced, extrovert, relaxed and entirely professional. But Paddy seemed to have just that little extra. Certainly I recall regarding him with more than a little awe and wishing I could be like him.

'When I arrived at 65 Squadron, largely because wartime pilot training had been condensed in time and content, I felt that formation flying meant being in roughly the same area of sky, moving at about the same speed in approximately the same direction. In short, I amounted to more potential danger to my colleagues than I did to the enemy. At no small risk to himself, sheer dedication to the job in hand and a capacity for patient leadership Paddy changed that in a few concentrated hours. I have to add that by the end of it I was also afraid that he would invent a new pungent comment on my capacity to handle a Spitfire in close proximity to his and broadcast it across the radio for all to hear. A fighter pilot's fighter pilot.'

Pilots from 65 Squadron, Kirton-in-Lindsey late Feb/Mar 41; Paddy Finucane far right. 3rd from right is the CO, Squadron Ldr Gerald Saunders; to his right is Fg Off Tom Smart.

Meanwhile there was other news of interest in the Finucane family. Ray had been accepted for aircrew and was on a wireless operator course at Yatesbury, Wiltshire, with training as an air gunner. On the afternoon of 12 April Brendan borrowed a Magister from the communications flight at Kirton and flew down to Yatesbury, via Desford, to pick him up.

'Hold tight. Here we go.'

'Where're we going?'

'We'll drop in and surprise the family.'

Thirty minutes later they were over Richmond on the way to Heston airfield a few miles north of the borough. The Maggie droned over Richmond town centre, the large splash of green of the Old Deer Park and Kew Gardens providing a bearing to Twickenham Road leading into Lower Mortlake Road where Castlegate was the second turning on the left with 26 the first house in the road.

Brendan rocked the wings and pointed down:

'That's it.'

Kevin, the youngest brother, looked up from the back garden to see them circling at 200 feet. Brendan banked the Maggie steeply and Kevin recognised Ray almost

Mechanic helping a pilot from 65 Squadron into his parachute, Kirton-in-Lindsey, Spring 1941.

standing up in the cockpit, waved back and went into the house with the news so that they were expected home.

Low flying over Richmond was a relaxing change from the sort of flying he'd been doing recently but back at Kirton things were on the move and there was no time to relax otherwise. On 14 April he was promoted to flight lieutenant and appointed to command A Flight in 452 Squadron which was being formed at the other side of the airfield; the first of the RAAF fighter squadrons in the UK for operations over Europe.

He did one more sortie with 65 Squadron on 15 April, a wing sweep with 266 and 402 Squadrons over Boulogne. On the way back late in the afternoon midway between Calais and Dover at 14,000 feet he shot a Me 109 into the Channel, following it down from a steep dive and pulling out low over the water as his victim went in.

This ended a successful tour of duty with 65 Squadron. Saunders recommended Finucane for the DFC and signed his logbook with a rating as a fighter pilot of 'exceptional'.

At the Spitfire operational training unit at Hawarden, now renumbered 57 OTU, Fred McCann, from Hobart, Tasmania, who had finished his advanced training at Calgary, Canada, noted the names in his diary of the others with him — Truscott, Willis, O'Byrne, Chisholm, Lewis, Cox and Eccleton — as they completed their conversion to Spitfires, got a final word of encouragement from Hallings-Pott, went into Chester for a drink and got the train to Hull with a change at Manchester. Truscott and O'Byrne won all the money at pontoon and poker on the way down and

at Manchester, while the rest were scratching around for tea, Bluey disappeared and turned up again with a bottle of scotch which they polished off well before they reached Kirton.

Keith Truscott, aged twenty-four, from Melbourne, Victoria – 'Bluey' because of his red hair – played the game hard on and off the airfield, a former soccer star and all-round sportsman who had nearly failed the basic flying course on Tiger Moths at Essendon, Victoria, and was still not an immaculate flyer, a bulky, ebullient extrovert, popular and loyal, whose personal qualities clearly marked him out during later flying instruction as a fighter pilot.

On leave sporting the DFC ribbon. Paddy Finucane was awarded the DFC 13 May 1941, a Bar to the DFC 9 September 1941 and then a second bar 26 September 1941 by which time he had been promoted to Flt Lt.

They were the second batch of Spitfire-trained men on 452 Squadron. Truscott, Jay O'Byrne (Launceston, Tasmania), Ray Holt (Cracow, Queensland), Bill Eccleton (Sydney, NSW), Don Lewis (Melbourne, Victoria) and Don Willis (Melbourne) were pilot officers. McCann, Barry Chapman (Charlesville, Queensland), Keith Chisholm (Manly, Sydney) and Ken Cox (Melbourne) were sergeant pilots.

Fighter pilots in typical attire.

The first group had already arrived at Kirton mostly, from 57 OTU, several days previously: Pilot Officer Ray Thorold-Smith (Young, NSW) and eleven sergeant pilots – Paul Makin, Adelaide, South Australia, (transferred from the RAF), Ian Milne (Wirrabara, S Australia), Ed Walliker (Wamambool, Victoria), Dick Gazzard (Sydney, NSW), Jim Hanigan (Sydney), Arch Stuart (Grafton, NSW), Pat Tainton (Sydney), Alex Roberts (Lismore, NSW), Andy Costello (Charters Towers, Queensland), Raife Cowan (Brisbane, Queensland) and Barry Haydon (Brisbane).

These were the original members of 452 Squadron and were frequently told they were to regard themselves as ambassadors for Australia as the first Royal Australian Air Force fighter squadron in the UK, recalls McCann. He would have been among the first batch to arrive but had pranged a Spitfire landing from a training flight at Speke, Liverpool, and ran into a drainage ditch in fog on the airfield which was a sea of mud. Their dispersal was a Lockheed Hudson packing case and they were glad to see Kirton in Lindsey with its acres of green grass, clear skies and quarters in a permanent RAF mess with hot water and electric heating. No sooner had they arrived at Kirton than those already there appeared and took them to their various messes. Great to see them again, recorded McCann, who paid Raife Cowan the money he owed him since their training days together in Canada!

These men had come a long way to fly and fight for England. With Finucane they were to become an élite fighting force – but it was not all plain sailing in the beginning.

452 Squadron June 1941; of the 16, 10 would be killed during the war, two would be captured and one evaded. L to R: Paul Makin, Ken Cox (+23 Jan 44), Arch Stuart (POW 18 Sep 41), Paddy Finucane, Ian Milne (POW 20 Sep 41), Jim Hanigan (+7 Sep 41), Fred McCann, Ray Thorold-Smith (+15 Mar 43), CO Bob Bungey (+10 Jun 43), Don Willis (+18 Sep 41), Alex Roberts (Evaded 11 Jul 41), Don Lewis (+22 Jan 42), Graham Douglas, Andy Costello (+5 Jul 41), Bluey Truscott (+28 Mar 43), Dick Gazzard (+19 Aug 41).

4

Flight Commander

Finucane grinned at McCann standing in front of him with his uniform dripping with a mixture of green aircraft paint and oily water: 'I appreciate the colour but it's not St Patrick's Day and could you go somewhere else because I like a tidy dispersal!' The half-gallon can had been left in the cockpit after a paint job at the maintenance hangar and the lot had showered down on McCann when he did a slow roll. To cap it all, the paint had locked the canopy solid and had to be levered open by a fitter with a screwdriver when he landed mad at the world – and ran into Finucane coming out of the flight offices.

Poor servicing initially was only one of the problems Finucane found in getting a new squadron off the ground.

They were crazy days [he recorded] when I helped to form 452 Squadron from a clerk and an office table. They were raw lads … but they put their backs into it while we were collecting enough aircraft and pilots to man the squadron for operations. My first impression of them was what a bunch!' But I very quickly lost it. The eagerness, keenness and ability of those boys stood out a mile. What a squadron that was, and still is. Since the first batch arrived in this country when we needed them most I have met and lived with a lot of Australians and my estimation of them all is that they are a wonderful bunch of fellows.

He seemed a little aloof at first and there is a lot of truth in Truscott's comment: 'We had to teach Paddy to play the fool when he came to us. The poor man had been with an English squadron so long he was trying to act dignified.'

They all called him Finney before the more general Paddy was accepted and McCann had it about right when he said Finucane mixed well with the sergeants as well as everyone else. From the start he got on well with Truscott although they were exact opposites in terms of personality. The Australian humour was of the needling type and as Finucane's own sense of comedy was never far below the surface he adapted quickly to the Aussie patois – probably on the basis of 'If you can't beat 'em … ' – and he rapidly discarded any idea he may have had of standing on rank, realising it would be useless if he wanted to get the best from the Australians, and as a result closely identified with them in a way he never did with 65 Squadron where he had had to concentrate on learning the fighter pilot's trade himself.

Once he had got over the initial shock of being called 'Finney' by the sergeants he never allowed them to forget what they were there for, including Truscott who later said: 'I owe a great deal to Paddy Finucane. He and I shared a room and Paddy would work out attacks with me. He thinks an attack from dead astern is the only way of making certain you get your man. Of course you have got to be good to get on your opponent's tail like that but Paddy could and thanks to his coaching I am able to get there now and again.'

Truscott was being untypically modest in that statement about his own capability and doing Finucane less than justice because he owed him just about everything for the tuition in fighter tactics. It was always the main conversational gambit. Finucane couldn't keep off the subject for long and had a terrific regard for Truscott who reckoned Finucane was the 'best bloke he'd met outside Australia', which was the apogee of praise.

Finucane's affinity with the Australians on 452 Squadron was due in part to his shrewdly recognising early on that they called for a totally different approach to what he was used to. The strongly marked individualism of the Australian character would have not responded to the conventional pre-war-trained regular RAF officer.

McCann: 'When we got to Kenley he often brought Lewis, Truscott or Thorold-Smith to the Red House (our billets just outside the Kenley main gate), pick up a few of us and take us into Croydon for a few beers at The Greyhound and we could sing all the way there and back – songs like 'Mountains of Mourne', 'Rose of Tralee' and 'Alouette'. Paddy's favourite song was 'Indian Summer'. He would puff on his pipe and discuss tactics and people's personal problems over a few beers, joke and tell us funny stories, and we would be driven home happy to belong.

'He was a great punster and we all tried our hand at punning. The punishment for a bad pun was to 'take one' which consisted of a blow, often hard, on the upper arm and a particularly poor pun was worth two or three blows.'

The Distinguished Flying Cross for Finucane's work on 65 Squadron was awarded on 25 April with a citation which said he had shown great keenness to engage the enemy and destroyed five enemy aircraft... 'His courage and enthusiasm have been a source of encouragement to other pilots of the squadron.'

In A Flight he had McCann, Willis, Lewis, Chisholm, Cowan, Milne, Makin, Gazzard, Roberts, Haydon, Thorold-Smith and Holt. The squadron now had some aircraft – early Spitfire Mk Is – and Finucane started working them up to operational status. Only Roberts and Tainton (both transferred from 607 Squadron) and Milne (from 254 Squadron) had any squadron experience but having at least flown with an RAF squadron was a start which the others did not have and they had to be trained from scratch.

Before Finucane could get properly started on A Flight he unexpectedly got temporary command of the whole squadron with an aptitude amounting almost to genius for getting off on the wrong foot. There was certainly an echo of the bad starts at Sywell, Montrose and Henlow in what happened on 3 May when he flew a formation air drill display for War Weapons Week.

The first commander of 452 Squadron was Roy Dutton DFC and Bar, an experienced pilot with nineteen enemy aircraft destroyed who was posted in from a flight commander post on 145 Squadron, Tangmere, to form the squadron. They were flying a close formation over Scunthorpe and then Brighouse, Yorkshire, when Finucane got too close to Dutton's aircraft and in the sudden shock of collision his propeller chopped off most of the CO's tail unit.

A fragment of the elevators was still intact and Dutton found by opening the throttle he kept the nose up slightly but had no stick fore and aft control. He came down in open country near Halifax at 180mph and smashed through a brick wall: 'Directly the control column was whipped forward from my hand Paddy said over the R/T quickly, "I have cut your tail off, leader – bale out." I think I replied something like, "So it seems", and

UD-C of A Flight 452 Squadron comes in to land over B Flight's dispersal, Kirton in Lindsey Spring 1941.

452 over Kirton in Lindsey, Spring 1942.

Pilots of 452 Squadron, Kenley, 1941. Paddy Finucane is third from left; to his left is Fg Off Keith 'Bluey' Truscott, Ian Milne & Fred McCann; to his right are Dick Gazzard and Alex Roberts.

that was that, and busied myself with trying to bale out but could not get the canopy back and by the time I did I judged I was too low to jump and just went down with it.'

Finucane led the rest of the flight back – there were six Spitfires – after circling the wreck and seeing no sign of life. George Potter, the station adjutant at Kirton-in-Lindsey heard later in the afternoon what had happened, and that Dutton was back at 4·30pm, and raced over to the officers mess to find 452's battered but otherwise intact CO slumped in an armchair in the ante-room: 'I called a steward and said, "Never mind about opening time – let's have some drinks."

'I think I was the first officer to see Roy after his return from hospital with only a small plaster on his forehead (after a miraculous escape) and I know that I was the only other officer present when Paddy came in, stared unbelievingly and said, "God, sir, I thought I'd killed you." Roy said, "You won't get my job that way, Paddy" and as on many other occasions I was very happy to buy the celebratory beer.'

Dutton had a swollen face where an eyebrow was stitched back on, cracked ribs, and walked with difficulty. He was weary and in no mood for tearing off a strip and recalls saying, 'What the hell did you do that for, Paddy?' Finucane's reply is unknown but the most likely explanation is that he was flying a Spitfire with the only metal propeller on the squadron (they were all early Mk Is) which gave him an extra turn of speed, and Dutton, a pre-war Hendon air drill flyer with 111 Squadron, had the flight in a very tight formation.

At the time he would, understandably, not wholeheartedly have agreed with Potter's assessment of 452's A Flight commander: 'Deservedly popular and respected and absolutely brimful of inborn leadership.' Dutton, knocked out when the straps broke, had been dosed with rum at Halifax hospital while they treated his injuries which included a back injury that later caused trouble when he was SASO to 249 Wing in Italy.

He went on sick leave from Kirton leaving Finucane, as senior flight commander, as temporary squadron commander in full charge of the training programme for 452 Squadron. From being a deputy flight commander three weeks ago he now had responsibility for twenty-three pilots, sixteen Spitfire Mk Is and around 130 NCO and airmen groundcrew.

After the crash 65 Squadron's humorists put up a sign-written notice, '452 yards to Bend 'em Brendan and his demolition squad', probably the work of Tommy Smart; Finucane decided to leave it where it was because there was a fair number of taxying and landing accidents during training. Truscott clipped the top of a 65 Squadron Spitfire at its dispersal, Alex Roberts damaged a Spitfire taxying, Ed Walliker belly-landed with undercarriage trouble, Jay O'Byrne and Andy Costello both crashed and Raife Cowan, undershooting on the approach, put himself in hospital with a broken arm.

The groundcrews got a rocket for being slow on the turn-round time in getting the Spitfires into the air. One of them was corporal airframe fitter Ivor Easton: 'The

Pilots of 452 Squadron clay pigeon shooting-sitting nearest the shooter is Don Willis.

ground crews' training programme was not going too well initially so Paddy had the NCOs assembled in the flight offices next to 452's hangar; he told us so in no uncertain terms that he was charged with the training while they worked up to operational standard but that they wouldn't be for a long time at this rate, finishing with the words ... "so pull your fingers out and get on with the job." This was the first time that I and most of the others present had heard the expression and there was much conjecture as to its derivation! There was no doubt that he meant it and from then on the aircraft serviceability improved. He did a very good job of working up the squadron to operational pitch.'[6]

He was joined in 8 May by Graham Douglas, a Scots former flying instructor, as B Flight commander, but Douglas had very little experience as a fighter pilot and the responsibility for 452's training remained with Finucane. Douglas, aged thirty-four, had done a few weeks' flying with 74 Squadron led by one of Fighter Command's ablest squadron commanders, Sailor Malan, and could draw a comparison with what he found on 452 Squadron: 'Paddy was just what was needed to get the squadron on its feet. He was a terrific morale booster. There was a general feeling on 452 Squadron that God was a poor second to fighter pilots,' said Douglas.

How much of this was due to Finucane's leadership and the fact that the Australians already thought they were good to start with is an open question, but he had good material to work on. McCann said: 'Our morale was high and we did not consider ourselves inferior to any other squadron.' But Finucane was the only pilot among the 25 with combat experience, regarded 452 as 'his' squadron, and put the same amount of energy and drive into it as he did in becoming a fighter pilot himself.

He drove the lessons home in the air. McCann: 'I did a practice tail chase dogfight with Paddy. He just got behind me and stayed there saying, "You're dead, Mac." When we landed he did a post mortem and gave me quite a lot of suggestions on evasive and attacking manoeuvres. One in particular stuck in my mind – "If in trouble keep turning and work your way down to the deck." '

The squadron had re-equipped with Spitfire Mk IIs by the third week in May and Finucane collected his, serial P8038[7], from 303 (Polish) Squadron, Northolt, on 21 May. P8038 was the first of four Spitfires to get the shamrock emblem – the others were Mk VBs – as Finucane's personal insignia and although not his idea he adopted it on successive aircraft. Jimmy Firth, aged twenty-nine, from Wakefield, Yorkshire, his airframe rigger, and 'Speedy' Moore, the Canadian engine fitter, were discussing it among themselves and not making much of a job of chalking the oudine when one of A Flight's engine fitters, Maurice Pownall, a former lithographic artist, took over.

Using green camouflage dope, he edged it in black with thorns sprouting between the trifoil leaves prominently on the left forward cockpit fairing panel. Finucane approved and the shamrock stayed. Pownall had done some training charts, showing at a glance the number of hours flown by each pilot, cautioned by Finucane: 'Don't be too colourful, these are for a training course – not an art gallery!'

---

[6] Easton adds: 'He was considerate to groundcrews and I had him to thank for recommending my application for a commission in the technical branch.'

[7] Spitfire P8038 survived the war and was last recorded on its RAF Form 78 at Portsmouth Aerodrome on 27 September 1945.

Paddy Finucane stretching in his Spitfire.

Photo signed by Paddy Finucane-note mechanic on the right has Paddy Finucane's shamrock emblem painted onto his overalls.

Having got the groundcrew servicing sorted out, Finucane gave his whole attention to 452's proficiency in the air at the gunnery ranges at Sutton Bridge and Manby, in practice dogfights, formation, air drill, a battle climb to 32,000 feet and practice interceptions.

The great day when 452 was declared fully day operational by Fighter Command was 2 June. Finucane was well satisfied. Bob Bungey arrived as the new commanding officer on 10 June.

Finucane was able to hand over to Bungey a squadron already moulded into a fighting unit and which was to prove his most notable contribution to its success. Bungey, from Glenelg, South Australia, was twenty-six, lean and Hawkeye-faced with the healthy tan of the Australian open air type; he had flown light bombers with 226 Squadron in France and Hurricanes with 145 Squadron from Tangmere. He was not a great fighter pilot and his strength with 452 was his leadership and discipline which quickly won him respect, but he was not 'accepted' by the squadron until he landed with his wheels up and gave further credence to Finucane's 'demolition squad'.

Andy Costello, son of a Queensland sheep farmer who learnt to fly at his own expense, was the squadron's first casualty when he was shot down and killed by an intruder while making a night landing on 5 July.

The squadron flew its first circus operation on 11 July.

The events leading to this began on 8 February 1941 when Air Vice-Marshal Trafford Leigh-Mallory, commander of 11 Group, on instructions from the Fighter Command chief, Air Marshal Sir William Sholto Douglas, compiled a document headed 'Circus Operations, Operations Instruction No 6'.

Paddy Finucane in cockpit is greeted by the CO of 452 Squadron – Bob Bungey.

OI 6 and 7 which followed set the pattern for Fighter Command operations for the next two years. It began:

> The German Air Forces in Occupied territory have by day been comparatively undisturbed by offensive action on our part. The initiative has been entirely theirs until recently, to be active as and when they pleased. We have been forced continuously to stand on the defensive prepared at any moment to meet attacks of the enemy's choosing. The German Air Force has so far been defeated in major engagements against this country but their morale has held because they have had the opportunity to recuperate at rest in their bases where it has been unnecessary for them to be constantly on the alert against possible counter attack. As a result of our circus operations to date the Germans have now started putting up standing patrols and these show signs of increasing with each operation.
>
> Important targets exist in certain of the enemy-occupied Channel ports and in addition there are also many military establishments, concentrations of supplies, and a number of aerodromes or landing grounds in Northern France suitable for attack. Nos 2 and 16 Groups wish to take advantage of our ability to provide escorts in order to attack these targets by day. No 11 Group require these bombing operations to bring the enemy to action on our own terms under conditions favourable to our fighters.
>
> *Intention.* The object of these attacks is to force the enemy to give battle under conditions tactically favourable to our fighters.
>
> In order to compel him to do so the bombers must cause sufficient damage to make it impossible for him to ignore them and refuse to fight on our terms.

Fighter Command left the selection of targets to the group commanders and the bombers were to cross the French coastline at not less than 17,000ft. OI 6 then defined the fighter escorts:

Escort Wing
Usually three squadrons

The close escort squadron is to fly at 1,000ft above and slightly behind the higher or highest box of bombers throughout the attack and the subsequent withdrawal to safety behind the English coastline. They are not to leave the bombers except to repel attacks actually made on the bombers until approaching their respective home bases. The squadron to act as close escort is to be detailed by the appropriate sector commander.

The escort squadrons. The remaining two squadrons of the escort wing are to fly one on each flank, behind and not more than 3000ft and 5000ft respectively above the higher or highest box of bombers. They are to engage enemy aircraft which menace the formation of bombers.

High Cover Wing
In certain circumstances a wing of two or three squadrons may be detailed as high cover to the bombers, in addition to the escort wing.

The high cover wing is to fly behind the escort wing and with their squadrons stepped downwards at intervals of 2,000 to 3,000ft from not less than 30,000ft, and to the flanks of the escort wing:

Squadron	Height
Top high cover	30,000ft or higher but in visual contact with squadrons below
Middle high cover	27,000ft
Lowest high cover	25,000ft
Higher escort	22,000ft
Lower escort	20,000ft
Closer escort	18,000ft
Bombers	17,000ft

Invariably the leader of the high cover wing is to lead the lower or lowest squadrons.

High cover squadrons, other than the top squadron, are permitted to reduce height to attack enemy aircraft in the air. The squadron flying at the top and acting as "above guard" to the other squadron or squadrons is to maintain a protective position above the other squadrons and only fight if forced to do so for the protection of the remainder.

After the bombing attack the high cover wing is to continue to give cover to the bombers and the escort wing during the withdrawal until the former with their close escort have re-crossed the French coastline and are well set on their course for home. They are then to provide high cover to the two escort squadrons of the escort wing who also become free from their escort duties to seek out and destroy enemy aircraft.

Mopping Up Wing

A wing of two or three squadrons may be detailed as a mopping up wing. At a height of between 25,000ft to 30,000ft, and by careful timing, they are to arrive off the French coast in an "up sun" position, at the same time and place as the bombers and their close escort squadron will re-cross it.

Their role is to protect the bombers and their close escort squadron during their return to the English coast, thus freeing the high cover wing and escort squadrons to enable the latter to carry out their main role of engaging enemy aircraft.

When the bombers are safely across the Straits the mopping up wing should, if possible, sweep towards the French coast to assist the other two wings, particularly during their homeward journey.

Details followed on the height and rendezvous for the components of a sweep and stressed that strict R/T silence was to be maintained except for instructions from the controllers and brief acknowledgments from wing leaders, and instructions on method of approach to the target and withdrawal after attack.

Fighter squadrons are reminded of the importance of maintaining visual contact with the bombers and other fighter formations and remaining in close mutual support. Fighter formations must, however, be flexible – Hendon formations are vulnerable.

The object of circus operations, from a fighter point of view, is to destroy enemy fighters enticed up into the air, using the tactical advantages of surprise, height and sun. It is important for all fighters to maintain good air discipline and only leave their formations if ordered by the formation leader. Such orders should only be issued in an attack against enemy aircraft or if a particularly favourable target is sighted under conditions where those detached to attack can be protected by the remainder of the formation.

The experience of previous operations show that our casualties in the past have almost invariably been inflicted upon the straggler and those pilots who still disregard the dangers of flying alone 'down sun', without constantly turning their aircraft to left and right, and who fail to keep a sharp lookout above and behind.

Leaders of squadron and wing formations are to ensure that their pilots realise the vital importance to each of them of not straggling, and that they endeavour to regulate their speed at all times to assist in eliminating straggling.

Signal arrangements would be stated in circus operations orders and Manston and Hawkinge on the Kent coast would be available with servicing parties for refuelling for those needing it on the way back. Circuses would only be ordered under suitable weather. This would be decided by 11 Group commander and the bomber group commanders and the group controller would obtain hourly weather reports from the fighter airfields on the day.

At zero hour minus thirty minutes the group staff officer would request the Royal Navy to position rescue boats in the Channel, having previously notified the air-sea rescue organisation of the day of the sweep. Lysander aircraft crews would be ordered on standby at an advanced base, such as Manston, and one Lysander would patrol under 3,000 feet with fighter escort when the air-sea rescue boats were in position.

Sholto Douglas replied to Leigh-Mallory on 12 February 1941 'concurring generally with the dispositions you intend' but

> ... it has been clearly agreed by the air staff that the purpose of these operations is to destroy enemy fighters under circumstances favourable to our own squadrons. Our bombers are present only for the purpose of forcing the enemy to come up and fight and they must therefore conform to the requirements of our fighters in pursuit of the main aim of the operation. The wording of the "intention" paragraph of your instruction should ... make it clear that the object of the operation is to bring about a fighter battle.

Leigh-Mallory issued Operations Instruction No 7 on 16 February 1941 to become the law on the sweeps for Fighter Command.

Sholto Douglas, a first world war fighter pilot, recalls in his memoirs[8] that offensive fighter patrols over the Western Front were expensive and had doubts about the sweep idea which he put to the Chief of the Air Staff, Sir Charles Portal, and envisaged heavy losses. He is vague in his memoirs about what caused him to

[8] *Years of Command:* Marshal of the RAF Lord Douglas of Kirtleside.

change his mind but no doubt it was the subtle pressure of Portal, the less than subtle pressure of Churchill, and the hardest pressure of all to resist – political expediency, when Nazi Germany invaded Russia on 21 June 1941 and the circus operations then acquired the role of pinning down German fighters on the Channel coast to prevent them reinforcing the Luftwaffe on the eastern front.

Thus in mid-summer 1941 a month before Finucane and 452 Squadron moved south to Kenley to take part in them the sweeps were stepped up dramatically in scale and intensity. But the original sweep formations were totally inadequate for the job and new fighter components were defined by Sholto Douglas in a letter to his group commanders:

Escort
Escort Cover
Target Support
Freelance Forward Support
Rear Support

Each role now had a full fighter wing of three squadrons assigned to the task; instead of one squadron for close escort as defined in OI 7 of February 1941 there were now three, and the original concept of six Spitfire squadron components of a sweep was now a minimum of eighteen squadrons considered necessary to do the same job.

The circus operations were Fighter Command's main effort but other innovatory operations flown, with new codenames entering the fighter vocabulary in 1941, were:

Ramrod: Bomber escort job but (unlike the circuses) the primary aim was to destroy the target

Fighter Ramrod: The same, except that fighters escorted cannon fighters against a selected target

Roadstead: Bomber escort job in diving or low level attacks on ships at sea or in harbour

Fighter Roadstead: The same, but without bombers

Rodeo: Fighter offensive sweep without bombers

Rhubarb: Small-scale harassing operations by fighters using cloud cover

Intruder: Night flying squadrons only

As can be seen from the foregoing Fighter Command's new offensive role was vastly different from the defensive actions of 1940.

Circus 44 of 11 July 1941 was a diversionary raid for Circus 45 and their sole charge was one Blenheim of 60 Group as a decoy. The three squadrons in the 12 Group wing were 452, 65, and 266 with two 11 Group wings, Biggin Hill with 72, 92 and 609 squadrons, and the as yet incomplete Kenley Spitfire Wing of 485 and 602 squadrons.

'There was so much competition to fly on 452's first circus operation that we had to draw lots from a hat,' recalls Fred McCann, one of the unlucky ones.

They crossed the French coast east of Dunkirk at 2.45pm, after refuelling at

West Malling, with 266 Squadron leading at 17,000 feet, 452 the middle squadron at 18,000 feet and 65 top squadron at 19,000 feet. The wing split into fours over Poperinghe as ordered and headed towards Cassel.

Five miles west of Lille at 3pm the action started and Finucane reported:

> The squadron was flying in fours line astern and I was leading starboard section. I was looking behind when I saw ack-ack fire. Immediately above AA fire there were eight e/a.[9] They dived down to attack our section and I turned to starboard away from their line of approach. No 1 of attacking aircraft overshot and as he was passing me I cut on the inside of his turn and followed him down. When about 150 yards behind I gave him a short burst of three seconds. The enemy pilot baled out. The type of attack was quarter from astern.

The 452 Squadron intelligence report elaborated:

> This was verified by Sgt Hanigan (Red 3) and P/O Truscott (Blue 3) who saw

UD-W of 452 Squadron with Paddy Finucane about to climb into the cockpit.

[9] Enemy aircraft.

the e/a diving straight down at very high speed to within about 1,000ft of the ground. After this attack nothing further was seen of Sgt Roberts[10] in yellow section. He was not seen to drop out of the circus. After this combat the squadron was split up and made for base over the French coast passing over Gravelines where e/a were seen at a distance over the coast but too far away to be contacted. The AA fire was extremely accurate. The Channel was crossed at about 1,000ft by F/Lt Finucane, P/O Truscott and Sgt Milne who landed at Manston and refuelled at 1525 hours, proceeding to West Malling. Bungey and Douglas with blue and green sections crossed the Channel back at 18,000ft.

Sgt Hanigan (Red 3) lost contact with red section in the Channel haze, came down to 0 feet, missed the Kent coast and forced landed in Essex, out of fuel. The remainder of the squadron landed at West Malling at 15·25 hours. The weather was good except for the Channel haze and some cloud. Squadron's R/T worked perfectly. No cine guns were carried. E/a were camouflaged with frog-like markings in grey and green upon the Italian plan. The only member of 452 Squadron who opened fire was F/Lt B E Finucane DFC (Irish) red leader in the starboard section A Flight commander. He fired 90 rounds and had one stoppage due to a separated case. He claims one Me 109 (type unknown) destroyed.

452 Squadron pilots at Kenley. Left to right 'Pyfo' Dunstan, Ian Milne (in doorway), Keith Chisholm, Jack Elphick, Don Lewis,?, 'Bluey' Truscott, Clive Wawn, Jim Cowan.

[10] Alex Roberts baled out safely with a shot-up tail unit, initially evaded German capture and after some adventures eventually got back to England.

The 11 Group report on Circus 44 stated:

> **Biggin Hill Wing** … rendezvous over Manston at 14·35 hrs … on starting the
> sweep inland the wing saw many black specks coming from inland … Me 109s
> flying in no set formation and trying to get up-sun of Gravelines to intercept our
> formation on its way out. The wing leader therefore decided to go straight to
> Gravelines and as the wing approached the coast again three formations, each of
> 10 Me 109s, suddenly appeared. The first two enemy formations were allowed to
> go by and the third was engaged … in the ensuing dogfights six Me 109s were
> destroyed, two probably destroyed and a further seven damaged. One pilot failed
> to return. The wing reports that as it crossed the Channel many pilots observed
> three enemy aircraft behind and shadowing them … and a considerable number
> of enemy aircraft already up over enemy territory when the wing arrived.
>
> **Kenley Wing** … 602 Squadron failed to make contact at the rendezvous
> and have nothing to report. … 485 Squadron state that on nearing the coast
> towards Gravelines at 23,000ft they saw six Me 109s at two of which short
> bursts were fired without result. One pilot of this squadron failed to return.
>
> **Summary of casualties:** Enemy 7 destroyed, 2 probably destroyed, 7
> damaged. Our losses 3 pilots missing.
>
> **Conclusions:** An entirely satisfactory fighter operation, against which some
> 120 German aircraft took off, thus enabling Circus 45 (with bombers) to take
> place 40 minutes later with maximum surprise and a minimum of interference.

Finucane entered in his logbook: 'July 11 1941. Spitfire II P8038. Pilot self. Sweep
Northern France. 1 hr. 35 m. 1 Me 109 (c). 1st for 452 (RAAF) Sqn.'

On 21 July 452 Squadron was posted at short notice to RAF Kenley, a few miles
south of London, on a plateau at the edge of Kenley common in East Surrey to join
602 and 485 (New Zealand) squadrons forming the new all-Spitfire Kenley Wing.

Flying with 602 (City of Glasgow) Squadron was John Niven from Edinburgh, a
jazz-loving twenty-year-old fledgling who became a veteran of the sweeps within
weeks. Although sharing the same officers' mess with Finucane he hardly knew him
in the early days and was not yet a disciple of his, but was within months to become
one. He sets the scene:

> 'The squadron had been resting after the Battle of Britain at Ayre, where I
> joined it in April 1941, and flew to Kenley on 10 July nearly landing at Biggin
> Hill by mistake. I don't know what we expected the evening we arrived in 11
> Group – maybe a sector recco and a bit of practice flying to settle in. What did
> happen was that we were in the briefing room at 8 am the following morning
> and were over Le Trait with three Stirlings by 10 am.
>
> 'That first trip set a defensive pattern that was to stay with us for the end of the
> year. By the end of July we had done ten shows, seven of which were close escort
> to Stirlings or Blenheims and we accepted our role and its requirements – stick
> with the bombers. The other law of the sweeps was that a No 2's only duty was to
> cover his No 1. This was forcibly brought home to me on 21 July when we
> escorted three Stirlings to Lille. Before the long range tanks appeared Lille was a
> very long way for a Spitfire and one could guarantee a steady plastering all the

way there and back. I was Glyn Ritchie's[11] wingman when we were attacked by 109Es near the target. I pulled up and got a squirt at a pair as they passed the bombers and looking around a couple of seconds later saw a Spitfire going down, my No 1. That was all it took, a couple of seconds.

'There were some real press-on types at Kenley – Bill Crawford-Compton, Reg Grant (Dumbo), Mick Shand, Johnny Checketts of 485 Squadron, and Bluey Truscott and an Irishman called Finucane on 452. Once they'd latched on to a Hun they'd chase them down to the deck and halfway across France if necessary.

'It was not unusual to hear the Kenley controller, Cyril Raymond, over the R/T "Furnace (602), Keyhole (452) and Swanee (602), *Glita* calling – 20-plus bandits angels 20 over St Omer, 30-plus angels 15 from Fecamp, 30-plus angels 30 approaching from Béthune …"

'Significantly the first reaction was very often a calm Irish voice stating, "About 3 o'clock, Blue (Truscott), slightly above, about eight of them, going to pass behind – watch for those others, about twelve – no, fourteen, above them coming toward us." There would be a pause, then a high-pitched Aussie voice, "OK, Paddy, I got them." 452 would then disappear and the first visible sign would be an aircraft plunging out of the sky on fire and the R/T filled with excited Aussie voices and an occasional brassed-off New Zealander telling them, "For Christ's sake shut up and give the rest of us a chance." When Paddy became our CO the reason for the pause was underlined.'

Paddy Finucane congratulates Keith Chisholm; Bob Bungey (far right) looks on, Kenley, Summer 1941.

[11] Flight Lieutenant Ritchie commanded A Flight, the only original prewar member still with the squadron. R/T callsigns picked for brevity and clarity.

The New Zealanders of 485 Squadron certainly had some justification for their irritation because 452's R/T discipline, at least in the early days, left something to be desired.

Niven:

'There is no doubt that if there was any action going the Aussies were in it. The point to make here is not original, but it must have been the experience of every pilot on a sweep at one time or another and it was summed up by our Welsh Flight Sergeant Gwyllim Willis: "I did a 360 degree turn and bloody squadron had gone – in fact bloody sky was bloody empty except for me!" It was an incredible fact that you could be in a milling mass of aircraft occupying many cubic miles of sky, you pulled away and on looking around you were alone – the whole action just moved out of range in a flash. In much the same way an action could develop in the main gaggle and within seconds had moved on out of sight. Conversely the main gaggle could report having seen nothing and yet one squadron or even section could be fighting for its life. In short, nobody had the right to suspect or criticise any other squadron.'

The last sentence of Niven's is a reference to 452's almost immediate success with the Kenley Wing which gave the other two squadrons an inferiority complex.

Niven has an entertaining fund of human stories of Kenley squadrons on the sweeps: 'Bluey Truscott was an enormously thickset red-haired Aussie with a high-pitched voice, especially when he got excited (which was any time he saw a black cross or a yellow nose). There was only one other to beat him, a New Zealander on 485 Squadron whose voice went to a rising squeak until it disappeared into the audio range that only a dog or a bat could perceive. He was a real character who later on, it had been told, parked his old car in Regent Street. Spotting a provost marshal with a couple of MPs and suddenly remembering that his tank was full of 'red' petrol (100 octane from the airfield pumps) he set the car on fire! True? I think it was.'

Bluey Truscott and Keith Chisholm being debriefed by 452's Intelligence Officer, Plt Off Denys Lane Walters. In the background is Gp Capt Thomas Prickman, Kenley's Station Commander.

5

High Scores in August

Approaching the English coast on the way back – F/Lt Finucane, 452 Squadron
'How the hell did I get five aircraft in my section … Christ, break chaps!' This
happened just behind and above us and the Hun was bloody lucky to get away –
from 602 Squadron's *Line book (ie line shoot) compiled by John Niven*

There was now to be no let-up in the sweep offensive and at Kenley Finucane
entered into another successful tour of operational flying. Ray went to a couple
of parties at Kenley: 'Bren was relaxed with the Aussies. They were good-natured,
friendly and exuberant and there was a tremendous team spirit on the squadron.
They were a good outfit and they knew it. Bluey was a good friend of Bren's – he
had a handshake like a steamhammer and there was a lot of ribbing. Jostling at the
bar, Bren said, "They're a great bunch here. You can't teach them enough." '

Finucane was finding time for relaxation and he took Truscott into London some
evenings to meet Jean Woolford, a secretary at the Ministry of Agriculture. Jean
was nineteen and lived next door but one in Castlegate; the two families had known
each other for years and it was natural that Jean and Bren should get on well
together. He usually met her at her Kingsway office and they went on to Oddenino's
restaurant in Regent Street which was a favourite night spot in wartime blacked-out
London for the RAF. There was good food and music; the famous bandleader Lew
Stone made his name at Oddies. Bren never spoke to her about the war; there was
an understanding between them of close friends, and leaves were spent walking in
Kew Gardens, by the river or in Richmond Park.

Wing Commander John Kent, from
Winnipeg, Manitoba, arrived on 2 August
from the Polish Wing at Northolt to take
over as Kenley Wing Leader and the next
day, 3 August, flew with 452 Squadron
on a circus operation to St Omer. 485
Squadron was relatively inexperienced,
but like 452 it was bolstered by some
veterans who knew the form, notably one
of the flight commanders, Hawkeye
Wells. 602 was commanded by a
seasoned air fighter, Al Deere. In early
evening the wing crossed out over
Manston at 18,000 feet, reduced height
over the Channel to 13,000 feet to get
below cloud, went in at Gravelines and
set course for St Omer, where 602,
separated in the cloud over the Channel,

Jean Woolford, Paddy Finucane's fiancée.

rejoined. Near Ambleteuse five Me l09Fs in line astern shadowed the wing at 14,000 feet and three peeled off to attack.

Finucane reported:

'I was red 1 in formation. Ack-Ack fire was encountered after crossing the coast. At 1920 hours approximately warning was given that there were five Me l09s on our starboard side above us. They were flying in line astern and in the opposite direction. They half rolled behind us and made a very spirited attack from our starboard. I led my section away and attacked as e/a crossed our path. My first burst missed and I followed e/a into thin cloud. As I turned away I saw No 2 e/a go down in flames which red 2 (Eccleton) had shot down. I followed No 1 into thin cloud, followed him by his condensation trail, and as we broke cloud I was dead behind at 200 yards. I gave a long burst and he went down in flames. (F/O Humphrey[12] Black 1 confirmed).

Pilots of 452 Squadron in the Summer of 1941. The Spitfire in the background is AB842/UD-X named The Staffordian as it was paid for by the people of Stafford. The Spitfire arrived on 452 Squadron in August 1941was responsible for the destruction of six Me 109s before being shot down on 8 November 1941 when flown by Flt Lt Bluey Truscott who was rescued from the sea off Ramsgate. In the centre is Sgt 'Pyfo' Dunstan whose name can clearly be seen on his Mae West.

[12] Later Marshal of the RAF Sir Andrew Humphrey GCB OBE DFC AFC ADC, Chief of the Air Staff 1974-76 and for three months Chief of the Defence Staff – was with 452 Squadron 19 July – 17 August, 1941.

Soon afterwards I saw eighteen e/a above me milling around in a loose circle obviously following a leader. I had six other aircraft of the squadron behind me so I went into the attack. I picked on the end e/a, gave him a burst and he broke away. I picked out another one preferring to keep with the loose maul[13]. I gave e/a a two-second burst and saw bits fly off his tail unit. He went downwards vertically apparently out of control. I lost sight of him when he disappeared into a cloud layer at 2,000 feet.'

They met more determined fighter opposition on 9 August on Circus 68; five fighter wings escorted five Blenheims of 2 Group to attack the power station at Gosnay, four miles south-west of Béthune.

Kenley's three squadrons shared the target support role with the Tangmere squadrons 610, 616 and 41, led by Wing Commander Douglas Bader flying with 616 Squadron. The escort wing was 71, 222, and 111 squadrons from North Weald; escort cover wing was 403, 603 and 611 squadrons, Hornchurch; and the support wing of 306, 308 and 315 squadrons of the Northolt Wing.

There was 10/10ths cloud over the target and the bombers, unable to pinpoint Gosnay, went to the secondary target at Gravelines with their escorts fighting off Me 109s all the way. 452 led the Kenley Wing at 20,000 feet with 602 above and behind at 22,000 feet and 485 on the left at 27,000 feet. On the way to Gravelines the wing was over St Omer at 1T32 am when Finucane's A Flight went after eight Me 109s which he had quickly seen, closing to 100 yards with a four-second burst which sent the 109 flaming and spinning. Turning after another one, he fired, followed by Ray Thorold- Smith who closed to 50 yards with a full deflection two-second burst; the 109 half rolled and dived vertically with its tail unit shattered.

The action developed into a general dogfight: Keith Chisholm shared in another attack with Thorold-Smith – both seeing the German pilot bale out; then Chisholm joined Finucane and his wingman (Pat Tainton). Finucane turned sharply after Chisholm, seeing the sergeant's fire rip into the grey fuselage, then fired from 250 yards, sending the 109 down well alight from the combined onslaught.

Truscott, steep turning after three 109s, got one of them before it could get him after overshooting from an astern attack and gave it a five-second burst which shattered the tail unit: It was out of control and heading for the ground at a terrific speed,' he reported. Crossing the coast at low level and in heavy AA fire Truscott turned back to machine gun the harbour from 200 feet and was followed by flak for several miles out over the Channel.

The squadron suffered its first shock of casualties, Barry Haydon, Geoff Chapman and Jay O'Byrne, Bungey's wingman, who went down pouring smoke but was later reported a prisoner of war.

Finucane estimated that A Flight had engaged at least thirty Me 109s and 452's intelligence report put the figure at around a hundred taking part in the action.

Thorold-Smith, a quietly spoken fourth year medical student, before flying lured him into the RAAF, added to his combat report:

[13] Finucane was using a rugby term, meaning where the main action is.

'Due to F/Lt Finucane's successful leading, the starboard section attacked
with great tactical advantage and the section was not at any time broken up.'

Most of the other RAF wings had been in action and total claims for Circus 68 were
eleven Me 109s destroyed, seven probables and five damaged for the loss of five
pilots. 485 Squadron missed most of the action and 602 claimed one probable and
one damaged.

One of the other missing pilots was the Tangmere Wing Leader Douglas Bader
who baled out south of Le Touquet from 24,000 feet.

Arch Stuart got lost in cloud near St Omer on the 11th and came out of it over
Le Touquet airfield. He went down in a machine gun beat-up from nought feet.
McCann's diary for 12 August noted:

> Archie flashed over the aerodrome and saw a few targets, turned and made
> another pass – they were ready for him this time and opened up with the lot.
> Arch swears he will never make more than one pass at a ground target again!

The squadron began re-equipping with the new cannon-firing Spitfire Mk VBs.
McCann's diary:

> They were lined up by the duty pilot's watch office. Bungey demanded first
> pick and I followed hoping to learn from him how to choose an aircraft. He
> walked along the line of Spits and then said I'll have that one – the numbers
> add up to twenty and that's my lucky number![14]

Finucane's method was just as haphazard. He picked Spitfire AB852 because it had
the individual code letter W – and W was the first Spitfire he flew operationally,
and crash-landed, at Manston a year ago. From then on he flew the W for luck on all
future aircraft, and with the shamrock it became his individual Spitfire markings.
Although there is no direct evidence that Finucane attached any mystical symbolism
to the shamrock, he got Pownall to paint it on before flying AB852 on operations.

The success of Circus 68 had boosted 452's morale further and there were times
when Finucane did some beating up of the airfield. This was a phase which did not
last long, but the A Flight commander was known to come in with the motor full on
at nought feet over dispersal and go up into a series of tight climbing rolls after a
pass over the airfield. He was a good aerobatic pilot, fully master of his machine as
McCann recalls: 'We loved beating up anything although it was frowned upon by
the brass.' McCann's particular beat-up patch was the home of a family called
Brown that he knew on Woldingham Hill, which was practically in the Kenley
circuit, and they used to come out and wave; once he was so low that they wrote to
Fred complaining he'd blown the crocuses flat in their garden!

Don Lewis was coming home in bad weather when the controller warned him
that Kenley was about to be fogbound, saying, 'The door is closing' – Don called
back, 'Well put your bloody foot in it, I'll be ten minutes yet.' In the evenings they
piled into Lewis's old car, or Arch Stuart's even older Austin Seven, and went to
Croydon. Returning one night Lewis tried to drive into an air raid shelter mistaking

---

[14] Confirmed by 452's log, Bungey's VB had the serial number AB857.

it for the garage – the engine went in but Don stayed out, with a broken arm.

Finucane kept the flight together on and off duty. 'Is there room in that glass for a small whiskey?' he asked the barman and receiving an affirmative said, 'Then fill it up with beer.' McCann tried the same thing having a drink with Bill Crawford-Compton of 485 Squadron at The George, Croydon, but the barman was too quick for him: 'I drank it while Bill regarded me with amazement and the barman smugly.' Finucane knew the value of seeing they got relaxation. One night Eric Schrader and another pilot came into the room McCann shared with Jack Emery in the Red House, just outside Kenley's main gates. They switched on the light and shouted at the sleeping Emery, 'Break, Jack, there's a Hun on your tail.' Emery groaned, drew his knees up and showed great strain as the two jokers withdrew ashamed.

The Greyhouse, Croydon, and The Tudor Rose, Old Coulsdon, were two of 452's favourite pubs and Finucane always went with them, rounding up the sergeants as well, but going easy on the beer himself.

Finucane's sense of humour sometimes slipped. There was a record he disliked, 'Victory Roll' sung by Deanna Durbin, which was only played at dispersal, notably by Truscott, especially to annoy him. Grim-faced he strode into dispersal hearing the strains coming from the hut window after a sweep, snatched it from the gramophone and smashed it. Raife Cowan thought 'Waltzing in the Clouds' was unlucky, so they played that one often as well!

Bungey did not fly on 16 August and Finucane led the squadron. It was a Saturday and a very full day – three sweeps. The first, takeoff at 7 25 am, was to St Omer on Circus 73. Finucane reported:

> As we were leaving the coast near Gravelines 8-10 e/a attacked 485 Squadron. I climbed to cut off further attacks and saw 1 Me 109E half roll towards the ground. I took a quick burst from 250-300 yards and half rolled after him. I quickly overhauled him and gave a 2-second burst from 100 yards. Bits flew off e/a and he went into a spin. I broke off combat at 5,000ft. E/a was last seen by me at 3,000ft still in a spin and going down vertically, Black 1 (P/O Truscott) confirms this. He saw e/a at 1,000ft still spinning and considers it was impossible to pull out. The e/a was too low for him to attack without his a/c hitting the water.

After an early lunch 452, 602 and 485 were off again at midday on Circus 74, again to St Omer, but 452 made no claims.

Circus 75 – St Omer again – was an early evening take-off at 5.45pm. Kenley was the escort wing, covered above by the Biggin Hill Wing, with the Tangmere and Northolt squadrons as target support wings and forward support by Hornchurch. Eight Me 109s came at 452 at 9,000ft fifteen miles NE of Boulogne and Finucane led the Australians in a diving attack, firing a three-second burst from 75 yards at a Me 109 which went down pouring white smoke and flames. Finucane closed almost to collision when his reflector gunsight developed a fault – he estimated the range at ten yards – and blasted the tail from another one which plunged down without fore and aft control.

His wingman Pat Tainton sent another one down burning furiously and Finucane saw it hit the ground. Chisholm got two more. Arch Stuart got one, seeing it spiral into the ground; it was confirmed by Truscott who almost collided with Finucane as he pumped cannon and machine gun fire into a 109 which he saw crash into a field. The whole circus claimed ten destroyed, and 452 had got seven of them. Both 602 and 485 squadrons had seen the action but had nothing to report.

The pace continued throughout August. On Circus 81 to the power station at Gosnay on the 19th Kenley were escort cover wing to the Tangmere squadrons escorting six 2 Group Blenheims, with target support wings from Northolt and Hornchurch and Biggin Hill as rear support wing.

Fred McCann had personal reasons for remembering August:

'During August I flew twelve sweeps – all as Arse End Charlie, the last man in the formation. Twice when I was No 2 to Bungey it was like a holiday! The end man, No 4 in a flight, was the one who got shot at. The men in front did the shooting. We flew in three sections of four:

Douglas	Bungey	Finucane
Green 1	Blue 1	Red 1
Green 2	Blue 2	Red 2
Black 1	White 1	Yellow 1
Black 2	White 2	Yellow 2

'Each Spitfire in a section of two flew 250 yards apart; Yellow 2 was 7 50 yards behind Finucane. This, for AE Charlie, was a hell of a gap. Bungey insisted on it and said that if Yellow 2 was attacked he should be covered by Red 1 who would break into the attack and be in range to fire at the leading attacker providing the warning was early enough. Meantime, Red 2 and Yellow 1 were supposed to follow around after Red 1 – what a hope for Yellow 2 calmly waiting his turn to break while a Hun blasts away at him. We lost a lot of arse-enders who generally were the most junior pilots. I reckoned I was the most shot at bloke on the squadron but was too dumb to complain, or too junior.

'One thing it taught me – no Hun would shoot me down from behind provided I saw him before he opened fire; turn into the attack and he can't get enough deflection. The trouble with this is that most aircraft were shot down from behind and never saw the one that did it.

'We took off in threes, Blue 1 (Bungey) leading with Blue 2 and White 2, next Red 1 (Finucane) and Red 2 and Yellow 2, then Green 1 (Douglas) and Green 2 with Black 2, and last White 1, Yellow 1 and Black 1. This was the order so that section and flight leaders could lead in take-off. We changed to battle formation as we crossed the English coast, a manoeuvre worked out by Bungey that brought howls of laughter from other squadrons.'

Finucane got two more 109s on Circus 81 off Calais at 1110 am and left both his victims shovelling out smoke like a furnace at very low level over the Channel where they had little hope of pulling out. The dogfights started at 18,000 feet and were fought down to 4,000 feet and in the first he got in three bursts of two, three and one second from 200 yards, claiming it as destroyed, and in the second got in a four-second burst from 600 closing to 150 yards. Truscott shot a section of wing from another 109 and it went down vertically with equally no hope of recovery. Two more original members of 452 were lost, Bill Eccleton and Dick Gazzard.

Sholto Douglas, Stanley Bruce (the Australian High Commissioner) and Air Vice-Marshal Frank McNamara VC, from RAAF (Overseas) HQ, London, visited the squadron on 21 August as they began to attract wider notice.

McCann's diary:

Sholto Douglas congratulated the squadron on its offensive spirit and said, 'I'll keep sending my fighters over there again and again. Whenever the weather permits we'll go to the enemy and fight him until he quits.' Jack Emery turned to me and said quietly, 'We'll go over early to Fighter Command and breathe on the windows so he'll think the weather is duff.'

The next day, 22 August, Finucane got a Bar to the DFC with a citation which said he had led his flight with great dash, determination and courage … 'Flight Lieutenant Finucane has been largely responsible for the fine fighting spirit of the unit.'

The next big actions for 452 Squadron were on 26 and 27 August. Fred McCann recalls:

'The 26 August sweep was a real mix up. The bombers did not turn up and the fighters went on to see if anything else turned up. Something turned up all right-dozens of Huns. We were engaged almost immediately we stuck our noses over the French coast. We were split up and I found myself following Paddy and Pat Tainton.

'Ground control called us home but Paddy said: "We are being attacked from all sides and can't break off." Above were dozens of 109s which attacked in fours and sixes simultaneously from all over the place. I was following one Hun at one time and another was following me with Chis behind trying to knock him down without shooting me.

'Paddy called, "Keep climbing and turning, chaps – keep together – climb and turn." The 109 on my tail saw Chis and broke away. I had a shot at my Hun and he broke away – all the time this was going on Paddy was circling higher above us and directing us, calling out to certain aircraft to break from an attack

Paddy Finucane Summer 1941.

Paddy Finucane wearing pre-war flying suit.

and others to close up: "Reform on me, Keyhole squadron. I'm circling and rocking my wings." Arch Stuart was then the centre of attention from some Huns and called for assistance, said he was "very busy". Arch shot down a Hun and after that we reformed and withdrew under constant attack.

'After we landed Paddy hustled into dispersal waving an ops order. The same show was on again at dawn next morning. Same team, same briefing.

'Dawn shows were shockers. We were woken at about 4·30am, staggered down to dispersal for a short briefing, cup of tea, cigarette which tasted like straw, put on our kit and went out to the aircraft… '

Circus 85 on 27 August was to St Omer/Longuenesse airfields. Three Blenheims of 139 Squadron, 2 Group, were thirty minutes early over the rendezvous at Rye, Sussex, and finding no fighter escort sheered off home. As a result a powerful formation of four fighter wings with nothing to escort went into France without them, but the Messerschmitt 109s reacted in force as the Spitfires flew their allotted roles: Northolt Wing (escort), Kenley Wing (escort cover), Tangmere and Biggin Hill wings (target support).

This was a memorable Wednesday morning. Kenley were over Rye at 6·43am at 13,000 feet in a clear sky and 452 climbed over the Channel to 18,000 feet crossing the French coast at Ambleteuse at 7·12am.

McCann's 27 August diary:

> Got chased all over France, Dunkerque and the Channel today by hordes of 109s. Paddy saved my hide – flak terrific – Paddy got 1, Smith got 1 and I hit one. Recommended for commission with Chis, Bardie, Raife and Archie.
>
> We took off in the early light. Once more the bombers failed to rendezvous and we again flew in without them to St Omer – a popular spot! We flew into the face of the rising sun, blind spot in front, and that's where the Huns had the advantage. We got a bit of flak as we crossed the French coast with some straight dotted lines of red flak among them to show the Huns where we were. We went on for a few minutes – just long enough to get nicely in the trap and then I saw four 109s belting down on our tail. I called a warning, "Keyhole squadron break right" – then realised my R/T was u/s. We had been on radio silence until then, or so I thought! I got a snapshot at their last kite and he broke downwards – those 109s could roll over in a flash – then as I continued my turn tracer fairly sheeted over my cockpit.
>
> 'They had been in front of us – in the sun. I finished a 360 degree turn and had a look for the rest of our blokes – they were gone! I rolled inward and aileron turned – straightened up and had another quick look – saw a gaggle heading towards England and started to dive to bring myself under them. They turned towards me – 109s. I was attacked again from the sun – turn again – nothing – dive and aileron turn from 28,000 feet down to 10,000 feet level and in a turn – four of the bastards after me, turn dive, aileron turn, right to the deck – hedge hop – more tracer, turn, straighten, turn, straighten – every time I turned into them they peeled away and I got a little distance ahead; a beach with a ship high and dry – now they caught me and as I turned from one the other fired. I remember tensing as I expected to feel the shots – then I was right on the drink turning hard left and watching over my right shoulder as I out- turned him.
>
> 'Suddenly he moved sideways through the air and I saw strikes all over the cockpit and rear fuselage – down he went and Paddy whizzed past followed by Smithy. I completed my turn, taking a shot at another Hun as I did so, couldn't wait to see the result and turned out to sea again. Paddy and Smithy went past again and I turned after them – more 109s in the offing – we turned out to sea and headed for home. I was worried about fuel. Paddy and Smithy were well ahead of me. I flew so low that the water appeared to curve away under my

nose. Another attack, another break then I set out for England again, by now well behind Paddy and Smithy. The coastal guns opened up, the sea was a mass of splashes and spouts around and ahead of me and black bursts spotted the air in front. They hated to see me go – one more Hun attacked, red tracer floated past and he couldn't get down to me – then I was clear -throttle back and float home; over the white cliffs, they looked good, and back to Kenley. A few kites had already landed and I climbed shakily out of the cockpit.

'I went into dispersal and Paddy was there sitting by the stove. He said:

' "Pull up a chair and sit down, Mac – you look cold."

'I told him I was glad he had shot the 109 off my tail and he then told me the whole squadron was split up in the first attack and he and Smithy ('Throttle') were diving for the coast when they saw me having a rough time of it. Paddy dived on the leading 109 and Smithy took on the second one, putting themselves at a disadvantage to get me out of trouble. They were all firing at the kite ahead – five or six in a line, all firing except me, the leader. I filled in a combat report confirming Paddy's Hun. Paddy saw Smithy's go in.

'We went to breakfast. Jack Elphick hadn't returned. After breakfast Raife Cowan and myself were walking back to dispersal and had just passed the site of a bombed hangar – now used by the Coldstreams on airfield defence and guard duty (much screaming and ferocious crashing of boots) when Elphick flew over and landed. He had landed at Lympne short of fuel. To hell with dawn shows!'

This had been a high speed line astern tail chase low over the water – McCann followed by two 109s, Finucane, another 109 and Thorold-Smith – and things happened so fast that Thorold-Smith at first thought that Finucane had gone into the sea instead of the 109 he shot off his tail, and went back to search for him with a few of 485 Squadron and was relieved to join up with him a few minutes later. Back at Kenley Smithy had not claimed for it but Finucane later reported that as he broke upwards and away… 'I saw over my shoulder a Me 109 going into the sea… from the relevant positions of the three Spitfires it is inevitable that this was the Me 109 shot down by yellow 1 (Thorold-Smith). Yellow 1 then joined up with me a few miles off Dover.'

In his own combat report Finucane stated:

I picked out the leader and gave him two short bursts. Yellow 1 again warned me of a Me 109 behind me. I did a steep turn and lost yellow 1 and the e/a. Black 2 (Sgt McCann) who was being attacked saw e/a go over on its back about 30ft above the sea and says it was impossible for it to recover from this position.

The 11 Group report on Circus 85 said that not less than fifty enemy fighters were in the air. Denys Lane Walters, 452's intelligence officer, in his report to 11 Group said … 'I have no hesitation in claiming a further Me 109 destroyed by P/O Thorold-Smith, this after a very lengthy and thorough and lengthy post mortem … this amends the score to four Me 109s this day by this squadron.' Finucane's earlier victory was also at low level and the Me 109 went into the Channel after he hit it with cannon, Thorold-Smith's going the same way.

At the end of the month Finucane's score for August was nine destroyed and two probables, and 452 Squadron was the highest scoring squadron in Fighter Command with 22 destroyed and nine probables.[15] 452 had toppled the Polish squadrons at Northolt from their high-scoring perch in one bound; 303 Squadron with 33 destroyed headed the Fighter Command list in June 1941 followed by 308 squadron (John Kent's former squadron) with 21 destroyed in July. In August the nearest Northolt could get to 452 was 315 Squadron's 17 destroyed.

This was a remarkable achievement after only one month on operations and 11 Group's Intelligence Branch queried, and subsequently cleared, all 452's claims for the month after the squadron's success had given the other two Kenley squadrons an inferiority complex. For August 485 claimed four destroyed, one probable and one damaged and 602 four destroyed, two probable and three damaged.

Finucane was furious about the attempt by 11 Group – as he saw it – to discredit the squadron, as Denys Lane Walters recalls.[16] Events happened with a surprising lack of subtlety when he told the inquiring officer: 'This is one of the flight commanders, you'd better ask him.'

Lane Walters told me:

'Paddy seldom lost his temper but when he did it was hot. He said, "We have enough trouble fighting the enemy without getting shot at by our own side," and ending ... "I'm not going to be queried." He had a lot more to say about it and we sent that officer back to 11 Group with a flea in his ear. I was never called to an official inquiry, neither was anyone else on the squadron.' Lane Walters, a wine merchant before joining the RAF in November 1940, said: 'Paddy was the squadron. He was the man who did the shooting and on landing they all ganged up around him and I always tackled him first the moment he stepped out of his aircraft because, first, he was always in the thick of what happened and, second, because I knew I could get a clear picture from him of the action.

'Some of the others would tell you their life story and you still hadn't got enough details to make out a combat report. Bluey I sometimes had difficulty with. He was keen to get into the spotlight, used to being the kingpin on the football field, and I sometimes checked with other members of the squadron. Paddy was the exact opposite.

'This was The Great Australian Fighter Squadron and it may have been a bit difficult for the press to say that an Irishman was doing most of the work, but the Aussies knew he was and his popularity with them had to be seen to be believed. As I recall it, Squadron Leader Bungey kept in the sidelines while the query was going on.

'Bluey and some of the others spoke of getting Huns – but Paddy never spoke of killing anyone. It was his skill against another man's skill – and his skill won. It was completely impersonal. He never had any personal animosity towards anyone. He was simply shooting them down because they

---

[15] For 452's August scoreboard see Appendix D.

[16] Interview with author.

Paddy Finucane being debriefed by Denys Lane Walters, 452's Intelligence Officer, October 1941.

were the enemy and therefore had to be shot down. All the events are clear in my mind.'

Lane Walters later wrote to Mrs Finucane:

I shall always remember your son's very great personal kindness to me. At a time when people sought to criticise the outstanding success of the squadron and to cast doubts on the veracity of our combat claims Brendan gave me loyal and unselfish backing.

On top of this Lane Walters got a rocket from 11 Group for sending in late Thorold-Smith's combat report for his second claim on 27 August. Lane Walters replied:

'You've just been accusing these blokes of shooting a line and now you are complaining because one of them is too modest to put in a claim.'

Hawkeye Wells, 485 Squadron, had originally complained to Kenley station commander, Group Captain Tom Prickman, but did not initiate the inquiry with 11 Group. Wells, aged twenty-five, the pre-war Auckland and Provincial clay pigeon champion, took his marksmanship into the air and with the same results in 1941, and told Prickman he thought 452 Squadron 'had spots before the eyes'.

Wells said[17]: 'Pilots were complaining how do the Aussies do it when we fly on the same sweeps and have seen nothing. We were in visual contact with other squadrons when 452 reported it was all happening and this could happen occasionally but was very difficult to understand continually' Our morale was getting a bit low and I had a responsibility to correct this, but I didn't really know what to do so I phoned the station commander and asked for an interview. He said he was busy and asked what it was about so I told him there was resentment on 485 over 452's high scores, that I felt he should know about it and that this state of affairs should not be allowed to continue. He replied, "Sour grapes, Wells, sour grapes", and put the phone down.'

The rules on combat claims were tightened up after this and two of 485's own claims were downgraded from destroyed to probably destroyed on 21 September, whereas galling though it probably was for the New Zealanders, all of 452's were cleared as authentic.

The Kenley Wing Leader, John Kent, flying on the same sweeps in the dispute and used to Northolt's high scores, accepted 452's success with equanimity: 'I was not approached about the query and if I had been I would have discounted it. Paddy was a fine officer and fighter pilot who set a good example to his men, fully committed to the scrap as were the Poles who hated the Germans, but Paddy never had the hatred.'[18]

Tom Prickman, a former fighter pilot who had commanded Kenley since May 1940, told me: 'Paddy was very modest about his claims – never a lineshooter. There were a few about but he wasn't one of them. He was alert and thoroughly professional.'[19]

Events for Finucane were now about to take an even more surprising turn. He was totally unprepared for what happened next.

[17] Interview with author.

[18] Interviews with author.

[19] Interview with author.

6

Bader's Successor

Despite press captions 'New Fighter Pilot No 1', 'Bader's Successor', 'Squadron Leader "Ace" Finucane', Paddy has remained his natural modest self and his skill as a fighter pilot has not relaxed -from 452 Squadron's operations record book

August 1941 ended in a blaze of glory and on a sour note. September opened even more strangely. Douglas Bader was already a legend. Finucane read with disbelief at breakfast in the Kenley officers' mess on 5 September Austin's story on the Daily Herald front page linking his name with the famous Tangmere Wing Leader:

Wing Commander Douglas Bader, famous legless fighter pilot, has a successor.

He is Paddy Finucane, of 452 Squadron, otherwise Acting Flight Lieutenant Brendan Finucane, DFC and Bar, 21-year-old Irishman from Dublin and one of the youngest flight commanders in the RAF.

Bader and Finucane appear together in the RAF awards list issued yesterday. They both win a Bar to the DFC, making Bader a DSO and DFC twice over.

But Bader, the greatest fighter leader and fighter tactician that this war has produced so far, is now a prisoner of war.

I say that Finucane is Bader's successor because he has the same qualities which made Wing Commander Malan, top-scoring fighter pilot, say not long ago, 'Bader is the most brilliant of the lot.'

Bader built up his reputation as a leader and tactician when he commanded a Dominion squadron, the Canadian 242, during the battles over London last September.

Finucane leads a flight in another Dominion squadron, the Australian 452. During fighter sweeps over France his squadron has destroyed 22 Messerschmitt 109. Finucane has been responsible for nearly half of them.

Recently his score of German aircraft destroyed has risen rapidly to at least 15.

But as with all great fighter pilots he is not merely an aerial duellist. He knows the trick of manoeuvres so that the rest of his flight have a greater chance of shooting down their enemies.

Not long ago his squadron tackled 100 Messerschmitts over France.

Finucane with three other pilots held off 30 of them for 25 minutes.

Austin, known as 'A B' or 'Sandy' to his friends, was a 37 year old Scot, from Kilmarnock with a high professional standing as a war correspondent and an authoritative and knowledgeable background for writing about fighter operations. As chief press officer at Fighter Command HQ during the Battle of Britain he was directly responsible to Dowding for the command's press releases. After an initial confrontation with Dowding who didn't want pressmen cluttering up his HQ, Austin's integrity won him over to a position of mutual trust and respect, no mean feat considering Dowding's reputation for being 'stuffy'. Austin resigned at the end of

1940 partly in disgust at the way Dowding was treated and partly because he saw that Fighter Command's great role was over and wanted to report the war on all fronts.

What Austin now did with Finucane was put two and two together and make six.

An Air Ministry news bulletin on the sweep of 9 August stated that an 'Irish DFC' had shot down two of the five enemy aircraft claimed by an Australian Spitfire squadron. Another bulletin on 27 August said the Irish DFC had got two more. In between these announcements Bader's loss was stated officially on 12 August in accordance with Air Ministry policy of a three day delay until the fate of shot down flyers was known or guessed at. Then on 4 September came the latest RAF awards list naming Bader and Finucane as recipients of a Bar to the DFC.

Austin had no difficulty with his highly placed contacts at Fighter Command in confirming that the 'Irish DFC' was Finucane, and the fact that he was with an Australian squadron added colour to capture the popular interest.

Austin played a hunch but he was, perhaps intuitively, astoundingly right, as was later proved, although there was little justification for saying so in September 1941.

'Fighter pilot' to the public still meant Churchill's famous Few who had won the Battle of Britain, and the Air Ministry had a curiously ambivalent attitude of wanting good publicity but not naming the men responsible for it. The press releases were anonymous, usually referring to 'a flight lieutenant DFC', 'a Spitfire pilot' or 'sergeant pilot'. One of the exceptions was Bader who was named officially in a lengthy press release on 21 September 1940. How Austin, chief press adviser at Fighter Command, managed to name him is not known but his admiration for Bader in his book *Fighter Command* is made clear.

Thus the success of Finucane and 452 Squadron in August 1941 was a phenomenon that the Air Ministry public relations department initially found difficult to deal with. The ruling on anonymity was eventually rescinded by order of the Air Council in March 1942, but in the meantime there was nothing to prevent newsmen interviewing top pilots, with permission.

A young Irish air battle veteran at the age of twenty was a gift to the publicists and they made the most of it.

They were aided generally in publicising the RAF by Sholto Douglas. Dowding shunned publicity, but Sholto Douglas who succeeded him at Fighter Command thrived on it and was cooperative towards the press. He understood the problems of press relations and knew the value of publicity as part of the war effort. In 1941 Britain and the Commonwealth were still fighting alone in the air war over Europe and needed all the good publicity they could get, to cheer up the civilian population and impress the United States that Britain was winning. Pearl Harbour which was to bring the United States into the war was still three months away.

The two press releases that mentioned the 'Irish DFC' in August were no more than routine bulletins, although they contained some description of the dogfights by Finucane presumably obtained over the phone from him by the 11 Group press officer who was alerted by reports on the Group H teleprinter from Kenley of the terrific fights 452 Squadron was having.

They were, however, probably responsible for the following entry which appeared in Fighter Command's operations record book for 29 August:

Established Ace – October 1941.

The public relations section at this headquarters will be instructed that whenever any news is forwarded to Air Ministry for publication containing specific reference to Australian squadrons or personnel, a note is to be added requesting that the information be conveyed to the Australian Air Liaison section at the same time as it is released to the press.

Copies of combat reports were also requested to be sent to the liaison office at RAAF (Overseas) Headquarters at Kodak House, Kingsway, London. The publicity-conscious Sholto Douglas was happy to agree.

Thus it can be seen how events contrived to ensure that Finucane's achievements and those of Bluey Truscott and the whole of 452 Squadron got the widest possible publicity. And this, in fact, when it did happen – almost immediately following Austin's story – took them all by surprise. Truscott became a national hero in his own country as Australian papers took up the lead of the British press – and Finucane himself became as well known in Australia as he was to the British public from then on.

By inspired guesswork or professional flair, Austin[20] had done a good job in promoting Finucane by mentioning him with Bader who since 1940 had become one of the great legendary figures of the RAF. By doing so he ensured people sat up and took notice with the old journalistic ploy of names make news. Other newspapers had been playing the same name game – and having fun in the process – with other selected aces flying on the sweeps, notably with Sailor Malan, leader of the Biggin Hill wing.

On 6 July 1941 the *Daily Express* ran a headline 'Malan's 34th Air Victory' and said he was Britain's foremost fighter ace. On 7 July the *Manchester Guardian* headline was 'RAF's Leading Ace' over another Malan story which said his score was a new record of 35. The *Evening Standard* of 8 July had a story 'Malan Gets Bar to DSO' which said his score was 35, and on 9 July the *Express* came back with the headline 'No 1 Pilot Has Medal Doubles' – a reference to the fact that Malan now had two DFCs and two DSOs and was the first pilot to get this combination of awards in this war. In a diary piece on 7 July the *Express* compared Malan with Bader as they were both aged thirty, 'an old man age for a fighter pilot', the familiar ploy of using names but with more justification.

Flying decorations apart, Malan, a tough South African who commanded 74 Squadron with outstanding success before becoming the Biggin wing leader, was, in fact, the RAF's No 1 fighter pilot in terms of aircraft shot down. On Fighter Command's list of men with more than twelve victories he was at the top in July 1941 with a score of 32. The list was for internal use only and not available to the press. Second on the list was Bob Stanford Tuck, with 27 victories, and third was Ginger Lacey with 25. Bader was seventh on the list with 20.

Finucane was not on the list in July but he was in August with 14 victories. By September 1941 Bader's score was $22\frac{1}{2}$ (two from August) and he was fifth on the list while Finucane had jumped from 23rd place in August to eighth in September with 14 victories. Al Deere (602 Squadron) was fourteenth with 17 victories.

---

[20] Austin was a frontline reporter. Chosen to represent the whole of the British press to cover the Dieppe landings in 1942, he went in with Lovat's Commandos and became nationally famous. In the Italian campaign he covered the Salerno landings and was killed on 28 September 1943 in the battle for Naples.

So Finucane wasn't the No 1 pilot in September 1941. Malan was. But Malan was rested from operations by 2 August, the same day that John Kent (fortieth on the list with 13 victories) took over as Kenley Wing Leader, and did not fly operationally again for another eighteen months as other pilots made their mark on the Fighter Command scoreboard.

Twenty-third on the September list was James Rankin, the Scots commander of Biggin Hill's 92 Squadron, with 16 victories. Within twelve days in August he shot down six, two in flames in one minute, and under his leadership 92 Squadron claimed 53 destroyed since February. The *Daily Express* later in the year under the heading 'DFC Sweep Leader Wins DSO' named Rankin as 'the *true successor* to Bader in Fighter Command ... '

By now the bemused British newspaper-reading public must have been wondering who *was* the leading fighter ace, the RAF's No 1 pilot, especially as the *News Chronicle* on 25 September further complicated it by naming Finucane as only the third man to win two Bars to the DFC (one of the others was Stanford Tuck), under the headline 'Britain's No 1 Fighter Pilot Thrice wins DFC.'

There was nothing new in high scores by individual pilots and ace squadrons, notable among them the Polish squadrons flying with the RAF which, as previously stated, 452 Squadron ousted from the top place in August. All those on the list had won their spurs in 1940 and now passed on their knowledge – as Finucane did with 452 – to the newly trained men employed on the sweeps in 1941.

Such men were the nucleus who formed the backbone of Fighter Command in 1941. They were a tough cadre of battle-hardened pilots who had been through the Battle of Britain and were fitted by ability, temperament and experience to fill the flight and squadron commander posts on the squadrons in 1941 to carry the air war on to Northern France on the sweeps. At Kenley they were typified by seasoned and respected leaders like Al Deere and Hawkeye Wells, and Finucane who was younger by several years than either of them and in a slightly different category in that he was a late starter but more than made up for it when chance gave him the opportunity to mould the fledgling 452 into a fighting unit and lead by example in August.

By far the most famous of them all at this time, however, was Bader, known to the public through the press and throughout Fighter Command via the grapevine on the fighter airfields. In September 1941 while Finucane read that he was the successor to this legendary figure, Bader knew nothing about it and was making the first of a series of courageous escape bids from German captivity, and only later heard of Finucane on his return to this country in 1945.[21]

Bader took command at Tangmere on 19 March 1941, just three weeks after 65 Squadron went to Kirton, and Finucane thus only narrowly missed flying under his overall command. Had he done so the reaction between the two men, worlds apart in most respects would, to say the least, have been interesting. Unlike Bader, whose natural flying ability delighted his Cranwell instructors, Finucane's apparent lack of it was a continual headache to his instructors at Montrose. Bader won a flying scholarship leading to a permanent commission. Finucane barely scraped through to a short service commission. Bader's unique fight to get back into the RAF after the loss

---

[21] Letter to the author.

of his legs in a flying accident is too well known to need repetition, or bear comparison with Finucane ten years his junior and of a different generation and background.

The 'RAF Gets New No 1 Fighter Pilot' headline was journalistic hyperbole, no matter how well-intentioned it might be, and Austin's story had several serious flaws and inconsistencies, but from now on the publicity was inseparable from Finucane and could not be discounted, much as he disliked it. Apart from his newly-won DFCs and ability and reputation for getting among the stuff and shooting it down no comparison was feasible. Finucane was well aware of it.

While he was coping with the fact that it had made him a reluctant national air hero, life went on as usual at Kenley with some ribbing about it from Truscott and the others. He had flown two sweeps on 2 September, one to Ostend escorting three Blenheims when Don Willis and Arch Stuart both shot down Me 109s, and the second to Béthune at a high level 30,000 feet. On the 4th they went to St Omer, again at 30,000 feet; then air operations were curbed by bad weather from the 5th.

They were on what the official records called 'a bad weather state' for the next week. On the 7th Jim Hanigan and Ken Williams, one of the new replacement sergeants, were killed in a mid-air collision practising dogfights over Kenley. With Hanigan's loss, one of the old guard, it was forcibly brought home that the original founder members of 452 were thinning out.

Fog in the mornings and hot hazy weather with poor flying visibility in the afternoons continued to ground the Kenley squadrons.

Finucane decided to take seven days' leave. Everything had taken him completely by surprise, the continuous action of August, the query, and now the publicity. He was tired and feeling a reaction.

During August he had flown 46·55 hours, mostly operational including a strenuous total of 27 sweeps which was a lot of work for any one pilot. He had flown at the head of A Flight on every sortie, not missing out a day. This was a peak of operational hours he was not to repeat and was even higher than his total for exactly a year ago, August 1940, when he flew continuously from Rochford and Mansion with 65 Squadron and recorded 42·50 Spitfire hours in his logbook. On 11 September Hanigan and Williams were buried in 'airmen's corner' at Whyteleaf Church.

After attending the funerals he went home to Castlegate and had an unwelcome taste of instant fame. Everyone in Richmond now knew who he was. Adding to the family's congratulations the neighbours called in, and he went to the Brentford aero accessories firm, where Mr Finucane was now office manager, to be presented with a mantel clock subscribed for by employees. He went to watch a Twickenham rugby match with his father and was recognised by the directors who insisted he shared their box. At a Richmond cinema with his younger brother Kevin he was embarrassed at being recognised by the audience.

To cap it all, Bluey phoned excitedly on 15 September to say that a signal at Kenley from 11 Group announced the award of a second Bar to his DFC, and that Leigh-Mallory had added his personal congratulations. He had fought with marked success and destroyed fifteen hostile aircraft, said the citation and added … 'His ability and courage have been reflected in the high standard of morale and fighting spirit of his unit.'

Aware at Richmond of the beginning of public adulation, and not thinking too much of it, Finucane returned to Kenley on 18 September. Being back with the squadron, Bluey and the rest, was like a tonic.

The day was marred, however, by the loss of two more original members of 452 on Circus 99 to Rouen, Don Willis and Arch Stuart, although Truscott, Douglas and Chisholm each shot down and destroyed Me 109s. After the peace and quiet of Richmond and the tree-lined leafy seclusion of Castlegate it was back to the realities of the air war.

7

Circus 100B

Refreshed by the seven days' leave Finucane now wanted to get back on the sweeps as quickly as possible. He did not have to wait long.

Saturday 20 September 1941 dawned cloudy but the weathermen forecast fine weather by the afternoon, and on this premise Leigh- Mallory signed the Form D giving operational instructions to set in motion the whole complicated procedure of fighter operations for that day. By early morning before the mist had cleared from the airfields the teleprinters at 11 Group HQ, Uxbridge, began chattering out the details to be picked up by the teleprinters in the orderly rooms at 2 and 5 Bomber Groups, 12 Fighter Group, and six fighter airfields in Leigh-Mallory's own 11 Group to launch the biggest combined fighter-escort sweep yet mounted over Northern France.

It was a maximum effort. A three-pronged attack with three circus operations in one, involving seven complete fighter wings of 23 squadrons comprising about 270 Spitfires with a mixed bag of 18 Blenheim and Hampden medium bombers, each of the three circuses timed to cross the French coast simultaneously but at different points and head for different targets. It was ambitious and daring and it was hoped that by splitting the attack the German radar would not know which way to turn or the fighter controllers where to direct the Me 109s.

As the teleprinted Form D began spilling out in reams of paper at Kenley the scale of the attack became obvious. There were the usual Form D details of co-ordinated take-off times, rendezvous times and heights, times for crossing the French coast and where, heights and roles for the respective wings.

The line-up was Circus 100A target Hazebrouck marshalling yards with the Hornchurch, North Weald and 12 Group wings; Circus 100C target Rouen shipyard with the Tangmere and Northolt wing; and Circus 100B, target Abbeville marshalling yard, which included the Kenley Wing.

Kenley had the escort cover role which was the best job – Finucane disliked the close escort which restricted fighter action and therefore lost them the initiative – and they were above the close escort squadrons on this one.

The battle order for Circus 100B was:

Escort cover wing:	452, 602 and 485 squadrons
Escort wing:	72, 609 and 92 squadrons (Biggin Hill) and 607 Squadron (Debden)
Bombers:	5 Hampdens from 5 Group

The duty officer at Kenley ripped off the teleprinted Form D from the machine and immediately phoned the station commander, Tom Prickman, and the wing leader John Kent at breakfast in the officers' mess.

The weather was clearing as the met men had predicted, but in 452's dispersal hut it was as smoky as ever from tobacco and the small round stove in the centre of the crew room, flue pipe jutting through the roof, as Fred McCann recalls: 'Lockers at one end for flying kit, pilots relaxing in the centre, and the flight commanders' offices at the other end, posters on the walls warning "Beware of the Hun in the sun". There were eternal games of Monopoly, pontoon and poker and music from a wind-up gramophone and a radio. Pilots were playing cards, reading, dozing by the stove or outside poking around among the aircraft. Naafi or YMCA van with tea and cakes – four pence for a cuppa and cake – very welcome! From outside ripping and banging noises from gun testing at the butts and engines being run up (engines running up work us for readiness in the mornings).

'Paddy was in his office sorting papers, Smithy reading, the gramophone playing a recording of "The Last Rose of Summer" sung by Frances Langford, the beautiful voice and melody contending with the sounds from outside.

'The 'phone rang – Paddy answered and emerging from his office said, "Show on, chaps. CO will be here in five minutes, briefing in twenty minutes, Abbeville marshalling yards this time, escorting five Hampdens. Chis – [22] you're my No 2. Ian and Jack, yellow 1 and 2, Don and Paul, white 1 and 2. Chis – tell Chiefy[23] we want the aircraft ready for take-off at 14·50 hours and let me know about serviceability ... Where's me 'at?" (an Australian phrase borrowed from the late Andy Costello). Having located his cap ... "I'm going to the briefing room for a minute."

'A bustle of activity—pilots wandered out to tell their groundcrews. The CO came in – "Everyone wanted for briefing in ten minutes." 'Around to the wing briefing room, in came the other squadron, 602, a few jokes, the air blue with cigarette smoke and then Bungey came in and the station commander, Group Captain Prickman, – "Sit down, chaps" as everyone rose to attention.'

John Kent has been called to London that day so Bungey was acting wing leader.

'Bungey – "Here's the drill – the marshalling yard at Abbeville is the target and we'll be escorting Hampdens at 20,000 feet. 485 from Redhill will rendezvous with us over base at 14-50 – rendezvous with the bombers over Rye at 15·11 hours – crossing in at St Valery and at the target at about 15·41 hours. Biggin Hill and one squadron from Debden are the close escort – the weather? Here's the weather man" – (groans) – "and a briefing on our weather. You might get some ground haze over France but perfect visibility over the target."

'Special comments by squadron commanders and flight commanders – "Any questions? ... No – well, good luck." – "Happy hunting (from the Group Captain) Wish I could go with you" (inevitable comment).

'Back to dispersal to get flying kit ready. Last cigarette, get packet of French and German money from the intelligence officer, empty pockets, clean goggles, go out to the aircraft and get strapped in.' 'Everything OK, Firth?' The usual 'All OK, Sir' from Firth and Moore. His groundcrew as ever kept the aircraft on the top line. Firth helped him clip on the parachute pack. Finucane climbed into the cockpit of UD-W and Firth moved onto the wing to help him strap on the Sutton harness. As usual he felt a taut feeling in the pit of the stomach before take-off but this would soon go, and he felt a lot better for having the peace and quiet of home life at Richmond the previous week. Now there was nothing to do but concentrate on the flight ahead, all the preparations worked out to the last detail. Moore had connected the starter battery

---

[22] Sergeant Chisholm, Sergeant Milne, Sergeant Elphick, Pilot Officer Lewis, Sergeant Makin - A Flight.

[23] Flight Sergeant 'Gary' Cooper, senior NCO i/c A Flight groundcrews.

lead to the engine ignition system. Silence. It was always like this before a sweep, everything went dead quiet on the airfield as the seconds ticked away to zero.

Helmet and goggles on. He watched Bungey's aircraft in the next bay but one. 14·50 hours. The CO's propeller suddenly spun and the harsh sound of the engine broke the hush. This was the start-up signal. A thumbs-up to Jimmy Firth, the engine burst into deafening life, thin streams of smoke from the exhaust stubs, and he brought the throttle back to a tick-over, as Firth and Moore moved to the chock ropes and hauled them away from the wheels.

Firth moved back and mouthed, 'Good luck, sir' against the thunder of sound from Finucane's engine and the others all down the line which had now started up. He had slept at dispersal all night with about half the squadron's other airframe riggers, engine fitters and armourers on 24-hour duty. They had their own hut about fifty yards or so away from the pilots' dispersal hut at the back on the grass behind the blast bays where the ground sloped away on the Kenley escarpment to Whyteleaf Hill.

Firth and Moore stood back and watched as the aircraft moved out singly from the blast bays and into line along the perimeter road to the left for take-off from the main runway. The groundcrews had been up since before first light, untethering the Spitfires from their retaining ropes on iron rings embedded deep in the concrete, warming up the engines, supervising the petrol bowsers topping up with fuel, polishing the Perspex canopies, Speedy Moore with the cowlings off and generally fussing around UD-W, and giving the shamrock an extra polish for luck.

Bungey's aircraft was in front, followed by Finucane and his No 2 Sergeant Chisholm, then Douglas with B Flight's green and black sections of Raife Cowan, Pyfo Dunstan, Bluey Truscott and Bardie Wawn, following on yellow and white sections of A Flight. It was a complicated take-off order but worked out so that the CO and flight commanders could lead in getting airborne.

Finucane turned right at the runway threshold and waited for Bungey's section to go — then into line followed by Chisholm and Milne. Brakes on, final checks, advance the throttle, UD-W trembled with the full-throated roar of the Spitfire VB's 1,585hp Rolls-Royce Merlin, brakes off, then he was rolling keeping straight with plenty of rudder to counter the powerful pull of the propeller torque which tried to swing the aircraft to the right until they gained flying speed.

Denys Lane Walters, standing outside the now deserted dispersal hut, watched them take off in sections of three and climb away over Kenley Common and then went back inside to phone the ops room controller that they were all away on time. He had been the assistant Intelligence officer on 151 Squadron before posting to 452 but had never known anything like this before. During August he was the hardest worked IO in Fighter Command.

He came outside again to watch them forming up over the airfield and never ceased to marvel at the awesome sight of the Kenley Wing setting off on a sweep. 485 were over on time from Redhill and the New Zealanders formated with 602 who followed 452 in take-off order – thirty-six Spitfires in three separate squadron formations but in a cohesive Fighting unit, all flying in sections of four line astern. The sound of thirty-six engines beating downwards seemed to be absorbed by the ground.

Circus 100B, 20 September 1941 – Keith Chisholm, Ian Milne, Paddy Finucane.

The wing set course and headed out over Caterham for the rendezvous on the Sussex coast.

When they got back his job would be just beginning. Immediately they landed 11 Group and HQ, Fighter Command would want details. First a preliminary combat report giving time and place, number of aircraft, times, our casualties, enemy casualties, teleprinted through for each pilot's claim. This was to be followed – within three hours – by a composite combat report to Group HQ and repeated to Command HQ by teleprinter outlining briefly the engagement with times, heights and course of RAF fighters and the enemy and tactics used, names and nationalities of pilots making claims. There was a lot of technical detail to be included in the written reports (not later than five days afterwards) including gunsight range and span settings, deflection shooting, calling for specialised knowledge which only the fighter pilot had. Fighter Command was asking a lot of its squadron IOs.

Keith Chisholm and Ian Milne get airborne after Paddy Finucane, 452 Squadron, Summer 1941.

Lane Walters originally wanted to be an air gunner but was rejected because he was too tall for a rear turret. Strange to think that only a few years ago he was in charge of Fortnum and Mason's wine department in London.

The Biggin Hill Wing met the Hampdens at 14,000 feet over Rye and stepped up its squadrons at 16,000 feet and 19,000 feet with the Kenley Wing coming in at 20,000 feet and similarly stepped up in its squadrons according to the plan at briefing. Trouble started almost immediately they crossed the coast at St Valéry.

They were about five miles NW of Abbeville when Finucane saw twelve Me 109s cross from left to right a thousand feet above and were tackled by 602 Squadron; then it was 452's turn. Finucane broke away to fire – and miss – at a 109, then he rejoined the squadron, when the same thing happened again and there was a rush of aircraft from the left. This time he was weaving and was ready for a Me

109F in front of him at 150 yards and which had apparently not seen him. Warning Chisholm to watch his tail, he closed to 75 yards with a one-second burst of cannon which must have hit the engine or fuel tank because it immediately blew up – 'Me 109 went to pieces,' he reported.

Within seconds the sky was littered with the smoke trails of wrecked and burning aircraft – Finucane flew through the fireball of the one he had just hit – and the debris fluttered to the French countryside, peaceful below in the mid-afternoon sunshine, as 452 Squadron again, as so often in the past, was heavily embroiled. Not all the wrecks were Messerschmitts. Ian Milne of Finucane's A Flight had to bale out in a hurry, and two of 602's sergeant pilots went down with their aircraft – no one saw how or when.

Things were happening in a flash and Finucane, still shadowed by Chisholm, found they were on their own; a minute or so later he was grateful the chunky, tenacious sergeant from Sydney was still with him. He climbed back from 10,000 feet trying to locate the rest of 452 or at least some other friendly aircraft and in a series of steep turns, watching all sections of the sky, saw a 109 steeply banked for a quarter astern attack on Chisholm, who was following to the letter the order not to lose the No 1. Intent on covering his leader Chisholm neglected his own tail and Finucane's shouted R/T warning alerted him into a fast break on the other wingtip. The 109 was committed to the attack, overshot, and Finucane waited for him to go past then … 'I whistled on to his tail by rolling on the turn' and giving a llA second burst of cannon, seeing strikes on the wing root and engine. It lurched and went down with a white plume of escaping coolant from a shattered radiator staining the sky. He followed it down for about 1,500 feet and saw flames erupt as it continued down.

While Finucane was closing in for the kill, intent on the target, another Me 109 was turning in towards him from the left. At the last minute the 109 for some reason decided against the attack and the pilot broke away to the right which gave Chisholm, still right behind Finucane and sizing up the 109's tactics and wondering what it was going to do, the chance. In Chisholm's words in his combat report… 'this gave me a perfect quarter head-on attack with a plain view of the e/a.' Profiting from the German pilot's mistake Chisholm needed a burst of only half a second at a range of 50 to 75 yards which caught the 109 in the middle of the fuselage and it immediately blew up in a shower of debris and oily black smoke.

It was a good fighting partnership which proved the value of two fighter pilots who both knew what they were doing forming the pair as a fighting unit, effective in co-ordinated attack and at the same time giving mutual protection.

Chisholm had got close enough – and remained cool enough – to observe the Messerschmitt's unusual markings, 'duck egg blue spinner and under cowling and two crosses on each wing edged in red', which he entered in his combat report on the action.

Like all the highly successful fighter pilots Finucane was an opportunist, firing on the instant, and Chisholm had profited by his example flying closely in formation and seeing how he did it.

Incredibly, 602 Squadron reported 'few engagements' and 485 saw only one Me 109 which Hawkeye Wells fired at ineffectively, although there was clear visibility over France with some ground haze.

The Biggin Hill Wing went on practically unmolested to Abbeville where the Hampdens bombed from 14,000 feet.

Circus 100B was unusual in that there was no flak about, either over the coast or the target. This was an all-fighter action – with 452 getting most of it.

The squadron was being fought every mile of the way to the target. Truscott got a Me 109 and saw it go into the ground and shortly afterwards shot another one into the Channel on the way back. Pyfo (Pull Your Finger Out) Dunstan, one of 452's new sergeants, finding himself alone and on the wrong end of two attacking 109s, fired on a climbing turn and got one of them, also over the Channel. Jack Elphick got two damaged.

Finucane dived for the coast and took on the last one of a formation of Me 109Fs which was lagging, and it took violent evasive action which he followed firing from 150 to 200 yards with cannon and machine guns. He saw strikes and pieces fly off and it went down vertically … 'it was evident that fore and after control had been shot away. I came down to 12,000 feet and left e/a several hundred feet below me. E/a was spinning and I lost sight of him about 500 feet.' It clearly had no hope of pulling out before going into the Channel.

Finucane and Chisholm got back at 6.25pm – Firth and Moore looked up as they went over and heard the whistle from the open gun ports indicating they had fired – and Finucane immediately congratulated the sergeant on a good show. It had been a good example of a section of two working together and Finucane made it clear he thought highly of Chisholm as a wingman.

Group Captain Prickman came over personally to congratulate Finucane on his score of three destroyed in one afternoon, and 452's total tally of seven destroyed. Prickman had been in the ops room following the course of Circus 100B by the relayed R/T conversations and rushed back to dispersal immediately they landed, already knowing that 452 had a successful afternoon. He recalls discussing the results of sweeps with Finucane at the mess during evenings.

The press photographers were waiting. They had already got some pre-sweep shots, including Finucane's UD-W leading his section of three, Chisholm and Milne, with wheels retracting on take-off just above the runway at the start of Circus 100B. Now they superbly recorded the bustle around 452's dispersal site when the squadron landed with the early evening shadows lengthening on the concrete in front of the dispersal blast bays.

Bob Bungey was first over to give Paddy a helping hand out of the cockpit and offer his congratulations, as Speedy Moore clambered on the wing and the armourers were already whipping off the wing gun panels for inspection … this was recorded by the photographers in a fine series showing a fighter squadron returning from a sweep. Already alerted by the previous Bader/Finucane publicity the photographers homed in on Finucane — and the fact confirmed when he landed that he had just shot down another three was a bonus for the pressmen. They made the most of it and did a good job … most of the pilots crowding around Finucane … Bob Bungey in dark glasses now standing a bit to one side, keeping a lower profile, and letting the young aces get the spotlight. … Finucane clapping his wingman 'young Chis' on the shoulder … Finucane in roll-neck sweater, hat off, cigarette,

*Sgt Keith Chisholm of 452 Squadron relates one of his many combats with 452 Squadron to
Paddy. He claimed 5 German fighters plus another two shared and one damaged before
being shot down and taken POW 12 October 1941. Far right is Wg Cdr Johnny Kent, the
Kenley Wing Leader.*

Mae West over one shoulder, candidly and with a lack of stiff RAF formality on the
part of a beaming Tom Prickman, extending his hand to meet the group captain's
congratulatory handshake ... Denys Lane Walters going around and asking
questions for the combat reports ... a thoughtful Truscott and Chisholm giving their
versions to Lane Walters ... Wing Commander Kent, back from London, and
looking dog-tired, standing to one side ...

All this and more was recorded by the photographers in a remarkable series of
un-posed pictures which told explicitly more of the men in a fighter squadron at war
than the press bulletins could. The strain, the tension, the excitement – it was all
there on film. The great value of these photographs is that Finucane and the others
were too pre-occupied with the results of Circus 100B to notice the cameramen who
therefore captured the scene at 452's dispersal exactly as it happened.

As well as to the British press the pictures also went to Australian newspapers
where Finucane and Truscott became national heroes overnight. From now on there
was to be no stopping the publicity.

8

'Spitfire Finucane'[24]

The next day, 21 September, Finucane got two more on Circus 101 escorting twelve Blenheims to the power station at Gosnay. They were attacked by 109s on this mid-Sunday afternoon sweep at around 3.25pm before reaching the target and Finucane's first victim was seen by Chisholm (again flying as Red 2) to explode in mid-air and the second went down uncontrollably in flames. Chisholm himself also got one, as did Truscott and Bardie Wawn.

This immediately gave the *Daily Herald* a problem. The Monday morning editions were already rolling with the headline 'Finucane wants 3 for his 21st' – '21 for his 21st birthday' – when news came in of the result of Sunday's sweep and the headline was changed for later editions to 'Finucane wants just one more'. Australian newspapers were more explicit over the next few weeks with a selection of headlines: 'RAAF on top again – Australian squadron bags 6 Nazi planes'; 'Finucane gets 5 in 2 days'; 'It just blew to bits' – this was Chisholm explaining to Finucane his combat – in the *Melbourne Sun;* 'Australians triumph in air' *(Melbourne Herald);* and 'RAAF heroes and Irish leader'. Most of these stories were illustrated with the pictures taken on the day of Circus 100B.

But back with the more down to earth atmosphere at Kenley it was still a continuing success story with 452. Bungey, who again led the wing on 21 September, was awarded the DFC on the 23rd, and Truscott, whose score was now six destroyed was promoted to flight lieutenant on the 29th to command B Flight, replacing Douglas who was posted on getting a squadron of his own.

Douglas actually owned Redhill airfield — he ran a flying school there pre-war — but he kept quiet about this at Kenley, wary of Finucane's and the Australians' sense of humour.

It seemed now that 452 could do no wrong with Truscott joining Finucane as a flight commander and this was confirmed at the end of the month when the Australians were again the top squadron in Fighter Command. Morale was at a peak.

The eighteen destroyed for the month placed 452 at the head of the tabulated scoreboard of fighter squadrons at Command HQ, beating 308 (Polish) Squadron in the Northolt Wing, with sixteen destroyed, into second place. Biggin Hill, the press 'glamour station', previously noted for its high scores, was not in the running. For the first time attention was centring on Kenley because of the Australians' success and it continued to do so while Finucane was there.

Lane Walters left with regret. He was first sent on an 11 Group Intelligence course, promoted to flying officer, then posted to a quieter sector in 10 Group at Predannack, Cornwall, on 1 October.

The next day, 2 October, Finucane got his twenty-first air combat victory on a fighter offensive sweep along the coast from Mardyck to Boulogne with 452 and 485 squadrons from Kenley and the Tangmere Wing of 41, 616 and 129 Squadrons. The five squadrons were briefed to patrol along the coastline looking for anything that was going in the way of fighter action at 22,000 feet where they were bound to attract attention.

---

[24] Daily Mail headline 23 September 1941: 'Spitfire Finucane shoots down 20 Nazis'.

Messerschmitt 109Fs climbed to meet them as they were leaving the coast and 452 Squadron was quickly engaged at a point east of Boulogne where Finucane shot the wing off one of them. Using only one cannon (the starboard one jammed after a few rounds) he closed to 50 yards from astern and saw the 109's left wing break off after falling 500 feet and go on down into the Channel in two pieces. Two more 109s curved in towards him and his wingman, Raife Cowan, who shouted a warning and then shot one of them off his tail, while Finucane damaged one: 'I turned sharply inside him and as he passed fired a long burst. E/a went through my fire, slowly rolled over on his back and started to spin, slowly at first and then faster. I followed him down to 10,000 feet and as I had no ammunition left I turned for base.' At 6,000 feet five more pounced on him and Finucane, unable to reply with empty guns, got away by a series of barrel rolls and steep turns. Back at Kenley he confirmed that he had seen the one Cowan shot off his tail spin into the Channel three miles off the coast.

The Air Ministry officially named him in a press bulletin for the first time, resulting in 'Finucane gets his 21st' headlines the next day. Finucane showed what he thought about the publicity. Jimmy Firth and Speedy Moore got together with Pownall to improve on the shamrock on AB852, resulting in his initials being painted in with Pownall's customary fine brushwork, and on Firth's and Moore's suggestion, twenty-one swastikas circling the emblem. The result was a monogrammed minor work of art. The initials stayed, but the swastikas went.

Finucane considered they were a line-shoot. He was pleasant about it, but ordered the symbols of victory to be erased.

On 3 October Truscott returned from brief leave to take command of B Flight and the next day got the DFC for his six enemy aircraft destroyed since 9 August and Keith Chisholm, also with six destroyed, became the first Australian to win the Distinguished Flying Medal.

On the 4th, Bungey went on ten days' leave to marry an English girl, Sybil Johnson, of Wallingford, Berkshire – leaving Finucane in command of the squadron as senior flight commander.

On the 6th Group Captain Cecil Bouchier took over the Kenley command from Tom Prickman who went to 11 Group as Group Captain Operations, and Norman Ryder replaced John Kent as wing leader. Kent, the Canadian with the RAF, who won the AFC for testing barrage balloon steel cables by flying into them, was now awarded a Bar to his DFC and rested from operational flying as an instructor at 53 OTU. He was twenty-seven and 'at times felt a lot older. One was very conscious of the load at times', he told me. He worried about the young pilots under his command and used to go around the mess at night peering into their rooms to see if they were all right, and found Paddy talking in his sleep. 'I think he had had a basinful', commented Kent. John Kent destroyed two Me 109s flying from Kenley, on 7 and 16 August, but his subsequent resting was not too soon. He noted in his logbook for 22 September on an Amiens sweep: 'Felt very ill and had to return. Nearly hit sea as passed out and spun.' He did not fly again as wing leader.

At a farewell party in the mess ante room Finucane gave a speech on behalf of 452, thanking those departing and wishing good luck to the newcomers.

He was very sorry to see the quietly-spoken Canadian leave Kenley and also

Prickman who was always equable to him and the squadron. Among their affectionate recollections of Kent were the times when he visited their dispersal and shot at tins with a revolver, recalled by Fred McCann, and said that in the air they should get in really close before firing. Kent illustrated the point by telling of one pilot who got in so close he could use a Bowie knife! What a 'line', commented McCann.

There was also the 'line' recorded in 602's linebook; absolutely authentic, says John Niven, and noted at the time:

August 1941. Returning over the channel – unidentified voice:

'Hullo that aircraft in front of me – it's OK I'm right behind you.'

Wingco Johnny Kent's voice: 'Don't be a c … !'

The incidents appealed to Finucane's sense of humour. There was always a lot of laughter when he and Bluey were around. Thus in an atmosphere of humour and drama John Kent left Kenley on 8 October, staying around a further two days to help Norman Ryder settle in. Sholto Douglas ruled in October 1941 that fighter pilots should be rested after 200 hours but Kent, like other top men, ignored that until the limits of physical and mental capacity were reached or officialdom caught up with them.

Finucane recalled discussing the sweeps during evening drinks with Prickman in the pleasant ante-room with its tall windows overlooking flower beds and a tennis court. Prickman was always friendly and approachable and listened carefully to what he, Truscott and the others were saying about the results of the sweeps. He had not spoken to him about the query but knew that if he had he would have had the group captain's friendly but firm backing. All arguments on the wing were forgotten as 485 and 602 joined in with good wishes and anecdotes relating to the top changes in the Kenley administrative and flying command.

National attention continued to focus on 452 outside the boundaries of the airfield where their Spitfires were at constant readiness and the pilots keyed up on flying days when there was a sweep laid on. But after the sweep of 2 October the weather clamped, foggy in the mornings and later mild and misty with no flying visibility. There was a lull in operations and on the 8th, while Kent was packing his kit on his last day at Kenley, 452, with no flying to do except a few local practices, got two more distinguished visitors.

The visitors were Sir Charles McCann, agent-general of South Australia and his opposite number for Queensland. Sir Charles gave 452 a large Australian flag which now flew over the squadron's dispersal hut as a symbol of national prestige, leaving no one in any doubt where the Australians were at Kenley.

In the evening, as the squadron was still on 'stand down' and no prospect of a sweep the next day, Finucane took Truscott and some of the others to London's West End, to Oddenino's restaurant. He had been dating Jean Woolford there in the evenings, and it became a meeting place for 452 in London as well. Bluey hadn't yet got his DFC ribbon up so Paddy gave him one of his old ones – so that he could be properly dressed!

It was while they were at the bar at Oddenino's that evening that Alex Roberts turned up. After being shot down on 11 July he sent a cable to the squadron: 'Nearly got away – interned south of France, inform relatives. Good luck, Alex.' It was wonderful news that he was alive, but after that nothing more was heard. He later did get away and over the Pyrenees with a team of tobacco smugglers in an incredible series of adventures, then to Madrid and Gibraltar. He was the squadron's second battle casualty, after Andy Costello.

McCann recalls: 'A group of us were at the Oddenino's bar when there was the sound of an altercation at the entrance. A scruffy type in odd clothes stood there demanding admission. Paddy looked at him and shouted, "Roberts!" – Alex was home again. The other patrons thought it was poor of us to be entertaining such a tramp – pointed shoes, baggy trousers, scruffy knitted cardigan in awful colours, topped by the smiling face and curly hair of "The Problem Child" – his description after a series of taxying and landing accidents during early training days.'

Finucane, as was usual with him, worried a lot when anyone of the squadron was missing, although he didn't show it too obviously. The bar showed signs of being drunk dry despite what the patrons thought of smartly dressed air force officers and NCOs welcoming their guest who looked as if he'd been living rough for months. In fact, he had. The news travelled fast.

An Australian newspaper report of 10 October with the headline 'Captive Lismore Pilot Walks Out of France' said he had walked across the Pyrenees wearing a dinner jacket and dancing pumps. These were obviously the pointed shoes noted by McCann. Roberts got away from three carloads of German troops by muttering 'Bonjour, messieurs', pretended to be shell-shocked on another occasion and teamed up with a Polish officer. A French girl overheard foreign voices and informed the gendarmes who arrested Roberts and the Pole in a small cafe.

Roberts kept them entertained at the bar with these stories and Finucane filled him in on the success of his old squadron. They went back to Kenley happy after a good evening.

There were still no operations for the next couple of days – rain and mist shrouded the airfield on the 9th and 10th – and the Spitfires stayed in their dispersal blast bays. The pilots hung around, some like Truscott and Chisholm impatient to get going again; Finucane shared their view but was more thoughtful about it and not sorry for the respite although the restlessness was again getting at him. They'd done no operational flying since 2 October and his twenty-first air combat victory, and as he was now acting squadron commander with sole responsibility in Bungey's absence he got them into the air for some practice flying on the 10th when the weather cleared slightly.

Bungey, incidentally, had for some reason kept very quiet about his wedding. The Australian newspaper headline of 8 October 'Squadron Leader Weds Secretly in London' seems to have taken most of 452 by surprise, including Finucane. The newspaper said it was not known until 'today' that he was married at the weekend. 'The bride's name is not known even by Flight-Lieut Finucane who is acting as squadron-leader with Flight-Lieut K. Truscott as his deputy.' The fact that this relatively unimportant snippet made news indicates the high readership value in Australia of anything to do with 452 Squadron. Then on 11 October ...

The tannoy clicked preparatory to an announcement and blared across mist-shrouded Kenley, reaching the squadron dispersals, the officers and sergeants messes, the workshops, hangars, administrative offices:

'I am pleased to tell you that Flight Lieutenant Finucane, 452 Squadron, has been awarded the Distinguished Service Order, and I am sure you will all join me in the congratulations.'

Group Captain Bouchier, the new station commander, decided to make the announcement personally and had already congratulated Finucane who had been called to his office and was, as usual, surprised at getting a decoration.

Finucane felt awkward at the tremendous cheer that went up at 452's dispersal and the terrific pumping handshakes from Truscott and the others who came bounding over with serious or half-serious comments, according to their various temperaments. But there could be no doubting their pride.

He hadn't known Bouchier was going to make the announcement although aware that he did so as a morale-booster for the whole station, letting the clerks and admin orderlies know that they too had a share in the air war, and that the Waaf parachute packers and typists although usually remote from the squadrons had their part in it too.

He was glad that Bouchier spared him the embarrassment of broadcasting the DSO citation as well. It stated that 452 had destroyed forty-two enemy aircraft of which he had personally destroyed fifteen ... and 'The successes achieved are undoubtedly due to this officer's brilliant leadership and example.'

Finucane would have been less than human if he had not acknowledged the DSO as the personal recognition of his ability as a fighter pilot. But this was personal – an inward thing. In the narrow cramped cockpit of the Spitfire he was doing what he always wanted. It was the fighter pilot's world. Not given to too much introspection, for him it was the now, the present and the future, that counted, and the decoration was an outward sign of authority to what he knew was his role – the command of fighter pilots in war. Some of the best days as a fighter squadron commander were still to come.

As if the DSO was a signal for the restart of operations the weather cleared the next day, 12 October, for Circus 107 to bomb the docks at Boulogne with a more extensive fighter cover than usual – nineteen Spitfire squadrons from six fighter wings all drawn from 11 Group.

Some of the newer pilots had been flying with the squadron for the past few weeks – Jack Donald, Jock Ross, Eric Schrader, Jim Anderson, Eric Sly, Frank Coker were among the newer names replacing those lost in action. The older familiar names still with 452 included Chisholm, McCaan, Wawn, Cowen, Jack Emery, Jack Elphick, Thorold-Smith, Makin. The sweeps had taken their toll of the 'originals'. Some of the newer men, Sly, Ross and Schrader, were on Circus 107, bolstered by the veterans who had been through it before.

Kenley and Northolt were target support wings, with the escort wing from Hornchurch, escort cover North Weald wing, high cover Biggin Hill wing, rear support Tangmere wing. The bomber force was larger than usual – 24 Blenheims from 2 Group – for the important target. Boulogne was a heavy flak area, the docks a prime target to be vigorously defended. The Blenheims hit the docks unmolested by the Luftwaffe which was slow to react.

The Messerschmitts came at the target support wings on the way back with 452

Squadron involved and fights developed between Le Touquet and mid-Channel twenty minutes after midday. 452, leading the wing at 20,000 feet, took on the best part of fifty German fighters. Finucane was commanding the squadron and leading A Flight with red section as usual, and it was Truscott at the head of B Flight, who saw them coming – about thirty 109s at first on the right and at the same height; they turned to meet the challenge, just as another twenty came down out of the sun.

Finucane's combat report:

> I was Red 1 in Squadron. As wing approached Le Touquet control warned us of bandits in vicinity. Just before we reached the coast on the homeward run, Green 1 (F/Lt Truscott) warned starboard section of e/a. I turned to starboard and in front of the squadron and saw about 30 Me 109Fs coming down. I was out of range and continued to turn. On the port side of the squadron I ran into about 20 e/a. I picked one, and e/a turned to port. I continued my turn and opened fire with cannon and then mg, closing to about 20 yards. I saw strikes starting at the engine, go into the cockpit, and pieces fly off his tail unit. I straightened up, and saw my No 2, Sgt Chisholm DFM, engaged by four Me 109s and spin down. I followed for about 10,000ft but he was still spinning. By this time my Me 109 had burst into flames and I lost sight of my No 2. I called him several times but got no reply.

Chisholm parachuted from his stricken Spitfire into the Channel and was picked up by a German rescue boat. He was sent to Stalag 8b in Silesia where he met Douglas Bader and was involved in one of Bader's plans to capture and fly a Me 110 to freedom. Chisholm later escaped to Warsaw where he joined the Polish underground on counter-espionage and outwitted the Gestapo for sixteen months by bluff and smart disguises. Chisholm was responsible for British escapees, and, stopped for questioning on the Vistula embankment, he hurled a Gestapo agent into the river with a rugby tackle.

With the net closing he went to Berlin disguised as a German Army corporal – 700 RAF Lancasters raided the city that night – then through Brussels to Paris where he fought with the French resistance until American troops reached the city in 1944.

Roberts' and Chisholm's are 452's two great escape stories; Chisholm's audacity would fill a book on its own.

The day after Chisholm's loss, Monday 13 October, Finucane led the squadron into its highest score for the month despite the fact that Kenley were the escort wing, tied to the bombers with less freedom of action. He destroyed two 109s and damaged another, Truscott got two destroyed, Thorold-Smith one destroyed and one damaged, Jack Emery one destroyed and one damaged, and Eric Schrader claimed a probable which was upgraded to destroyed on 28 October. Schrader, from East Malvern, Melbourne, was flying in the Red 2 position, wingman to Finucane.

The weather had now cleared completely and the squadron took off at 12.35pm with exceptional visibility to the target, the ship lift at Arques. This was Circus 108A, six Blenheims escorted by six fighter wings. After the rendezvous over Manston they met heavy and accurate flak near Gravelines – but no enemy fighters.

Finucane was sure they'd be there. Arques was near the Luftwaffe lair at St

Omer. He was right. As the Blenheims started their bombing run the 109s came at the escort squadrons. Finucane warned the wing leader and got permission to attack. He got in a short burst at one then climbed back to the bombers, intercepting ten 109s: 'I let the first six pass and warned the wing leader of their presence. No 8 of the 10 presented me with a nice shot. I allowed plenty of deflection in a very broad quarter attack.' Finucane fired from 150 down to 70 yards, shot most of the tail unit off and it went down smoking with no control.

Between St Omer and Boulogne Finucane ordered the squadron to break seven times to break up attacks. As they approached the coast at 8,000 feet he got in astern of a 109 with a long burst of cannon: 'I must have killed the pilot because e/a went straight down into the sea about 2-3 miles from Boulogne.' In his third combat Finucane lost flying speed and stalled his aircraft trying to get a bead on a 109 above him, so he only had time to see his machine gun fire rip into its starboard wingtip before he fell out of the fight.

Jack Emery had been flying so close that Finucane's empty shell cases streamed past his cockpit and dented the leading edge of his right wing. Jack Elphick baled out but was picked up by the Dover lifeboat. Truscott fired at the baled-out pilot whose Me 109 he'd just shot down. As they walked towards the dispersal hut Bardie Wawn[25] said: 'You're a bastard, shooting at that Jerry in the parachute.' Truscott just smiled and said: 'He might have gone up tomorrow and shot you down.'

Fred McCann recalls that Truscott had seen a German pilot doing the same thing a few days earlier and vowed he would get the next one. Truscott entered it in his logbook, 'One Hun parachutist shot' but no one on the squadron said 'Good show' and he never mentioned it again.

Air Ministry named Finucane for the second time resulting in 'Finucane gets 2 more out of 20 in sweep' *(Daily Mail)* and 'Sweep pilot gets 23rd' *(Daily Sketch)* with other morning papers mentioning him based on the press communique issued just before midnight on 13 October.

Circus 108A cost the RAF eight pilots missing for total claims of 15 destroyed, four probables and one damaged. Finucane's score was now 24½ and 452 had now reached a total of 51 destroyed.

That night he and Truscott rounded up about ten of the others and they piled into two Standard trucks and headed through the blacked out streets of Croydon to The Greyhound pub to hold a wake for Chisholm. When there were no operations Chisholm used to spend the day complaining about the need to get on with the war unlike most of the others who were glad for a rest. He had left some Derby winnings in his locker with a note that the cash was to be used for a wake if he didn't get back. Bluey bought the first round and said that if young Chis had the hide to turn up alive he wouldn't get his money back, recalls McCann.

At 10.30pm walking back to the Standard vans they were in Katherine Street when Finucane decided to get rid of some of the excess beer drunk that evening – 'Can't hold out any longer' – and vaulted over Croydon town hall's stone balustraded parapet with an eighteen foot drop to the town hall basement on the other side unseen in the dark. He landed awkwardly on his right ankle and felt a

[25] Letter to the author.

stabbing pain, wondering for a second what had happened in the blackness of the basement, then shouted up a warning: 'Don't jump, I've broken my bloody leg.' But too late, Thorold-Smith had already followed and then McCann who hit a rafter which broke his fall on the way down. It was a dismal end to the evening which had been convivial; they were all good company as usual hiding the sadness they felt at Chisholm's loss. The accident effectively dampened any further high spirits.

Tony Seldon, the squadron MO, rushed Finucane to Sutton Emergency Hospital, in Brighton Road, where an x-ray showed a hairline fracture in the right heelbone. It was serious and was to have far reaching consequences. He spent a restless night in the hospital.

9

Fly Higher Next Time!

The orthopaedic surgeon Hubert Wood saw the x-ray the next morning and transferred Finucane to Horton Emergency Services Hospital, Epsom, which dealt with fractures and combat wounds. In view of what Wood told him he would be off the squadron for some time. Drowsy with painkillers, he spent the next two days mostly sleeping from the cumulative effect of the drugs and exhaustion of the past three months.

Ray Finucane, now a sergeant air gunner with 101 Squadron at Oakington, phoned on Thursday 16 October with congratulations for his twenty-first birthday. They kept in touch by phone about once a week but Finucane was in no mood for the usual banter and replied, 'Now I've lost my squadron.'

After a pause he added, 'I'm over that one, Ray. It was absolute balls!' It took Ray a moment or two to realise that he was referring to a fairground palmist in Phoenix Park, Dublin, who predicted in his early teens that he would die by the age of twenty-one. Ray knew he had thought about it because he mentioned it occasionally, but it was now dismissed from the conversation and they went on to talk about news of the family and RAF matters.

Ray recalls: 'He was furious about the accident and felt deeply the separation from 452 Squadron and operational flying. He hated the publicity of the past month and never really learned how to cope with it. He was always surprised when he got his promotions and decorations.'

Finucane found it difficult to be optimistic when Hubert Wood told him, 'This is quite a serious fracture, my boy, you are likely to be off flying for several months.'

Leigh-Mallory wrote:

Dear Finucane, My heartiest congratulations on your very well deserved DSO. I have watched your brilliant exploits with the greatest admiration and hope that your successful career may be a long one. Good luck to you.

Yours sincerely,
T. Leigh-Mallory.

Group Captain Prickman also sent his congratulations. Bungey sent the combat reports for the 13th and asked him to sign them because 11 Group were complaining about the delay!

The telegrams and fan mail letters started flowing in to Horton Hospital. A telegram from Bluey and the squadron said: 'Many happy returns you little Irish … We all hate your guts!' Another from a well wisher said: 'Fly higher next time.' The fan mail, mostly from the public, reached several hundred letters, many from women. One was signed by 'A Land Girl' who gave her address as 'Among the turnips, Wiltshire'; another signed herself as 'A Blonde Admirer, Miss Bette Davis.' Another telegram was from 'Ann – old friend of the Henlow dances – Many congratulations Paddy on DSO'. Birthday cards arrived by the score, some anonymous – 'From a Waaf fan', and others. The letters, without exception, expressed genuine concern.

Finucane wrote home to Castlegate telling them not to worry. The news of the accident had been headlined as also was the news of the DSO although this was not officially announced until 21 October. 'Air Ace Hurt in Fall' and 'Finucane's DSO on 21st Birthday' headlines coincided and made life somewhat difficult for Sister Ethel Turner who was running the ward with responsibility for the distinguished patient. Bluey and the squadron came in but she did not let them stay too long. Nurse Hughes was pictured sewing on the DSO ribbon. Jean Woolford came over with Mr and Mrs Finucane.

Doctors said he wouldn't be at Horton too long and was to be transferred to the RAF Hospital Halton. Dr Tim Culloty, the radiologist who took the x-ray at Sutton, wrote:

I hope you will have a better twenty-first birthday than you anticipated on Tuesday. I also hope that Horton was able to give you a more cheerful verdict than ours, but a fracture like yours has to be treated with respect, otherwise it may cause symptoms at a future date. I also hope that you are enjoying your enforced rest and trust you will soon be shooting them down again. The BBC had asked him to give a broadcast talk and this was planned for 15 October, the eve of his twenty-first birthday. He was clearly unfit to leave the hospital and in no condition to face a microphone only two days after the accident and the talk was now scheduled for a week later, 22 October. Freddie Grisewood announced him anonymously as 'a fighter pilot of the RAF whose name must be familiar to everybody. He is an Irishman. He was 21 last week. He has shot down 24 enemy aircraft plus a half share in another. He has won the DFC with two Bars and the other day was awarded the DSO.

Paddy read from the prepared script he had written some weeks previously, and approved by the Air Ministry, on The World Goes By Home Service programme at 6.45pm on Wednesday, the 22nd:

'I've been on about fifty sweeps and most of my victories have been gained over France. I've got my bag because I've been blessed with a pair of good eyes and have learned to shoot straight. I've not been shot down – touch wood – and I've only once been badly shot up (I hope that doesn't sound Irish!). And for all that I've got a lot to thank the pilots in my section. They are Australians and I've never met a more loyal or gamer crowd of chaps. They've saved my bacon many a time when I've been attacked from behind while concentrating on a Messerschmitt in front of me, and they've followed me through thick and thin. On the ground they're the cheeriest friends a fellow could have. I'm sure that Australia must be a grand country if it's anything like its pilots and after the war I'm going to see it. No, not flying or farming. I like a job with figures – accountancy or auditing.

'Perhaps that doesn't sound much like a fighter pilot. But pilots are perfectly normal people.

'Before going off on a trip I usually have a funny feeling in my stomach but once I'm in my aircraft everything is fine. The brain is working fast and if the enemy is met it seems to work like a clockwork motor. Accepting that, rejecting that, sizing up this, and remembering that. You don't have time to feel anything. But your nerves may be on edge – not from fear but from excitement and the intensity of the mental effort. I have come back from a sweep to find my shirt and tunic wet through with perspiration.

'Our chaps sometimes find that they can't sleep. What happens is this. You come back from a show and find it very hard to remember what happened. Maybe you have a clear impression of three or four incidents, which stand out like illuminated lantern slides in the mind's eye. Perhaps a picture of two Me 109s belting down on your tail from out of the sun and already within firing range. Perhaps another picture of your cannon shells striking at the belly of a Me and the aircraft spraying debris around. But for the life of you, you can't remember what you did. Later, when you have turned in, and sleep is stealing over you, some tiny link in the forgotten chain of events comes back. Instantly you are fully awake and then the whole story of the operation pieces itself together and you lie there, sleep driven away, reliving the combat, congratulating yourself for this thing, blaming yourself for that.

'The reason for this is simply that everything happens so quickly in the air that you crowd a tremendous amount of thinking, action and emotion into a very short space of time, and you suffer afterwards from mental indigestion.

'The other week I was feeling a little jaded. Then my seven days leave came round and I went back bursting with energy. On my first flight after getting back I shot down three Mes in one engagement, and the next day bagged two more. This shows the value of a little rest.

'It's a grand life and I know I'm lucky to be among the squadrons that are carrying out the sweeps.

'The tactical side of the game is quite fascinating. You get to learn for instance how to fly so that all the time you have a view behind you as well as in front. The first necessity in combat is to see the other chap before he sees you, or at least, before he gets the tactical advantage of you. The second is to hit him when you fire. You mightn't get a second chance.

'After a dogfight your section gets split up, and you must get together again or tack on to others. The straggler is easy meat for a bunch of Jerries. Luckily, the chaps in my flight keep with me very well, and we owe a lot to it. On one occasion recently I saw a Me dive on to one of my flight. As I went in after him another Me tailed in behind to attack me, but one of my flight went in after him. Soon half a dozen of us were flying at 400mph in line astern, everybody except the leader firing at the chap in front of him.

'I got my Hun just as my nearest pal got the Hun on my tail and we were then three Spitfires in the lead. When we turned to face the other Me's we found that several others had joined in but as we faced them they turned and fled.

'The nearest I've been to being shot down was when another pilot and I attacked a Ju 88. The bomber went down to sea level so that we could only attack from above in face of the fire of the Ju's rear guns. We put that Ju into the sea all right, but I had to struggle home with my aircraft riddled with bullets and my undercarriage shot away.

'I forced landed without the undercarriage and was none the worse for it. But it wasn't very nice at the time. Well, as I said just now, one day I'm planning to go to Australia and audit books.'

On 14 November Finucane was transferred to Halton, the RAF hospital at Wendover, Buckinghamshire, for a week, with his foot in plaster and a rubber heel to absorb shocks. Father Peter Blake, the RC chaplain on the station, recalls: 'He was excessively proud of being Catholic. I told him I was going to bring Holy Communion to him in the ward but he insisted on walking three-quarters of a mile to the church to attend the mass, despite the crutches and plaster boot. From talks I had with him it was clear that the faith was for him a great sustaining influence and he made it quite plain to me that he was not going to have communion in the ward and that it was important he should be at the church, despite having to hobble there.'

He had another x-ray on the foot and the doctors, he wrote home, were pleased with the result. On 22 November he was sent to the rehabilitation centre for aircrew in the former luxury Palace Hotel, Torquay, set in parkland a mile and a half outside the town. There was a quiet relaxing atmosphere and patients were given physiotherapy.

Paddy Finucane recovering from breaking his ankle in hospital at Torquay during which time he was awarded the DSO, the ribbon of which is being sewn on by Nurse Hughes.

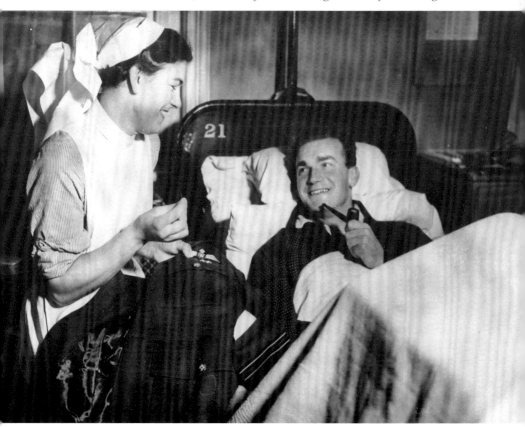

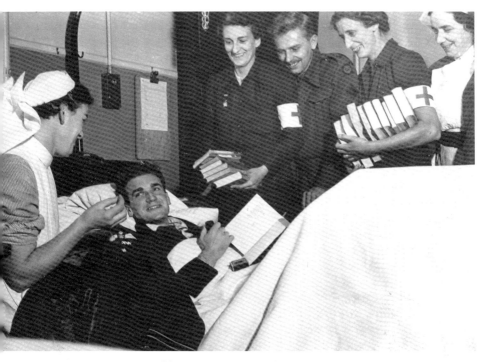

Nurse Hughes sews on Paddy Finucane's DSO ribbon

No sooner had he arrived at Torquay than he had to obtain permission to go to London for the investiture by King George VI of his DSO and two Bars to the DFC on Tuesday, 25 November. It was a family occasion with Mr and Mrs Finucane and Ray who recalls that Paddy told him, outside Buckingham Palace, that he had just heard he was to be given command of a squadron but he did not elaborate on this.

With the onset of winter, shorter days and worsening weather, Sholto Douglas curtailed the circus operations in a letter to his group commanders on 12 October – the day before circumstances curtailed Finucane's further flying on them – ordering them only, as a matter of air offensive policy, to be flown occasionally to keep the threat of attack effective.

The losses that Sholto Douglas had foreseen early in 1941 were now plain. The sweep offensive undertaken by Fighter Command in 1941 had cost 524 fighter aircraft and their pilots either killed or missing. This figure is given in HQ Fighter Command Intelligence Notes and Appreciation No 18 which also gives the command's total claims of enemy aircraft destroyed on the sweeps in 1941 as 731. But Basil Collier in *The Defence of the United Kingdom* states that in 1941 the Germans lost only 154 first-line fighters over France and the Low Countries and 51 of these were not attributed to British action, and a further eleven were lost over the UK. If Collier is correct the RAF, far from winning the air war over Northern France, was losing it at a disastrous rate. The sweeps were, in fact, among the RAF's hardest fought and least rewarding campaigns.

Above: *Investiture for the DSO with his Mother.*

Right: *Flt Lt Finucane at the investiture for his DSO. He sports a broken ankle-an accident jumping over a wall in the blackout. To his left is his brother Ray.*

The sweeps' intention from mid-summer of pinning down the Luftwaffe in Northern France also failed. In June 1941 the fighter component of Luftflotte 3 was reduced by half when Jagdgeschwader (JG) 52 and JG53 were transferred to the eastern front, leaving only JG2 and JG26 in Northern France. The nominal strength of a fighter Geschwader was 125 aircraft (in 1941 these were mostly Messerschmitt 109Fs and Gs) but because of losses and unserviceability JG2 and JG26 never had more than 150 combat ready aircraft available at any time[26] to oppose the Fighter Command sweeps. They reacted with vigour. JG26 was commanded by Major Adolf Galland. He and his men were 1940 veterans of the Battle of Britain and with the advantages now mostly on their side they got their own back for their defeat in the more famous air action of a year ago.

Some of the reasons for this become clear from a memorandum Leigh-Mallory

[26] Letter from General Adolf Galland to the author.

sent to his airfield commanders on 5 September revealing the 11 Group euphoria:

> Since it became possible to start regular offensive sweeps over France on 14 June 1941 we have averaged two to one aircraft destroyed in our favour – without taking into account 'probably destroyed' and 'damaged' aircraft, the fate of which cannot always be known over enemy territory. The average was as much as three to one after the first month of the fighting, but as the German warning system improved and his fighter pilots became more experienced and were reinforced, the fighting has become more even.
>
> It varies tremendously. Sometimes we have good days, such as Saturday August 16, when we destroyed 16 Germans for a loss of three of our own. On the other hand we have had bad days, such as 21 August when we had eleven aircraft missing and only destroyed one German aircraft, though in addition ten 'probables' were accounted for, confirmation being difficult owing to thick cloud.
>
> During August 101 German fighters have been destroyed and 48 probably destroyed for a loss of 74 British fighter pilots. Over the period of these circus operations from 14 June to 3 September 437 German fighters have been destroyed and 182 probably destroyed for the loss of 194 British fighter pilots.

The memorandum claimed that bombers could be escorted 'to the limit of fighter endurance with comparative impunity from fighter attack'… and have thus gained the initiative'… 'experience has shown that we can take in and escort in comparative safety sufficiently powerful forces of bombers to the important industrial objectives in the Lille-Lens-Béthune industrial area to compel the enemy to fight on satisfactory terms and consequently with favourable results.'

This was contradicted by an earlier paragraph:

> The German warning system has improved out of all recognition since these operations commenced. In the earlier operations our formations were generally reported as they crossed the coast and the German fighters were slow to take the air. Now German fighter formations are generally plotted over the St Omer, Lille and Béthune areas as soon as our fighters leave the English coast, and the fact that they are plotted means they have already gained a considerable amount of height. It is therefore more difficult for our formations to surprise the Germans and easier for them to surprise us.

The fact is it was not just 'more difficult' to achieve surprise. It was impossible. Few pilots who flew on the circuses would agree they could escort anything in comparative safety, or that they were ever in a position to fight on satisfactory terms, with comparative impunity or that they had gained the initiative. The Luftwaffe could attack at will. The documentary evidence for this is in the hundreds of combat and intelligence reports and the figures on losses and claims; but mainly in the recollections of the men who flew the sweeps, the circus pilots.

There was another penalty and the close escort squadrons suffered most. Throttled back to under 300mph to stay with the bombers it took vital seconds to accelerate a Spitfire to combat speed – while waiting to be attacked – and this was often enough for gaps to be blasted in the escort screen of fighters.

On the target maps in the fighter wing briefing rooms the routes to the French industrial towns became increasingly familiar. The targets now included power stations, synthetic materials plants and marshalling yards. Some, like Mardyck and Gravelines, were on the coast but the deeper penetrations to Hazebrouck, St Omer, Béthune, Lille and Lens inspired dread in many and a taut feeling in the guts common to all who flew the sweeps. Lille especially. It was at the extreme range of the Spitfire's petrol endurance and was always heavily defended.

Lille was a high priority sweep target. It included a power station, steel and engineering works and a locomotive works. If they had to fight their way out – nearly every time – they were short of fuel and had to break off combat early or risk coming down in the Channel with empty tanks. The dice were heavily loaded.

That Sholto Douglas was never proud of the sweeps is evident from his autobiography. He dismisses the circus operations in fewer than half a dozen pages and puts up a rather weak defence of criticisms by two eminent air force historians, and says that the sweeps in 1941 cost Fighter Command 426 pilots, although his intelligence branch shows nearly a hundred more were lost. Sir Arthur Harris, who became Bomber Command chief, was even briefer on the sweeps in his memoirs: one sentence.

On the Kenley Wing 602 Squadron lost twelve pilots from August to December 1941 and 452 Squadron had fourteen pilots killed or missing from July to November.

Paddy Finucane (centre) with NCO pilots of 452 Squadron. The only other pilot that can be positively identified is Mark Sheldon to Paddy's left who was killed in action with 76 Sqn RAAF 11 Aug 1942 and Jim Cowan to Paddy's right.

In November Finucane was the top scoring pilot on 11 Group's list of aces;[27] Bader was second. The fan mail continued; from the United States Illinois Senator William Finucane wrote: 'All the Finucanes in Chicago arc pulling for you to lead all other flyers in your group.'

After the investiture of his DSO and two DFCs by the King, Finucane stayed on in Richmond for a few days with the family and Jean Woolford. It was especially good to see her again. On the back of his invitation to the investiture he had pencilled – 'Take Jean dancing. I want to see how good she is.' With his foot still in plaster this was postponed.

The train was late getting back to Torquay and it was raining hard, he wrote home in early December. There was a dance on when he arrived but he was too browned off to enjoy it. He started getting fit again in the gym and at golf. For the past three days he had not smoked a cigarette and had only five pipes and it wouldn't be long before he was flying again, adding 'take care of my gongs'.

He did some clay pigeon shooting. No 3 Initial Training Wing was in Torquay with a range on the cliff tops overlooking the town. Trevor Field, the instructor, told me: 'Paddy was ready to listen to our theories about shooting at moving targets and gave his opinion on how our training fitted in with air firing.' Geoffrey Page was another fighter pilot there at this time and he had a drink or two with Finucane. Page told me: 'The RAF made a balls-up in siting the aircrew ITW near us. I had been shot down and badly burned and went into town with another chap who was in plaster. Some of these young chaps from the ITW saw us in a shop and I'll never forget their expressions – "Is this our future?" '

After talking to Trevor Field and trying out the firing range Finucane wrote home: 'I am glad to say that my eye has not lost its quickness nor my hand its steadiness.'

While Finucane was learning to relax again at Torquay the widely read *New Yorker* magazine published an interview with him by A.J. Liebling, a noted columnist, on 6 December – the day before the Japanese attacked at Pearl Harbour and brought the United States into the war.

The restlessness was getting at him again. He went home for Christmas – good to see Jean and the family again – but he was too unsettled to enjoy the festive season. On Boxing Night he appeared on the BBC's *Irish Half Hour* with the

Paddy Finucane clay pigeon shooting.

famous Irish tenor John MacCormack. After the programme he told MacCormack: 'John, I think I would rather be in the air than on it.'

Back to Torquay in early January 1942 and he went down with flu on the 11th. Doctors now passed his foot as perfectly fit and told him he was OK for flying. As soon as the flu cleared up he was going back to Kenley, he told them at Castlegate. But the weeks dragged on as the old year ended on a sour note and the New Year was a continual frustration. 'But for the flu I would be at Kenley now and doing some flying,' he wrote on the 15th.

> I am seeing a medical board tomorrow. The intense inactivity is setting my nerves on edge. If I do not get away from this place soon I will go completely nuts. If I do not get into action soon I will burst a blood vessel. The MO has promised to let me go as soon as possible.

Five days later, 20 January 1942, he wrote:

> I have arrived at Kenley and have settled down to the old way of life. It is great to be back with the chaps from the squadron. The Australians have left Redhill and now work from Kenley. I was posted back to the squadron yesterday as supernumerary. This means I can fly with them again. I am going to stay with them until a new job turns up for me. I spent most of today and yesterday getting square with people who want me to pay for things I have not got. I have been collecting my flying gear together and reading up all the latest reports. Have not been doing any flying due to the unsuitable weather. I will be at Kenley for a while.

On the 28th:

> I have not written to you for a week. I am terribly sorry but I have been very busy. I have been over France with 452 and then posted to a new squadron down here. I have been posted to command this squadron as squadron leader. These events have all happened in a flash and as a result bags of work has

Bluey Truscott, Paddy Finucane, Ray Thorold-Smith. All have the DFC and Paddy Finucane the DSO.

come my way. Not only flying but ground duties as well. This letter must be
very short because I am falling asleep over it. I will write more fully in a day.'

On the 29th:

I have now dug myself well in down here. In fact I am spoiled. I have my
own car which I drive about in a great deal. The mess here is a wizard old
house owned by Benson the watchmaker. My room is large and airy and has
a bathroom attached. The bath is a green one and nice and roomy. Nobody
else is allowed to use it except myself. The food is great and the chef is a
Czech who personally sees you eat all he puts before you. We have creamed
sweets for lunch and supper and are they good.

My job down here is going to be a tough one. Some of the boys are hard
nuts and need cracking. This will be done. This type of work suits me down
to the ground. I wonder who is going to win? The squadron or me. Really,
they are not a bad lot but need careful handling.

I have a great deal of office work and administration to do. This makes
life rather interesting. I have been doing a fair amount of flying and have
already done a few sweeps. These remind me of the fine times we had last
summer. I often wish those days were back again instead of this continual
bad weather.

I have very little news to tell you. All my work has been routine and so
nothing unusual has happened. I am coming home soon for twenty-four
hours leave. Love to the children.

His new command was 602 Squadron and the station commander now was a fellow
Southern Irishman, Victor Beamish.

10

Squadron Commander

Group Captain Francis Victor Beamish DSO and Bar DFC AFC hit Kenley with the impact of a blockbuster.

He was posted as station commander at Kenley from 11 Group HQ on 25 January 1942 and on the same day promoted Finucane to squadron leader and gave him command of 602 (City of Glasgow) Squadron, and promoted and appointed Truscott to command 452 Squadron.[28]

Beamish, from Dunmanway, Cork, was thirty-nine and one of four rugby playing brothers in the RAF. He commanded North Weald fighter station in 1940, was reputed to have followed his squadrons into action and threatened to shoot down anyone he found holding back, tackled a formation of twenty to forty Me 109s on his own in a head-on attack, and had spent most of 1941 at Group HQ as Group Captain Operations continually badgering his chief Leigh-Mallory for a return to an operational command.

Thickset with icy blue eyes and close-cropped head, Beamish was not the sort of man anyone easily argued with; they usually came off second best. Beamish ignored personal instructions from Leigh- Mallory not to fly on operations and headed his new Kenley command in the air whenever he felt like it.

He gathered the pilots of the three squadrons in the Kenley Wing together in the mess and said: 'The reason for this station being here is for you to fly from and shoot down the enemy in large numbers. Every one of you has got to realise you have to get into the fight and to do this properly you have to be totally fit. I don't want to see any of you driving around the airfield in cars. You will walk or go by bicycle. If any of you don't pull your weight and get into the fight you won't be around here too long.' [29]

Finucane got on well with Beamish from the start and took over his new command at Redhill on 26 January. The airfield was in the stockbroker belt of Surrey and the officers' mess was Barnridge, a red brick Victorian mansion set in parkland, owned by the wealthy Benson watchmaking family whose Rolls-Royce was still in the garage, laid up for the duration.

Aware of the strong auxiliary tradition of 602 Squadron and its roots in Glasgow, Finucane immediately took steps to show that he respected the squadron's customs. He revived the squadron badge of the Scottish lion rampant in red on 602's Spitfires in white shields for A Flight and orange for B Flight on the engine cowlings. With the shamrock on his own aircraft he thus flew with national emblems of Ireland and Scotland which may have seemed a bit Irish to some!

John Niven:

'A favourable haunt from Redhill was The Chequers pub near Crawley. Late one night we had just about drunk the bar dry and a group of us were in the gents singing Hun marching songs including the 'Horst Wessell and 'Wir

[28] Bob Bungey was posted to command RAF Shoreham.

[29] Recalled by Max Charlesworth, 602 Squadron.

*In the background is the emblem of KG 30 from one of 602's victims shot down
16 October 1939.*

Paddy Finucane took command of 602 Squadron in Jan 42 when based at Redhill; shortly afterwards the Squadron moved to Kenley.

Fahren Gegen England'. The local bobby was called in and asked us politely to be more patriotic or leave. This, of course only made the boys bellow louder and the law became officious and slung us out. When we got back to the bar Paddy asked us what the hell was going on. Max Charlesworth explained that four uniformed constables and two plain clothes men had ejected us! By the time we got to the van for the trip home it had escalated yet again to two flying squad cars and twelve bobbies with rubber hoses. By the time we got back to camp it was six Bren gun carriers and a battalion of brown jobs with Tommy guns.

'In the morning, too bloody early, Paddy dragged us into the sky to do somewhat bleary formation and some head-splitting tail chases with remarks like "Bring your bloody section in close Yellow 1 – would you like a vector?" (course to steer) – and "At least we all seem to be going in the same direction!" So much for exaggeration and curse all Irish COs!'

Joe Parker, an A Flight mechanic, got the order to paint the shields and the shamrock:

'It was not unusual to have a 'snap' visit in the dispersal rest room which at times was a mixture of a high- class doss house and an untidy reading room. Paddy would appear unheralded and with one sweep of those steely eyes take in every detail and airman present. There was no need for an order from any NCO present to call the lads to attention. Paddy's presence made itself felt and the in-built radar in a flight mechanic's forage cap gave warning that full alertness was called for. A few sharp commands and an observation or two and he would depart to other regions that he felt might benefit from personal inspection. There were never repercussions from these tours of Paddy's. He knew his instructions would be carried out without question.

'He gave and received respect from everyone. His integrity was unquestionable and his concern for and pride in the squadron was readily apparent. He reorganised the Naafi morning break at dispersal points. He had observed the scramble when the cry went out "Naafi up" and was annoyed at the queuing up of the lads after dashing after the tea wagon. He contacted the Naafi manager and got co-operation so that the wagon stopped at convenient points to where the men were working. This ended the undignified melee and was more to the liking of Paddy's tidy mind.'

'The squadron was paraded as per the book, B Flight on the left, A Flight on the right, HQ in the centre when Paddy was introduced to the squadron,' recalls B Flight airman Alex Davis. 'Before he addressed us, in typical Irish form, he told us to break ranks and gather around him informally and he gave a talk which went down very well with the lads.'

Anxious as usual to get some action he was impatient at Redhill as the weather continued non-operational. Heavy snow in January was followed by freezing rain which waterlogged the airfield, then more snow and ice. Along the hedgerows and small trees forming the airfield boundary behind dispersal, the narrow winding road, not much more than a lane leading to Nutfield village, the frost formed intricate patterns of white lace, beautiful to look at, but mostly grounding the Spitfires.

On 12 February the deadlock was broken by the most dramatic British naval-air action of the war; the Channel Dash escape of the German battle fleet, the *Scharnhorst, Gneisenau* and *Prinz Eugen* from Brest to Norway. Beamish took off in a snow shower from Kenley with Robert Finlay Boyd, the wing leader, as his wingman just after ten o'clock and half an hour later was directly over the fleet.

No one knew better than Beamish what was involved or appreciated the situation more. On Christmas Day 1941 as Group Captain Operations at 11 Group he had sent the following signal to all 11 Group airfields:

> Operation Fuller may take place at any time. Until further notice the maximum release for day squadrons is two hours. Sectors on their release days must, until darkness, have their squadrons at two hours recall.

Operation Fuller was the codename for action to be taken against the German fleet's breakout from Brest which was anticipated by British air and naval intelligence since early 1941. It is a strange quirk in Beamish's character that while he was prepared to ignore instructions not to fly on operations he would not break the comparatively minor rule, in this case, of breaking radio silence to warn 11 Group. So it was not until he got back to Kenley just after 11 o'clock that he reported the sighting. Not that it would have made much difference; the British forces were asleep.

Since 0845 hours massive radar plots in the Channel approaching the Dover Straits were being received in the filter rooms at Fighter Command HQ and 11 Group. Dover Naval Command had also received them. It was not until 11.25pm that Leigh-Mallory was recalled from an inspection at Northolt, Bomber and Coastal Commands were informed, and Operation Fuller began. The ill-fated Fleet Air Arm crews of Eugene Esmonde's 825 Squadron were ordered to take off within a quarter of an hour from Manston on their suicide mission in their six antiquated torpedo-carrying Swordfish biplanes against three capital warships, twenty-five destroyers, and numerous E boats. 11 Group promised fighter cover. Only one squadron, 72 Squadron from Biggin Hill, made it in time to see the massacre of the Swordfish.

Within five minutes of Operation Fuller starting, at 11·30am, 602 Squadron at Redhill was ordered off on a Roadstead operation, a strike against shipping. Finucane wasn't told what it was about. He took the call from operations which ordered him to take off immediately to escort some Beauforts. This was cancelled and then another show laid on. The controller was not even sure which squadron he was to escort. Finucane led 602 off and they were halfway to the rendezvous on the Sussex coast when he got the recall signal from Kenley and led the squadron back to Redhill. 602 pilot Max Charlesworth told me: 'We all wondered what ops were playing at. We just thought we were being buggered about.' Finucane got back on to Kenley operations and got nothing out of them; he was told to get lunch and then bring the squadron to readiness.

The squadron's experience was general. The Fighter Command and 11 Group records reveal an incredible mix-up, bungling and what must have approached near-panic in the RAF and Naval high command. Orders were being cancelled and countermanded at a moment's notice without informing the units concerned. Finucane still thought later in the day that he was to escort the Beaufort squadron but this job was later given to 41 Squadron without anyone informing either him or the Beauforts' CO.

Finucane and 602 were sitting down to lunch in Barnridge's oak-panelled dining room when Kenley rang through putting them on fifteen minutes' readiness. Frank Decmar, the Czech chef, recalls Finucane saying: 'Bloody hell! First it was no flying, now it's on again. We are going to finish our lunch first.'

Back at the airfield tension mounted. It was obvious something big was on. Finucane's Waaf driver, Trixie Kay, a fresh complexioned country girl aged twenty-three, heard a loud angry Irish voice over the station tannoy: 'Get back to your kites, men, never mind the bloody Naafi van!' The van drew away. Sergeant Bill Lathey, an A Flight groundcrew NCO, also remembers this, and the reason for it, as the queue broke up like startled rabbits. Trixie recalls he was the only CO to use the tannoy in this way. She was new to the MT section and he was embarrassingly blunt in giving her confidence – 'Get out of first gear' – as she negotiated the narrow country lanes between Barnridge and the airfield. She also recalls his kindness in bringing her cups of tea if she had to be kept waiting outside the mess.

Just before Beamish's Christmas Day signal, at 8.35pm on Christmas Eve the duty air commodore at Fighter Command HQ sent a memo marked 'immediate and secret' to Sholto Douglas:

Admiralty appreciation suggests cruisers may leave Brest at any time. Cruisers may break south or possibly move up Channel. Bomber and Coastal Commands holding appropriate striking forces at readiness. Request your concert with AOCs-in-C concerning fighter protection measures for coastal and bomber forces operating at short range.

However the Beauforts the Kenley Wing was supposed to escort were not at Manston at the arranged time. Wing Commander Tom Gleave, commanding Manston, wrote to 11 Group that three different Beaufort squadrons landed at Manston after waiting for their fighter escorts, unaware of what the target was, and giving extracts from the controller's log to prove it. Just after one o'clock Finucane got the scramble order.

Within three minutes he was in his aircraft and starting up, the propeller blast whipping up puddles of melting snow on the concrete and creating a miniature snowstorm in the slipstream. The Kenley Wing, not finding the Coastal Command Beaufort torpedo bombers over Manston, went out over the Channel alone. Finucane led the squadron down on two armed merchant ships and raked them with cannon and machine gun fire. Further out they went down again at two others thought to be destroyers. Max Charlesworth recalls: 'I flew over the superstructure of a ship into a curtain of flak from all directions and could see it splashing on the water. I got separated from the squadron in the murk, the cloud base was nearly on the water. Still dodging flak, I went home thinking uncharitable thoughts about the Navy – I thought the ships were British, we'd never been told to expect anything that big in the Channel.'

Raife Cowan, still with 452 Squadron, told me: 'We broke cloud at 200 feet and at sea level the ships were a dramatic sight – their astonished comments over the R/T – every ship in the fleet seemed to open fire at us as shrapnel peppered the water and huge spouts from heavier shells churned up the surface. We strafed a destroyer in line astern.'

Back at Redhill the station's log noted that seven of 602's pilots had used their cine-camera guns and the objectives attacked could be clearly seen – the films of Finucane and his wingman Pilot Officer Johnson were particularly good. The whole of 11 Group had been committed to provide fighter cover for bomber and coastal aircraft. 452's log summed up the 'feeling of baffled disappointment among the squadron when it was realised that the German warships had reached safety.'

The Fuller Inquiry opened at the Admiralty, London, headed by Mr Justice Bucknill, with Air Chief Marshal Sir Edgar Ludlow- Hewitt, inspector-general of the RAF, and Vice-Admiral Sir Hugh Binney.

Finucane attended on the fourth day, Thursday, 19 February. He and Bluey went to London together. He told what happened as far as he and 602 Squadron were concerned after Truscott had given his evidence and Ludlow-Hewitt turned to him and asked: 'Have you anything to add to that, Squadron Leader Finucane?'

Finucane: 'Nothing very much, sir, except that my first orders were that I was to take eight Spitfires from my squadron to Le Touquet, with four Hurricane bombers of 6 or 7 Squadrons, proceeding to Le Touquet under 6 or 7 leadership, to attack two transport vessels down there. We got into our kites and we were called back and they said "Take twelve Spitfires and the whole of 6 or 7 squadron, rendezvous Manston or Rye again and go to Le Touquet and attack 25 vessels leaving harbour there."'

Ludlow-Hewitt: 'You were really put on to this roadstead operation in the first place?'

Finucane: 'Yes.'

Ludlow-Hewitt: 'And that was cancelled and then you were put on to the second one?'

Finucane: 'Yes. For the second one we got airborne and were halfway to Rye when we were recalled, and we refuelled and then I was told to have a quick lunch and bring the squadron to readiness. We were back to readiness about half past twelve and I rang up operations asking for some gen and they could not give me any information, and then at five minutes past one I was told to scramble my squadron and to rendezvous with the rest of the wing at Kenley. My squadron was airborne at eight minutes past one. We rendezvoused Kenley at twelve minutes past one and we set course about 23 minutes past one for Manston. I picked up the bombers at Manston. I made it about 41½ minutes past one when we got there. We did a circle of Manston. I saw one of the Spitfire squadrons and the Hurricane bomber squadrons going out to do the job. My impression was that I was still to escort 6 or 7 Squadrons, but my later instructions were to go wherever 452 Squadron went so I went with 452 Squadron. We crossed the English coast about 13·45 plus three minutes, about 13·48, and then we set course and we climbed roughly up the coast.'

Ludlow-Hewitt: 'And then you went with them?'

Finucane: 'Yes, then I went with them. Then we orbited around and made a circle round somewhere near the French coast.'

Ludlow-Hewitt: 'At a height of… ?'

Finucane: 'About ten thousand feet. I looked down through a gap in the clouds and saw two boats on the sea. I think I recognised what they were and I informed Squadron Leader Truscott. We took a look around for enemy aircraft, there were not any in sight and we went down through this gap, heading south, and I took on the destroyer nearest the French coast and Squadron Leader Truscott took on the other one about one hundred yards apart. We beat up those destroyers and we left them smoking.'

Ludlow-Hewitt: 'You were really working with that wing?'

Finucane: 'Working with Squadron Leader Truscott.'

Ludlow-Hewitt: 'At what time was your squadron told to scramble?'

Finucane: 'At five minutes past one.'

Ludlow-Hewitt: 'And you were airborne at 18?'

Finucane: 'Yes.'

Ludlow-Hewitt: 'You did not see anything of any attack made by the Beauforts?'

Finucane: 'No, sir.'

Ludlow-Hewitt: 'And you did not see the big ships?'

Finucane: 'No sir, we only saw the destroyers.'

Ludlow-Hewitt: 'Did you do another sortie that day?'

Finucane: 'No, sir.'

Truscott: 'No, sir.'

Truscott earlier said: … 'We went through the cloud base, the cloud base was about 1,000 feet, and we then picked up the destroyers near the French coast and each squadron attacked a destroyer … Squadron Leader Finucane's squadron attacked one and I led my squadron to attack the other… both ships were smoking and the last couple over them reported no return fire … ' Beamish, one of the most important witnesses, gave his evidence on the first day, and said he and Finlay Boyd were at sea level chasing two Me 109s at full throttle and … 'The next thing we saw was that we were over the fleet.' He and Boyd then beat up an E boat, were chased by more 109s at sea level, were too low to use the R/T, and got back to Kenley at 11·19am. It was 'complete chance' that he and Finlay Boyd found the fleet… 'I thought it was one of the quiet days of the war.' Beamish flew with Finlay Boyd as a section in the subsequent Kenley Wing sortie over the German fleet and told the inquiry that he also went down to strafe a destroyer. Finucane and Truscott shared the general disgust as they left London after the inquiry and returned to Kenley. 602's Spitfires were back there temporarily as bad weather over the past few days had made Redhill completely non-operational again.

The next day, 20 February, low cloud hung over the airfield and Finucane decided to break the monotony by flying a rhubarb operation. This was a two-man patrol and a type of operation flown in bad weather when pilots could seek out targets of opportunity on their own. Niven: '602 had its own selection of swing records – Woody Herman' 'Fort Worth,' 'Jailhouse', 'Too Late', 'Woodchopper Ball'; Glen Miller's 'In the Mood', 'Sunrise Serenade', 'Moonlight Serenade' and so on. There was, however, a 'must' for 602. The last record to be played before take-off on every sweep was Miller's 'Under Blue Canadian Skies' – it was a sort of good luck charm, and at the other end of the superstition scale the playing of Miller's 'Adios' was taboo before a sweep. The boys really believed that if it was played someone would get the chop. This just happened. The Boss getting clobbered sealed it.'

Finucane went into dispersal and said to Dick Lewis: 'Dick, come on, let's see what's happening on the other side.' Lewis, aged twenty-nine, from Kojunup, Western Australia, had put his age down to become a fighter pilot, had just got back from leave and jumped at the chance to get some flying.[30]

Finucane led him off at 10·55am and headed out over Manston and low level across the Channel to Dunkirk where he strafed a small ship and then turned back flying south down the coast. He turned back to meet two aircraft he saw taking off from Mardyck but lost sight of them and dropped down again to sea level.

Two minutes later two aircraft came straight at them. They were Focke-Wulf 190s. This was Finucane's first encounter with Fw 190s and if one of the German pilots had been using cannon instead of just machine guns it could have been his last.

Lewis broke R/T silence: 'Two bogies at nine o'clock.' Finucane acknowledged and turned into them. He had already seen them and did a steep right turn for a full beam attack and saw his fire chew bits off the second one. The German pilots were experienced and flying in close formation. They came in again.

In the Fw 190A the Luftwaffe had a new and more powerful weapon. Its 1,700 hp radial engine gave it a top speed of 418mph, some 50mph faster than the Spitfire VB's R-R Merlin which delivered a top speed of 369mph. The VB was more manoeuvrable and had a tighter turning circle than the 190s, but they had to be caught first.

Lewis recalls: 'They went over the top of us. Paddy then said over the R/T, "Turning right", which we did.' Before Finucane could get into a firing position he saw the enemy pilot's guns firing. The first burst went over the top of him but the

[30] Letter to the author.

second was on target. Six machine gun bullets went into the fuselage, wings and main spar of the Spitfire's tail unit. One bullet sent a piece of fuselage in his right thigh. He radioed Lewis: 'I've been hit. Going home.'

Finucane went down to sea level feeling dizzy from loss of blood. Lewis formated behind and slightly to one side as the Fw 190s made six more astern attacks. Lewis turned into them, followed twice by Finucane who relied on Lewis to warn him when to break. On the last attack they came in from opposite directions. Lewis got one of them on the tail unit and saw it go into the Channel. Finucane also saw it and radioed, 'Good show. Good show.' They were now at mid-Channel and the other 190 gave up.

The weather was bitterly cold and it started snowing. Finucane felt his grip slackening on the controls. The right wing dropped and he was going down. To shock him out of it, Lewis radioed: 'You silly bastard, pick up that right wing.' Finucane replied, 'OK. OK.' Lewis led him down on the main runway at Kenley, he taxied to 452's dispersal, and then lost consciousness.

Sister Ethel Turner was still in charge of B Block at Horton Hospital. She said: 'What, you again!' Finucane grinned faintly. He was not in a mood for banter. The other nurses, Susie Lilley and Grace Clarke, were also still there and fussed around to make him comfortable. The wound was superficial and he was operated on to remove the pieces of fuselage. On 2 March he went home to Castlegate on six days' sick leave.

11

Friday the Thirteenth

Finucane returned to 602 Squadron at Kenley on 10 March. The early spring weather, sunny with clear blue skies and cold winds, freshened the grass and the trees and shrubs behind the dispersal huts were coming into hesitant leaf. The Spitfire VBs thundered in the blast bays on hill throttle as the flight mechanics ran them up for testing. It was a comparatively quiet time. Finucane decided on some entertainment. Niven:

> 'Paddy dragged most of the boys along to the gun alignment bays to take pot shots with our Smith and Wesson 38s. This was great fun and we were popping away when Paddy disappeared in the van and reappeared shortly afterwards with a load of Thompson submachine guns and 303 rifles with tracer and explosive ammo. With the tracers and explosive stuff it was like the entry of the gods into Valhalla. All spectacular hell was let loose and the village of Whyteleaf must have thought the invasion had started. While everyone had a hell of a time blazing away there was not the slightest danger to life or limb – Paddy's presence was enough to discipline the whole affair and even the youngest sprog sergeant showed a complete sense of responsibility under his tolerant eye.
>
> 'Our nervous tension was released after about an hour of this more than it could have been after a dozen boozy parties and we would have swum the Channel and taken on the Huns on the deck. There was, of course, an aftermath, one bloody awful rocket, for it transpired we had shot off most of the Tommy gun ammo in the south of England and even the army was screaming. The Boss took it in his stride, stuck his chin out a bit further and told the powers that be that he'd decided his boys needed this sort of training and what the hell was all the fuss about! And that was that – no further trouble at all.'

The quiet time ended on 13 March with Circus 114 to the marshalling yards at Hazebrouck. Kenley were flying as high cover wing.

Finucane fought an Fw 190 from 23,000 feet down to 8,000 feet at mid-afternoon inland from Cap Gris Nez, gave it a two-second burst of cannon and machine gun fire and saw it crash, confirmed by one of his NCO pilots, Sergeant Paul Green. Climbing back to the dogfight at 20,000 feet, he shared another one with Pilot Officer Johnson, and, after an astern attack

Paddy Finucane showing off his chess skills.

Back from a sortie.

with a one and a half-second burst followed by two shorter bursts, saw it crash near a railway embankment. Eric Bocock nearly collided with the parachute of the baled-out pilot whose Fw 190 he had attacked with cannon from astern.

Fighter Command's loss/claim ratio alarmed Portal, the Chief of the Air Staff, who asked Sholto Douglas for evidence to back the claims for Circus 114; he received extracts from three combat reports which included Finucane's and that of 602's B Flight commander, Bocock.

Portal's letter of 14 March was headed 'personal' and therefore not official:

> In the fighting yesterday we claimed eight German fighters destroyed plus four probables for the loss of six and I see from today's German communique that they claim to have lost nothing.
>
> I do not know how they get away with this in their own air force and I think I may be asked questions about it from that point of view. As you well know I have implicit faith in the genuineness of the claims put forward by your pilots and in the system of confirmation you use, but it would help me if you could obtain for me a report of the actual evidence of the destruction of, say, two or three of the best authenticated German casualties.
>
> I am sure you will take care not to suggest to anyone in the Fighter Command that I have any doubt about their veracity.

Sholto Douglas replied on 16 March:

> I enclose a report by my Group Captain Intelligence giving extracts from the

Paddy Finucane speaking to pilots. The lack of 'Australia' flashes on the uniforms and that Paddy Finucane is a Squadron Ldr would indicate this is 602 Squadron, Kenley, 1942.

combat reports of three pilots who claim to have destroyed German fighters on 13 March.

You will see that, in the first two cases, the enemy aircraft was seen to hit the ground by two pilots; in the third case the enemy pilot baled out and nearly collided with the British pilot who shot him down.

Portal replied on 17 March that the evidence was 'entirely convincing'.

The third evidential combat report enclosed with Sholto Douglas's reply was by Finucane's friend from 65 Squadron days, 'Ski' Drobinski, now a flying officer DFC and with 303 Squadron, Northolt. Drobinski saw his 190 go into the ground, witnessed by a sergeant pilot.

Fighter Command's claims for Circus 114 were later amended to ten destroyed, not eight as Portal stated. As the results of the day's combats had already been sent to the press and the BBC in an Air Ministry bulletin Portal's embarrassment is easy to understand. The press bulletin said:

Fighter Command, for the third time this week, carried out this afternoon a large scale offensive sweep into occupied territory. A small force of bombers was escorted to attack a vital marshalling yard. Many dogfights between our Spitfire squadrons and German fighters took place and, although full details of this operation are not yet complete, it is known that at least eight enemy fighters were destroyed. One wing led by Group Captain Beamish DSO and

'Shooting a line'.

Bar DFC went in over the target ahead of the bombers and swept the area almost clear of the German fighters. Then when the bombers with the fighter escort arrived the greater part of the air fighting was over.

This was the first operation in which Squadron Leader Paddy Finucane DSO DFC and double Bar had taken part in since being wounded a week or two ago. He celebrated his return to the squadron by destroying two Fw 190s.

The total claims made by 602 for that day were four destroyed (Bocock got a second one), John Niven got a probable and John Dennehey and Johnson each claimed a damaged.

The rest of the claims for Circus 114 were: 303 Squadron, two destroyed and one probable; 316 Squadron, one destroyed; 452 Squadron, one destroyed; 72 Squadron one destroyed and one damaged; 401 Squadron, two destroyed and one damaged.

The claims for Circus 114 highlight one of the problems of post-war research. According to the Luftwaffe Quartermaster General's Returns (copies are on microfilm at the Imperial War Museum, London) there were no losses over Northern France that day. The sole casualty recorded is a Me 109F of I/JG 26 which made an emergency landing with thirty per cent battle damage.

The thirteenth of March 1942 was a Friday – unlucky for some, but not, according to their own records, for the Luftwaffe. There is evidence to suggest in RAF records that the claims procedure in Fighter Command, and especially in 11 Group which was still doing most of the fighting as it did in the Battle of Britain, was

being tightened up in 1941 and 1942. Portal must have felt some disquiet to have approached Sholto Douglas on it in the first place. But he asked a 'political' question and he got a political reply. Sholto Douglas showed his disdain for the question mark that Portal had tactfully raised over his command by the shortness of his reply. All this high level correspondence, however, was marked 'personal', thus ensuring it did not go on the official records, a point no doubt kept in mind by both parties. It is only preserved now, at the Public Record Office, Kew, because someone thought to keep a small file of the fighter chief's unofficial correspondence intact.

Finucane, of course, knew nothing about all this high level stuff. He never had any doubt about his claims on Circus 114, or any of the others, and his combat report describing his victories on 13 March are clear and explicit.

He reported that the weather was clear with no cloud and unlimited visibility at 23,000 feet over the target area and on the way back from Hazebrouck when the action started.

> I saw about 10-15 e/a about 2,000ft below and in combat with 452 Squadron. I decided to wait until enemy aircraft had broken off combat with 452 Squadron. I continued to orbit slowly to starboard and when enemy aircraft broke off combat I attacked from the sun. I picked one Fw 190 and we went into a series of steep turns. I took a very few short bursts at him. I sat on his tail until he straightened out. I was about 150 yards behind him and gave a burst of two seconds with cannon and mg. Aircraft did a half roll and went straight into the deck. I broke off combat at 8,000 feet. Red 2 (Sergeant Green) confirmed this.

*Believed to be Sgt Paul Green (+25 Apr 42), Plt Off Sandy Sampson (?),Paddy Finucane 602
Squadron early 1942. However, Sampson joined 602 Squadron after Green was killed in action.*

Finucane had already ordered 602 Squadron to close up on him, already planning
the attack and preparatory to going down on the 190s, circling above in the sun and
waiting to pounce at the right moment to get the enemy at a disadvantage. On the
second combat:

> I saw a Spitfire doing an astern quarter attack from starboard on a Fw 190.
> E/a pulled inside the Spitfire. I hopped on to e/a's tail and closed to 150
> yards. I gave a 1 second burst and then two short bursts. Enemy aircraft did a
> half roll. After 2,000ft enemy aircraft did an aileron turn and started to pull
> out. A thin stream of white smoke came from the aircraft. E/a did not pull
> out but continued to dive at an angle of approximately 30 degrees until it hit
> the deck near a railway embankment.

Finucane also found out an interesting piece of information which he added to his
combat report to help RAF Intelligence: 'I found at 18,000 feet a Spitfire could turn
twice as well as an Fw 190.'

Eric Bocock was also a very wily fighter pilot, as his combat report shows:

> Red leader (Finucane) manoeuvred us into position and then led us down to
> attack... . Enemy aircraft took extraordinary evasive action consisting of a
> series of fast right hand rolls. I held on to him and fired in short bursts ... I
> held him by coarsening my pitch and finally hit him from dead astern at
> about 250 yards with cannon.

Smoke and flames sprouted from the 190 and he saw a large object detach from it...
'I nearly collided with it. As it passed I saw it was the pilot with his parachute just
opening.' Coarsening the pitch of his propeller enabled Bocock to fly slower and
keep the 190 in his sights without overshooting in a high attacking speed – cool
thinking in the heat of combat.

The sweeps had posed a problem for the RAF Intelligence branch. Hits on an enemy aircraft by the Spitfire VB's cannon were unmistakable, often devastating, but as RAF fighters did in the Battle of Britain, some German fighters undoubtedly got back to their bases with severe damage. Much depended on the pilot's degree of observation on the damage. The difficulty now was not so much the problem of duplication, several pilots claiming the same aircraft in the heat of combat, as of establishing whether the 109 or 190 got back to base now that they were over their 'own' territory. The RAF Intelligence people had a big headache, not only at command and group HQ, but at squadron intelligence officer level as well.

For Finucane 13 March was his first day of fighter action in a full scale dogfight – after the inconclusive and unsatisfactory mid-Channel skirmish on 20 February and since the last of the great days with 452 Squadron, in October 1941.

He had lost none of his old skill, despite the long lay-off, and this day had tested it as the Fw 190 framed in his reflector gunsight, with the span setting at 40 feet, wavered 150 yards ahead and then went down as he thumbed the firing button. He had flown with the same old precision, the Spitfire as usual answering to a sure touch on rudder and ailerons to bring the target into line. With the better weather he found his spirits rising.

While he was on sick leave three extremely good men had been posted into the squadron. Flight Lieutenant Bocock was one of them, to command B Flight – and the others were Flight Lieutenant James 'Ginger' Lacey DFM and Bar, and Sergeant Bill Loud, aged twenty-two, from Dorset, son of a butcher, who applied to join the RAF in that trade, but they made him a fighter pilot instead. Loud was a natural fighter pilot. Within two years he was a wing commander with a DSO and two DFCs: 'I remember the first time I flew as Paddy's No 2. It was my third flight. Paddy saw three Fw 190s below, put a wing down and went tearing after them, over on his back and straight down. I had no idea and couldn't keep up and I lost him. Later, Johnny Niven, then a flight commander, called me in and said: "You are no bloody good if you can't keep up with him." Paddy shot down an Fw 190 on that show.

'This introduced me to the hard facts of squadron life. I was just out of flying training when I arrived on 602. At dispersal someone called me into a tiny office. Paddy looked up and said, "You are Loud? I am Finucane. I hope you will be happy with the squadron." That was all, a man who didn't waste time or words. I was awed and impressed by the man and his style. I saw him shoot things down when we thought they were out of range and before we could recognise them as German aircraft. He had wonderful eyesight and was a wonderful shot.[31]

Finucane said to Lacey: 'Hullo, Ginger, call me Paddy, everyone else does. You're taking over A Flight.' Lacey replied: 'Thank you very much, sir. "A" has always been my letter and I won't have to learn a new one. I was in A Flight on 501 Squadron and commanded A Flight at 57 OTU.' Lacey, with a score now of twenty-seven, had been the highest scoring sergeant pilot in the Battle of Britain.

On 14 March Finucane shared in the destruction of a Ju 88 returning from a sweep to Le Havre with John Dennehey and Sergeant Green of red section. Out of ammunition they left at sea level fifteen miles from the coast shot to pieces and with one engine blazing.

[31] Interview with author.

Also on the 14th Truscott, commanding 452 at Redhill, got a Bar to his DFC with a citation stating he was 'a skilful and courageous fighter pilot… has shown a fine fighting spirit… ' and his score of air combat victories was now eleven enemy aircraft destroyed.

On 17 March at Fighter Command HQ, Bendey Priory, Stanmore, Middlesex, Sholto Douglas wrote to his group commanders ordering officially a resumption of the sweep offensive. He wrote that the 1941 offensive was halted in November to conserve fighter resources but that the 'present strategic situation demands a change in this principle.' The German air force on the Russian front was now weaker – particularly in fighters – and one way to help the Russians was to further weaken the Luftwaffe fighter force in the west.

> It had therefore been decided to renew our daylight circus operations over France. The general policy underlying these operations will be to send escorted bombers to attack important objectives with the object of inducing German fighters to accept combat with our own covering fighter forces.

'You will realise,' he told Leigh-Mallory and the AOCs of 10 and 12 Groups, 'that owing to the drain on our fighter resources particularly for overseas, there is still need to avoid heavy wastage due to operations such as those covered by this directive. The difficulty of regulating operations to ensure low wastage rates is realised, but so far as possible these operations should be so planned and conducted that the losses sustained by our fighters are not normally greater than those inflicted on the enemy.'

At the height of the sweep offensive in the summer and autumn of 1941 Fighter Command's punishing losses had caused Sholto Douglas, as is clear from this letter, to call a halt, not entirely because of the weather. That he clearly expected heavy losses again in 1942 is evident from the above paragraph which indicates that he expected the sweeps to break even in terms of results, but might be lucky to do so, and in fact could be on a loser from the word go. Within two months the deeply worried and embattled fighter chief was to produce statistics of claims and losses which confirmed his worst fears as the sweep offensive got under way in the spring and early summer of 1942, and the Spitfire squadrons on his fighter airfields formed up in the same pattern as in 1941 to bait the Luftwaffe over Northern France.

Sholto Douglas's misgivings and disquiet were to be felt at the highest level as his statistics on fighter losses and claims on the circus operations went to the Air Minister Sir Archibald Sinclair and the Prime Minister, Winston Churchill.

It was under these adverse conditions that the skill and extraordinary talent of Squadron Leader Brendan Finucane DSO DFC, officer commanding 602 Squadron in the Kenley Wing, again thrust him to the forefront of the fighter aces but not, as in 1941, again without some controversy.

The 17 March 1942, St Patrick's Day, was also the day that ended the fighting partnership of Finucane and Truscott, and Finucane and 452 Squadron. Truscott was posted to Australia for home defence against the Japanese. He was 'fittingly farewelled' in the bar of the Railway Hotel, Nutfield, Redhill; Thorold-Smith was awarded a DFC and given command of the squadron which was posted from Kenley on the 23rd, and later to Australia. The great days of the Kenley Wing partnership were finally over.

12

Freelance

The right heel was still occasionally causing him trouble and on 19 March Finucane limping slightly with a swollen ankle went to see the squadron MO, 'Doc' Harry Hands, who gave radiant heat treatment, massage and a crepe bandage. Next day the swelling had gone down and it was much improved and he went to a dance that night in the officers' mess, where the slight exercise caused it to swell again.

On the 23rd Finucane chose a new Spitfire VB, serial number BM124, to replace the one, BL584, in which he got shot up on 20 February. He had been mainly flying AD536 since getting back from sick leave. Joe Parker painted on another shamrock and the B Flight shield in orange. Finucane was still particular about the letter W. Because it was a late letter in the alphabet W was in B Flight although he always led with his customary red section in A Flight, as on 452. The shamrock was back in its normal place on BM124 on the main cockpit fairing, an important point. It had been painted in error on the main fuselage tank panel on BL584. With the squadron code letters LO-W was now 'the Boss's kite'.

The squadron was on dawn readiness at 5.35 am on 25 March. Finucane picked up the phone. The Waaf on the switchboard sounded dozy. She'd been up all night on the late shift, what did he expect? After some friendly banter he got the operations controller. At 7.35am A and B Flights were airborne on a practice flight. It was a perfect spring morning.

Max Charlesworth, aged nineteen, a former bank clerk from Leicester flew in A Flight's yellow section. Midway across the English Channel his sense of foreboding increased and he thought, 'Christ, we're going right into France.' His earphones picked

Spitfire Vb BM124, paid for by the Queen & people of Tonga, joined 602 Squadron 16 Mar 42 and became Paddy Finucane's personal plane. He destroyed a Fw 190 on 26 Mar, Bf 109 destroyed, one probable and one probable Fw 190 27 Mar, Fw 190 damaged 4, 10 & 15 April, Fw 190 destroyed 26 April, Fw 190 damaged 28 April, Fw 190 destroyed 17 May, Fw 190 probable on 8 June. On 8 June, he damaged a wingtip landing at Redhill but never flew it again. After a long service, BM124 was struck off charge in April 1946.

up a metallic resonance which usually meant they were being tracked by German radar. 'Kenley operations called us on the R/T and said "What are you doing over there so near the French coast?" Paddy acknowledged: "OK OK, practice flying." ... "Coiner squadron, keep your eyes peeled, chaps." None of us needed any second telling. The Irish tone was cool, clipped and very precise. I didn't doubt he was looking for an unauthorised battle. Since he became CO you knew that if you were flying with him and there was any action about Paddy was sure to find it. Some of the chaps did get a bit worried at times! We very quickly learned he was a daring squadron commander at a time when they were scarce – and it produced exciting results.

'We went right up to the French coast and flew down it at nought feet to the cliffs at Cap Gris Nez – they looked a bit like Beachy Head but they bristled with multiple quick-firing flak, guns and we flew straight through the barrage at sea level. The guns were actually depressed to get at us and the flak was churning the water.'[32]

Charlesworth entered the flight in his logbook: 'Formation. One hour. CO had us east of Mansion and we swept down on the Channel and came in at Dover.' In theatrical shaky handwriting he added: *'Practice flying only!!!??!!'*

Charlesworth gives this portrait: 'Fresh complexioned with piercing blue eyes that always looked straight at you, with a firm boxer's jaw and his head slightly lowered giving the impression he was peering at you. Paddy was a great opportunist in the air. Many times we were in action when other squadrons on the same sweep were not. He was disciplined but also expected his chaps to get at the enemy and was always disgruntled if we came back without seeing anything. There was a reserve about him, and I never saw him lose his temper. But you could sense his tremendous offensive spirit, a sort of restlessness, a religious zeal almost.

'He looked what he was, a dedicated fighter pilot, flying boots battered hat at a slight angle, battledress with a roll-neck pullover, scarf, pipe, hands in pockets strolling around dispersal. I thought he was a bit of a loner. He was reserved but had a built-in self confidence. He was not a glory-seeker but he had his enemies within the Service. If he had a blind spot it was that he always thought everyone else was as press-on as he was.'

Ginger Lacey said: 'Paddy had this habit of initiating pilots by taking them out at low level across the Channel and flying along the cliffs at Gris Nez. He usually left the routine practice flying to his flight commanders. No one ever got hit but by God it frightened them! Paddy didn't believe in chatting, he believed in action not talk. Some who went on the Gris Nez trips muttered, "Christ, never again!" But Paddy's style was not nattering in the crew room and he would simply take them out and say, "Let's go!" He knew they would get a baptism of fire that way. He led by example. Never told anyone, just said, "Let's go." That was his idea of an unofficial flight.

'I never knew anyone who was not on edge and I said to Paddy: "You are going off on edge. You are out of your mind, Paddy, you are an idiot. You are not proving anything." I used to say, "This is not for me, I wouldn't have gone." Paddy replied: "I'll teach the buggers it's not all beer and skittles!"

'He was right in a way because flak guns didn't have one per cent chance of hitting a Spitfire at low level going at 350 knots.

[32] Interview with the author.

'Paddy told me: "This is something they will not learn at an OTU. They are going to be fired at," and I think he told newcomers to the squadron: "We are going to see what this war is all about."

'I thought at the time that he was putting on a front as a squadron commander, going out of his way to make everyone see that he was the boss and was going to prove it – but he didn't need to.

'There was never any doubt about who was in command. We got on very well together, although I think he was wary of me at first but I said, "I am happy to be out of instructing and on to ops again and that's all I'm interested in. You're the CO." I was a pre-war Volunteer Reserve sergeant-pilot while he was a regular officer, and I therefore would expect him to get ahead faster.

'I said: "For Christ's sake, Paddy, come along and have a drink." He would say: "We have to fly tomorrow and I'm not very good when I've had a few." I replied: "Alcohol is a friend of mine, and you don't leave out friends!" But he didn't drink much and dropped out very quickly. His sense of humour never wavered. I would say airily: "You youngsters . … !" and when were were alone "Boy Finucane" but he took it all in good part. It was good fun and lightened squadron life. I liked him and we got on well.'[33]

Whatever Ginger thought, Finucane really *was* a freelancing fighter CO. There was no 'front' about it. If there was no action about he went back looking for it. The flight on 25 March was unauthorised. But he and Group Captain Beamish saw eye to eye.

He had Beamish's tacit approval for the unofficial 'practices' and the group captain looked the other way providing he wasn't told about them first. Permission would have had to be refused. 602's CO obligingly said nothing to Beamish or anyone else about where they were going until they got there.

Finucane stamped a highly individualistic style of leadership and command on 602 Squadron, and his presence and personality as well as its success under his leadership gave a remarkable élan to the squadron. It obviously had something to do with his reputation as a freelancing fighter CO and ability to get among the stuff and shoot it down, but there was a personal quality, a magnetic aura of

Paddy Finucane in pensive mood.

[33] Interview with the author.

invincibility, which no one in contact could fail to sense. The unofficial sweeps disguised as practices may have been a controversial use of command authority and it would be too easy to present Finucane as a loner at odds with authority. But he was not. He was a disciplined officer who set a good example to his men on the ground and in the air. As Lacey noted, there was never any doubt about who was in command. Finucane always had a firm grip on what was going on, closely identified with the squadron and the men he commanded, and had a good working relationship with the station commander, Beamish. He was not the 'rather wild Irishman' that Sholto Douglas later seemed to think he was. But he could be bloody-minded, stubborn and impulsive – and he was not always right.

Apart from Niven, Lacey, Loud, Lewis, Bocock and Charlesworth already mentioned there were some very good flyers on 602 Squadron when Finucane commanded it: John Dennehey, from London, a keen and steady type, had the occasional beer, just got engaged and was well liked, but could be excitable; Roland de la Poype, a Free French officer, naturally known as 'Popeye'; John Niven was a jazz-loving Scotsman from Edinburgh, rapidly building up operational experience and leadership qualities. These were all pilot officers. Among the sergeants were the Welshman Flight Sergeant Gwyllim Willis, Joe Kistruck, Arthur Strudwick, Flight Sergeant Len Thorne and Les Scorer.

Bocock, 'a good type', did ground duties conscientiously, was a good organiser and flew keenly and well. He was posted to 602 from 72 Squadron, the only squadron which provided fighter cover to 825 Squadron's attack on the German fleet on 12 February, had shot down an Fw 190 and seen the hopelessness of the Swordfish biplanes attacking the *Gneisenau*. He was awarded the DFC on 27 March.

Circus 116A[34] was laid on for 26 March. Kenley Wing was flying escort cover to 24 Bostons of 88 and 107 Squadrons attacking the docks at Le Havre, with 41 and 129 Squadrons of the Tangmere Wing as escort. Considering that Le Havre was a long sea crossing and the bomber component was larger than usual the fighter cover – only five squadrons – seems miserly, especially as the aim was actually to destroy the target. The Kenley squadrons left at 3.20pm and refuelled at Tangmere, joined the Tangmere Wing and the Bostons over the airfield. There was high wispy cloud and a slight haze but visibility was good.

The Bostons swung into the target when about five miles seaward and abreast of Le Havre at about 12,000 feet. Me 109s and Fw 190s curved in towards the fighter escorts in individual attacks as the Bostons on their bombing run saw hits on an armed raider and the docks. The bomb bursts were clearly visible in the perfect weather. Finucane's combat report states:

> I was Red 1 leading 602 Squadron. We rendezvoused with bombers and set course for Le Havre. Before reaching target 10- 15 enemy aircraft were seen flying above in pairs and singly. I led 602 Squadron to cover bombers after leaving target and took up positions on starboard side. I saw two enemy aircraft attack four Spitfires from astern. Red 3 (P/O Dennehey) followed me down and we attacked enemy aircraft. E/a turned towards coast and we positioned

[34] 602's log says Circus 116A but the 11 Group report calls this operation Ramrod 17. A ramrod differed from a circus in that the main aim was to destroy the target, not just provide the bombers as bait.

Above and overleaf: *Paddy Finucane watches his Spitfire being re-armed, Kenley, Spring 1942.*

ourselves astern. I gave a one second burst more in hope than in anger, followed by a two seconds burst of cannon. A puff of black smoke came from engine. Enemy aircraft did a nose dive, and went into the drink. I saw three enemy aircraft above and broke off combat. I warned Red 3 P/O Dennehey to watch for splash as enemy aircraft hit the drink. He saw the splash.

His victim was an Fw 190. John Dennehey noted in his logbook: 'Le Havre. 24 Bostons. Dived on 2 190s. CO fired at 500 yards. Went straight in. Enjoyable show.'

Max Charlesworth, Yellow 3, had lost his section as the squadron orbited to the left of Le Havre and joined up with Finucane and his wingman, Colin Tait. Charlesworth saw a Me 109 climbing to reach 602 and it stall turned and attacked red section head-on. Charlesworth fired a three second burst from 500 yards closing to 300 and saw no hits, but Finucane saw it emitting white smoke and Charlesworth claimed it as damaged.

As well as being a successful fighter action 88 and 107 Squadrons had, in air force jargon, thoroughly 'pranged' the target although only twenty-two Bostons reached it. Dock No 7 was left covered in reddish brown smoke and a direct hit was seen on the dock entrance at Bassin Vetillart. Other dock areas was straddled with bomb bursts. One Boston crash-landed back in England, another was destroyed by flak over the target and a third forced-landed at Tangmere with a wounded pilot after the observer and air gunner baled out near Shoreham. A reminder that the bomber crews also ran risks.

When they got back at 4.50 there was a press reception waiting at dispersal. 602's log noted

During this operation and after Mrs Laela Laid of Life magazine came to glamorise the squadron. Highlight: The CO playing chess for American consumption. Poker to while away the waits in which Laela showed much dexterity in refraining from stripping the squadron of their hard earned dibs.

Laela, the poker-playing Yank newswoman, was quite dishy, Max Charlesworth recalls: 'We all tried to chat her up except Paddy who stood on his dignity as the CO.'

Life was renowned for the high quality of its picture presentation. The photographer, Oswald Wild, was a top professional and the result was another series of superb photographs of an RAF fighter squadron at war, fully comparable to the agency photographs of 452 Squadron the previous year. He also stood around unobtrusively getting candid shots immediately before and after 602 took off and landed from Ramrod 17 on 26 March of this Thursday afternoon. The squadron was too busy to notice the camera and Finucane's take-off sequence is recorded and the landing with his Glasgow flight mechanic Alan 'Jock' Wilson hurrying up to meet LO-W at the wingtip as Finucane taxied across the grass and up to the concrete.

Dennehey, Charlesworth, Lacey and all those who flew on Ramrod 17 are shown gathering around 'the Boss' as he unfastened the Sutton harness, climbed out of LO-W, handed his parachute to Wilson. The shutter was still clicking unobtrusively … as soon as the propeller stopped the groundcrews swarming over LO-W, armourers on the wings, Wilson the wing root helping Finucane out… Finucane illustrating with his hands held up at a high angle indicating the difficult shot at the Fw 190 … explaining the combat closely watched by Niven and Lacey … 'Bo' Bocock is standing on the fringe looking thoughtful, he didn't fly on Ramrod 17 and missed the whole show …

Paddy Finucane taxies in LO-W of 602 Squadron, Kenley, Spring 1942.

LO-W of 602 Squadron, Kenley, Spring 1942.

Paddy Finucane is attended by two mechanics, 602 Squadron, Kenley, Spring 1942.

Pilots of 602 Squadron at dispersal, Kenley, 1942.

Paddy Finucane assists moving his Spitfire into its allotted parking space outside the 602 Squadron hut.

602's pilots gather round Paddy Finucane in his Spitfire.

Charlesworth had seen the fantastic angle at which Finucane had fired with cannon at extreme range of 500 yards – which Finucane admitted was fired 'more in hope than in anger' – and went over to congratulate him: 'That was a bloody marvellous shot, sir.' Max told me: 'I saw these two 190s attacking the wing. I pulled up the nose and all I saw was these two aircraft. They were going up vertically like a rocket and I was right behind Paddy – he was actually in my gunsight – as he went up and over the top to get one of them. I could see Paddy's guns firing and I think he actually fired at the top of his climbing turn, stalled with the recoil of his guns and spun out. I was also firing, there was a bang in my engine and it stopped with the cockpit filling with smoke. I rolled out and down with a dead engine but it picked up and I headed for home.'

Wild, still hovering in the background and moving among the parked Spitfires and bustling activity of the groundcrews, got one of the finest character studies on film ever recorded of Finucane.

As the late afternoon sun slanted across Kenley shadowing the concrete with the outlines of men and aircraft Wild moved in to capture with a fast shutter speed Finucane's moment of quietness, his thoughts turning inwards perhaps to the German aircraft breaking up under his guns half an hour ago and the Boston exploding in the flak barrage over Le Havre. Finucane looks a man alone, a loner, which in a way he always was.

Around Finucane in Wild's photographs is another of 602's 'characters', Colin Tait, fair-haired, another Australian in the RAF, humorous, sober and steady, known as Shortarse to the squadron, he was Finucane's wingman on Ramrod 17.

A more marked character was 'Ossie' Osborn. He looked like the Abyssinian ruler Haile Selassie, more than a passing resemblance, which led to the squadron wags christening him in a way which resulted in another gem in 602 Squadron's linebook:

Large dogfight over the French coast – voice 'Break Ossie, break left!'

Disgusted Australian voice – 'Which f*****g Aussie?'

P/O John Niven – 'The Abysinnian Bastard.'

Further gems – some of which caused acute embarrassment to the pilots concerned, and possibly still do as memories dull the savageness of the air war, but the humour remains constant and shines through the bloodthirsty atmosphere of a fighter squadron constantly in action – all were recorded meticulously by Niven at the time with gleeful authenticity:

P/O Maxie Charlesworth, taking a Waaf home after a party, temporarily and most unusually at a loss for words, felt a box of gramophone needles in his pocket and taking one out said, 'Would you care for a gramophone needle?' Quick as a flash the Waaf replied, 'No thanks, I don't play.'

Sgt Les Scorer:

'The armourer has just told me I had one bullet left in the guns – I must have missed one out!'

P/O John Dennehey on his first show broke away on his own as we were coming home and went whistling off into France again. Al Deere waited for him coming in and tore him off a hell of a strip. His excuse was 'I saw some funny red flak and went back to see what it was.' Al's reply was 'You're f*****g lucky you didn't find out.' (Red marker flak was used to direct Hun fighters)

P/O Maxie Charlesworth's first sweep when we got mixed up with about 150 Me 109s. His R/T packed up after the first report and when he got home he remarked, 'By God you types certainly know how to keep R/T silence.'

Sgt Griffiths, 485 Sqn, owner of a very high pitched voice, got badly shot up over Gravelines and gave a running commentary as he lost height over the drink. His voice rising gradually to an incredible squeak saying 'I am now at 800ft and my engine is on fire – will I bale out?' About 35 transmitters went on simultaneously to tell him and the Kenley ops room receiver was nearly wrecked by the invective.

The mirth of the squadron humorists was typical of 602. Lacey was not the only mickey-taker around at the time on Finucane's squadron, not by a long way.

Leading the Kenley Wing on Ramrod 17 at the head of 485 Squadron was Group Captain Beamish. Since taking command at Kenley he hardly ever saw his desk. From 27 January he had flown ten operational flights, including the action against the German fleet and eight circus operations at the head of his Kenley command. When not flying he was touring the station, talking to the pilots at dispersal, frequently chatting with Finucane. Apart from his exploit in joining the much younger men in beating up a destroyer on 12 February, he destroyed Fw 190s on 9 and 14 March and strafed two E-boats. Ramrod 17 was his ninth sweep from Kenley; he got an Fw 190 and Me 109E, the second in a low-level seaward dice when he followed the German pilot down to 200 feet and narrowly missed flying into the Le Havre cliffs:

... in a turn I got an Fw 190 in my sights and gave him a three second burst and saw him enveloped in smoke, but I immediately left him as a Me 109 presented a target. F/Lt Grant and P/O Gibbs of 485 Squadron confirm that the Fw 190 exploded in the air and what remained went down in a smoking mass.

The Me 109E which I then attacked gave off white and blue streams of smoke and dived vertically down. I followed it down with my No 2 until it was less than 200ft when Wing Commander Boyd warned me of a Hun on my tail and I pulled away. P/O Gibbs confirms that the Me 109 was dead and still falling vertically just over the cliffs north of Le Havre under 200ft.

This was Beamish's last combat report. Two days later on 28 March he was killed leading the Kenley Wing. He disappeared without trace. John Dennehey's logbook entry: 'G/C last seen gliding over the drink 13,000ft.'

The operation on this day was a Fighter Rodeo (fighters only) and considering there were no bombers the Luftwaffe reacted in force. This was the first time they tangled with the Fw 190s in large numbers – more than fifty 190s and 109s were seen in the biggest dogfight most RAF men remembered since the Battle of Britain. It was a late afternoon show. Kenley Wing was airborne at 5pm to join the Northolt, Biggin Hill and Hornchurch Wings to patrol the French coast at 20,000ft from Cap Gris Nez, St Inglevert, Ambleteuse, Gravelines within sight of the Luftwaffe at Calais Marck airfield.

Finucane clobbered one in his usual style by getting on his opponent's tail and blasting him from dead astern – in this case from about 200 yards, seeing strikes on port wing root and engine, pieces fly off and flames from the engine. John Niven, close behind, flew through the debris and noted in his logbook 'windscreen covered with petrol spray'. The 109 half rolled and spun, followed down by Sergeant Jimmy Garden in Finucane's section who saw it spinning in from 1,000 feet. Having seen nine 190s coming down he waited until they were below, got on the inside of one of them in a tight turning circle and shot off part of its tail unit… 'I sat on his tail' and the 190 went down vertically streaming white smoke as he watched it for about 5,000 feet. Finucane finished his scoring by firing at another Me 109 as another Spitfire from 457 Squadron joined in also firing. Finucane finished his attack from 7 5 yards and the 109 went down in flames.

The first he knew that Beamish was in trouble was when he heard him calling on the R/T for a fix home. Someone advised 'steer 310' but it was learned later that Kenley operations did not receive the call.

After they got back at 6·10pm Finucane had 602 airborne again at 7pm to 'scan the drink' for Beamish.

Kenley's operational log recorded:

It is doubtful whether the loss to the Service of such a leader as was G/Capt F V Beamish can be over-estimated. No such doubt exists, however, as to the sincere regret and sense of personal loss which prevailed at Kenley when, at the close of Saturday March 29th 1942 it was realised that hopes of effecting a rescue must be abandoned. His indomitable courage and outstanding skill as a fighter pilot combined with a great capacity for leadership and a rare sincerity which lay behind and prompted all that he said and did endeared him to all those who were privileged to serve under him. Here, indeed, was a man!

This was true – but they all knew that sooner or later Beamish, stubbornly continuing on when age had blunted his reflexes, would buy it sooner or later. Human nature being what it is, officers at Kenley now handed in their cycles insisted on by Beamish and those entitled to personal transport went to the MT section to claim it.

With Beamish out of the way a senior officer at Kenley now queried both Finucane's claims for 28 March of one Me 109 destroyed and one Fw 190 destroyed and got them downgraded to probably destroyed.

13

Day of Reckoning...

Finucane went to 11 Group HQ, on 31 March to sort things out. Surprisingly the decision went against him. Both claims had complied with Fighter Command's definitions of the damage to an enemy aircraft needed to claim it as destroyed.[35] There is the evidence of Niven's logbook: 'Got in defensive circle then followed CO after some 109s. Windscreen covered with petrol spray,' and the NCO pilot's evidence of seeing it spinning in from 1,000 feet. From Finucane's description of the 190 combat he had clearly shot away the elevators and this was sufficient to claim a kill.

There is evidence to support the view that the senior officer at Kenley who started this had a strong dislike of 602 Squadron and Finucane in particular. It is still recalled with distaste by Charlesworth, Niven and others. Niven said: 'On one sortie I reported a 109 below and Paddy told me to go after it. I did but overshot, then Paddy came down and blasted it out of the sky. He told me to watch for it and I saw it spiralling down and crash. This officer then did his damndest to get us to say it was not a kill.[36]

Charlesworth said: 'I was in the bar one night with Ken Murray, an Australian pilot. We had been there all the evening and were both well oiled when this officer came in late at night and the three of us had the bar to ourselves. He started criticising 602's and Paddy's claims. Both of us were junior pilots talking to a senior officer and some words were exchanged ending with us telling him to stuff himself. Shortly afterwards myself and Murray were posted.'[37]

It is clear that this affair would not have got off the ground had Beamish still been around. From the evidence of those who knew him he was a good judge of men and fully approved of Finucane who had an identical full-blooded attitude to the air war.

That there was known to be over-claiming in Fighter Command, especially 11 Group, at this time is confirmed by Group Captain Harry Broadhurst who was then station commander at Hornchurch. Like Beamish he was one of the 'flying Group Captains' and led his wing in the air on the sweeps: I knew Victor personally when he was at 11 Group and when I mentioned high claims on other wings he just looked at me and said nothing. I think Leigh-Mallory sent him to Kenley to look at their high scoring and he was killed in a determined attempt to show that what his chaps at Kenley were claiming was right. I also knew Leigh-Mallory quite well. He was a very able air force commander but he could be a bit pigheaded at times – but then at times you had to be. Leigh-Mallory called in Reg Grant of 485 Squadron (who was in Beamish's section on 28 March) who gave an unsatisfactory reason why he failed to cover Beamish. The Kenley Wing was not in Leigh-Mallory's good books that day – he was very upset over Beamish's loss. The Fw 190 was making things difficult for Fighter Command and we had trouble in shooting anything down. I told Leigh-Mallory we should make more use of cine combat film to confirm kills. We could see there was going to be a day of reckoning.'[38]

[35] See Appendix C

[36] Interview with author.

[37] Interview with author.

[38] Interview with the author

CO of 602 Squadron early 1942 – LO coded Spitfire in the background.

It is difficult to see why Leigh-Mallory thought Reg Grant had defaulted in covering Beamish. Grant, an experienced flight commander with a DFC, had shot down Beamish's two attackers, but one of these was downgraded to probably destroyed as well as Finucane's two claims.

Finucane at the end of March 1942 with $29\frac{1}{2}$ enemy aircraft destroyed was the top scoring and highest decorated pilot still flying on operations in Fighter Command. Ginger Lacey was second with 27 destroyed. 602 Squadron at Kenley now had the unique distinction until 25 April when Lacey was posted of having the two top aces, one as CO and the other as a flight commander, a combination which was never achieved by any other fighter squadron.

Malan, the only one with a higher score ahead of Finucane on Fighter Command's list of aces,[39] was still top but was not yet back on operations and Bob Stanford Tuck, third on the list, was shot down and into German captivity in January.

April was to be another eventful month for Finucane – and for Fighter Command – and ending on a happier personal note for him with his engagement to Jean Woolford. They had known each other for more than four years and the friendship had deepened to a permanent personal level. He was flying with his usual flair during the month and had six more combats.

The first was on 2 April on a Kenley Wing only sweep along the French coast. At 17,000 near Cap Gris Nez he attacked two Fw 190s with cannon and mg and was then caught from behind by two more that got hits on his starboard wing forcing him to take violent evasive action. He sent the cine camera gun film and his combat report to the Air Fighting Development Unit. It came back with this assessment:

[39] See Appendix F.

Burst 1: 1³/4 seconds Range 375 yards. Attack 30° from above on the starboard. Good line of fire but insufficient deflection allowance. Target appears to be turning and climbing.

Burst 2: 4 seconds Range 240-125 yards. Attack 20° from above on the starboard. Line of fire good, but with slight wander in aim throughout burst. Deflection allowance fairly good and is gradually decreased as attack closes to nearly astern.

Remarks: Good shooting in both bursts and a number of hits would be scored.

Finucane claimed one Fw 190 damaged.

On 6 April Group Captain Richard Atcherley OBE AFC took over the Kenley command as station commander. Atcherley was a colourful character – known as 'Batchy' – a fighter pilot member of the winning Schneider Trophy team in 1929, achieving the first lap of 331mph, and the same year won the King's Cup handicap air race at 150mph in a Gloster Grebe. He was a stunt flyer and aerobatic ace who as a flight lieutenant in the thirties flew in the US National Air Races at Chicago and Cleveland entertaining the Americans with 'crazy' flying. From the command of a night fighter squadron in 1940 he went to Norway to command a small fighter force operating from a frozen lake at Narvik. As station commander at Drem, he devised a new system of flarepath lighting. He was another one of the 'flying group captains' and soon started flying with the Kenley Wing on the sweeps – to the consternation of the wing leader.[40]

He quickly was told about the bickering but said, 'We don't want any arguments on the "Wing" and was always friendly to Finucane and 602 at dispersal and in the mess, and nothing like a CO administering a rocket.[41] But from now on Finucane had all 602's combat reports independently signed by other members of the squadron on all claims. On 4 April John Dennehey drew white smoke from an Fw 190 but Finucane would not even allow him to claim it as damaged because Dennehey forgot to switch on his cine camera gun and there was no confirmation on film.

Max Charlesworth: 'At dispersal Paddy looked a bit serious. He got us together and said: "You are probably aware that other squadrons think 602 is over-claiming. We have to be very careful about our claims and don't claim anything unless you are sure you have got it." Paddy was baffled by this query but the rumours had been filtering through to us and the squadron was suddenly uncomfortably aware of it. Paddy brought us face to face with it and said, "We will have to tighten up a bit."[42]

Finucane was clearly rattled when he flew up to Bourn, near Cambridge, the next day 5 April to see Raymond who was newly- commissioned with 101 Squadron. He put one wheel over the edge of the concrete on landing, lurching as

---

[40] On his fiftieth birthday in 1954 Atcherley was the first jet air marshal to break the sound barrier.

[41] Letter to the author from Ralph Sampson.

[42] Interview with the author.

the wheel skidded on the mud and straightening up with a burst of engine back on to the runway to taxy over to park near the Lancasters, the Spitfire dwarfed by the four-engined bombers. The bomber groundcrews had sly grins because they recognised the highly-decorated young squadron leader who stepped out of the aircraft with the shamrock insignia; the erratic landing was also seen by some of the Lancaster crews and Ray who came bounding over. Big grins of welcome:

'How are you, you old bugger?'

The usual firm handshakes. 'How many trips you done?'

How many sweeps?'

They had a drink in the bomber mess with some ribbing over 'fighter boys' landings'. Then Ray and Bren went into Cambridge for a meal. 'He had great admiration for the bomber crews,' Ray told me. 'But he always said, "Fighters are for me." A favourite joking remark was, "You have longer to be scared than me" and, "How do you manage to sit there on those long trips?"

Back at Bourn Finucane did a 'fighter boy's take-off in LO-W and then in a short flying display using the whole length of the bomber runway for a series of slow rolls 'just to show them he was still a good pilot.'

It had been a minor incident 'but he would not leave without correcting a bad impression,' Ray told me.

While Finucane was at Bourn, Lacey was in temporary command of 602. Ginger was also a 'rebel' – probably one of the reasons why Finucane liked him – and there occurred a diverting incident: '11 Group phoned to ask if we were going to do any rhubarbs and I said very probably, until I looked at the rhubarb map (targets were phoned through from group) and saw there were two to the flak sites at St Omer airfield. I went into the chaps and said, "Any volunteers for a rhubarb but don't all rush until you know what they are." I told them and they all said, "Go away. Don't be silly". I went back to the phone and said, "The flak sites, no go", was told that Leigh-Mallory had personally picked the targets and I said, "Leigh-Mallory knows as well as I do that rhubarbs are done by volunteers – and there are no volunteers." Minutes later the phone leapt from the hook of its own accord and a voice barked, "Leigh-Mallory here. Get me the CO." I said he was away and we wouldn't do the rhubarb, repeated they were volunteer jobs with no volunteers and added "If you care to order us to go then we'll go." L-M said, "This shows a low standard of morale on your squadron." I said, "Yes, but it shows a high standard of intelligence" and L-M rang off furiously.'[43] Coincidentally (?) Sholto Douglas wrote to L-M within a week on 12 April:

> I do not want to fetter the initiative of younger pilots and I look on rhubarbs
> as a chance for the enterprising young section leader to show what he can do.
> I do however want group commanders to see that fighter effort is not wasted
> on ill-planned and undisciplined rhubarb operations.

Finucane would have backed Lacey. Arthur Strudwick recalls group phoning with a rhubarb target when the weather was just right – low cloud – but Paddy elected not

[43] Interviews with the author.

to go and felt that it was not worth the risk involved. This does not accord with the thinking of a rash CO. Finucane had by now stopped the unofficial training flights to Gris Nez which he had initiated to keep the squadron on top line readiness, but were now unnecessary with the increase in fighter action.

The April weather was setting in cold, wet and windy after being on dawn readiness at 6·24am on 7 April the squadron was released at 10am for the rest of the day. Most of the pilots went to London with Finucane in the evening to meet Jean Woolford at Oddenino's. Finucane met Jean at her Kingsway office and took her to Oddies to meet 'his chaps'.

Finucane still liked to do a spot of freelancing as his combat reports indicate. The weather cleared on 10 April and the Kenley Wing went on a fighter rodeo to St Omer. Finucane and his wingman Colin Tait 'became separated from the wing' as he put it, and went steaming off on their own towards Mardyck at 20,000 feet. Warning Tait to stay with him, he peeled off, unseen by an Fw 190 below and on his right, closing from the port quarter and opening fire when dead astern at 270 yards. The first burst missed but the second burst of cannon drew a large red flash from the engine, the 190 skidded violently and glided along the coast 5,000 feet below. Tait signed the combat report as witness.

In the space reserved on the combat report for 'enemy casualties' Finucane wrote '? Camera-gun proof ' and it went to 11 Group like that where someone on the Intelligence staff crossed it out and wrote 'damaged'.

On 13 April Finucane made one of his very few tactical errors, led the squadron into a trap, and they were 'bounced' by higher flying Fw 190s from 30,000 feet over the French coast between Cap Gris Nez and Boulogne. 602's log noted: 'Squadron airborne by 1415 – all, repeat all, think it a miracle they returned from the rodeo.' What happened was that 602 Squadron was sandwiched between fifteen Fw 190s below, which Finucane saw and led the squadron into a diving attack, and another forty Fw 190s above, which he didn't see until too late. To dive away was impossible; the 190s were much faster and their massive radial engines gave an extra 40mph in a dive and the squadron would have been shot to pieces before they reached the deck. The squadron was still at around 23,000 feet. Finucane did the only thing possible – he ordered them into a defensive circle steep turning on one wing covering each other and turning into each attack as it happened getting in snap bursts at the fleeting targets hurtling down and fractionally in their gunsights.

Max Charlesworth:

'After some sweeps when we'd had no action the Kenley ops controller said at debriefing they were plotted all around us. Paddy said, "The next time it happens I'm going back to look for them." And that's what he did. We hadn't fired; he wanted to get stuck into some Huns and we went back into France to intercept any of them approaching us from behind.

'We all heard the controllers telling us there were Huns all over the place but we hadn't seen any, and returning over the French coast Paddy called the wing leader and said, "I'm going back." The squadron pulled around and we went back in alone. There was no immediate sign of enemy air activity but the R/T was still warning of enemy concentrations and I was feeling the tension, getting twitchy and sweating despite the cold. Paddy ordered, "Coiner squadron, keep your eyes peeled, chaps." Suddenly he saw them below and ordered us straight into the attack.

'I think it was Ossie Osborn who first spotted the contrails above us 6-7,000 feet higher. We saw four lines of 190s in line astern keeping directly above us. I had my eyes on them and saw three of the contrails suddenly cease and everyone on the squadron knew what that meant – three were on their way down. We were at a serious tactical disadvantage. Paddy very calmly took charge of the operation and got us into the defensive circle. We were short of fuel and the odds stacked up against us.

'The 190s were queuing up in to attack us – coming down in pairs and threes and pulling up and away over the side of us. Paddy judged the right moment between attacks to call out "Blue 1 and Blue 2 – break, head for home." He judged the right moment in the attacks "Yellow 1 and 2 – turn into them – now" as three more came slanting down. We could see the gun flashes on their wings as they fired. All the while he was turning into them himself and getting in a burst of fire. He kept complete control and direction of the battle, anticipating where the next attack would come and ordering a section to face it. The discipline and Paddy's presence held us together. The squadron did not break and we fought our way down to 10,000 feet. He knew that the angle and diving speed of the 190s was too great for us to get a hit, but by turning into them they could be put off their aim, and he continued directing us even when under fire himself. This was generalship of the highest order.[44] 'Paddy's section was the last out. I heard him say, "OK, let's head back" as he opened the taps, half rolled and went for the deck.'

Max entered in his logbook:

'This day we really fell for it… every Fw 190 in France leaped onto our necks … due to excellent leadership by Paddy we all got out OK. Didn't fire.'

Niven's logbook:

'… defensive circle for 15 minutes … 190s attacked from all angles. Radiator temperature rose to 135 degrees … broke out of circle and dived home. Was followed to Dover.'

Finucane simply entered in his logbook: 'Rodeo. 1hr 30 mins.'

Most of them flew at fifty feet over the Channel on the way back, some chased by the 190s to within three miles off Dover. Before the higher flying 190s got among them Niven destroyed a 190, and de la Poype and Willis each damaged one.

One hundred miles away in London while Finucane and 602 were fighting their way out from 20,000 feet over the French coast, Sholto Douglas was at Air Ministry in King Charles Street, Whitehall, talking to the Air Minister Sir Archibald Sinclair about fighter losses and claims on the sweeps.

---

[44] Interview with author

The next day, 14 April 1942, Sholto Douglas wrote to Sinclair:

My Dear Archie,

With reference to our conversation yesterday, I sent you as promised a tablet showing the losses we have suffered as compared with the number of enemy aircraft shot down for the last six weeks, ie since we started once again to carry out offensive operations.

You will see that we have destroyed 67 enemy aircraft (plus 40 probables) for the loss of 65 of our own aircraft and 56 pilots.

As you will see therefore, we have up to the present broken about even.

Sinclair replied on the 16th:

My dear Commander-in-Chief,

Thank you for your letter of the 14th April and for the interesting statement which you enclosed about your own and enemy casualties. I showed it to the prime minister. He was satisfied.

It means hard fighting but I remember in May or June 1940 your predecessor saying to me we could not afford to go on shooting down Germans at a ratio of only two to one in our favour. Today there is no doubt that equal losses in an air battle mean a reverse for the Germans – your figures indicate that you have done better than that.

The disquiet over air losses was obviously making itself felt higher up or Churchill would not have been brought into it. Sholto Douglas knew what they were up against. The Fw 190A was taking its toll, much harder to shoot down than their old adversaries the Me 109Fs and Gs, and his correspondence and Fighter Command records refer to the need for an improved version of the Spitfire which came on the scene later in 1942 as the Mk IX. The trend worsened in early summer.

Sholto Douglas had another table of figures prepared from 13 April to 9 May.[45] The figures were 70 destroyed and 54 probably destroyed for the loss of 109 aircraft and 95 pilots.

So, added to the list Sholto Douglas sent to Sinclair showing the balance sheet from 1 March to 12 April, Fighter Command had lost from 1 March to 9 May a total of 174 Spitfires and 151 pilots for claims of 137 enemy aircraft destroyed and 94 probably destroyed.

Fighter Command Headquarters Intelligence Notes and Appreciation No 18 dated 19 June 1942 gives the figure of 205 enemy aircraft destroyed for 242 RAF fighter losses in the first five months of 1942.

Sinclair's reply to Sholto Douglas on 16 April is a remarkable admission and it is unclear how he arrived at it. Churchill had other aspects of the air war on his mind which probably accounts for his uncritical acceptance of the figures. Uppermost in his mind no doubt was Bomber Command's first 'thousand' raid in May which shifted the emphasis away from the fighter to the bomber.

The sweeps over Northern France in 1942 were a Fighter Command sideshow.

---

[45] See Appendix G.

The command's night-fighting squadrons with new AI equipment and developing expertise among the crews were performing a more useful – and vital role. The sweeps bear no comparison to the deep penetration daylight operations of the UK-based 8th United States Air Force which precision-bombed targets in Germany and occupied Europe from 1943 onwards heavily escorted by long range Mustang fighters especially designed for the job, which the Spitfire VB never was.

According to Sholto Douglas's memoirs the picture was even blacker than the figures on the Fighter Command files indicate: 'Over a period of about four months during that spring and early summer of 1942 we lost three hundred and fourteen fighters and bombers, with the Germans losing only ninety aircraft.'

Sholto Douglas's memoirs contain another oddity of the sweep period which would not merit mention here except that he calls Finucane '… a rather wild Irishman who was making a name for himself as one of our outstanding fighter pilots of that time … ' which is a strange way to refer to a pilot who headed the list of 11 Group top scorers in 1941 and had the triple distinction in 1942 at the age of twenty-one of being the youngest wing commander to command a wing in Fighter Command while still the highest scoring and highest decorated operational pilot. There was nothing 'wild' about Finucane.

Finucane did not lead a deputation, as he claims, to meet him at Kenley to complain about Batchy Atcherley flying with the wing (it was Hawkeye Wells who did the complaining) and the account is incorrect. He is also wrong when he says that Atcherley, the day after being shot down into the Channel, presented himself at Fighter HQ, to be ticked off for disobeying orders not to fly on operations and that Atcherley's only injury was a grazed wrist when a cannon shell shot off his watch into the sea. Atcherley was in hospital for three weeks. It was Harry Broadhurst who got the ticking off: 'The watch incident was mine, not Atcherley's … The description of the incident is accurate … but the watch fell out of my left hand flying glove, and I still have it.'[46]

Atcherley's flying with the wing caused Hawkeye Wells, then wing leader, 'to have the only serious row I ever had with him'[47] when Batchy insisted on going as his No 2 so 'keen to bag a Hun', but was inexperienced on the sweeps and nearly collided with Wells twice while looking around for something to shoot at. Wells' threat to complain to the AOC led Atcherley unwisely to ignore the wing leader's advice and follow the wing out on his own and he was shot down the second time he did it.

In perfect spring weather, clear and cloudless, the Kenley Wing was off at 6·40am on 16 April on Circus 126 to Dunkirk and they swept inland for 25 miles via Birques. This was one of the shows when Atcherley was flying as wingman to Wells, who was promoted in March to command 485 Squadron and was now acting wing leader. Finucane, leading 602 at 26,000 feet south of Mardyck, saw three Fw 190s ahead and a thousand feet below him but they half rolled away before he could get within range. He was luckier with the next one, the last in a section of four, and gave it a two second burst with cannon and mg from 230-260 yards and it lurched into a half roll and dived away trailing grey smoke. Niven's logbook records: 'S/Ldr Finucane made a mess of one. I saw hit on ground which may have been it.'

Charlesworth noted in his logbook:

> 'Took off 6-40 before sun up. We climbed to 28,000ft and swept in behind Dunkirk and saw about ten Fw 190s altogether. CO got one. Damned cold but weather excellent.'

Finucane claimed the Fw 190 as damaged.

The April weather was unsettled, and on the 22nd after a cloudy morning the squadron was released in the afternoon when Finucane flew to Eastleigh to see the folks at Swaythling. It was an odd experience to land a Spitfire at Eastleigh after all those years ago. It was also something of a sentimental journey. After calling in on Eileen and Steve Physick and the children in Harefield Road he went over the road to see Ada McKinnon. She was of Anglo-Scots parentage and he called her Maxie. It was good to renew old acquaintances, childhood friends from the pre-war holidays. When he was in sick leave in March he came down by train and they had dinner at the Polygon Hotel – miraculously still standing in the devastation of Southampton city centre after the 1940 winter blitz – and it was a pleasant evening: 'It was typical to call in unannounced. I looked up from the front garden to see him walking casually along Harefield Road, still the same old Bren, good fun and good company.'[48]

Len Thorne, aged twenty-one, a former bank clerk from Slough, flew as Red 3 on Circus 137 to Abbeville on 25 April:

> 'Group Captain Corner[49] was my No 2. Red section attacked a pair of e/a, then four, then a single Me 109 at which I got in a long burst and nearly ran out of ammo. Approaching the French coast Corner and I were attacked by two 190s. Despite repeated calls to break he failed to turn with me and was hit, going down with smoke. He pulled out, headed for home, and the smoke stopped. Paddy called on the R/T, "Close in Furnace Squadron, we can get this Spitfire home." At mid-Channel I saw tracer going over and under both my wings and pulled hard around to avoid two more 190s belting at me. I gave them the slip and caught up with Corner in time to see him go into the sea. He baled out too low for his parachute to fully open. It was a mistake for a man as valuable as Corner to have been permitted to join in such a hazardous operation. There was an inquiry and I submitted a report to Fighter Command but no blame was attached to us. We were all depressed by his loss. My friend Sergeant Paul Green was also lost on this trip.
>
> 'Again flying as number three to Paddy on 26 April. As we left the French coast the first enemy aircraft were climbing from the sea inland

[48] Interview with author.

[49] Hugh Corner was another of the flying group captains, a distinguished medical officer with the Air Force Cross who flew with squadrons to study aircrew psychology, was popular at 602's dispersal but Finucane aware of his age (43) asked yellow section also to keep an eye on him. John Dennehev, the fourth member of red section, Paddy's wingman, noted in his logbook that Corner baled out within eight miles of Dungeness. Corner was to have been promoted to Air Commodore as principal medical officer at Fighter Command.

heading north east and Paddy fired a short burst at an Fw 190 which was in a climbing turn to starboard. I tightened my turn and as he ceased firing I pulled the nose up as the 190 was now above. I gave a short burst of about 1½ seconds and saw part of it going in and around the 190. My airspeed was down to 140mph and I could not hold the deflection and my fire dropped behind the 190 which rolled on his back and went vertically down. Breaking to port, I rejoined Paddy who attacked the second 190 which was diving slightly and under Paddy's fire emitted a cloud of white smoke. As Paddy ceased firing, I steepened my dive and fired from dead astern at about 500 yards when the 190 was going down almost vertically. He was held in my fire for about one second as I continued the dive for about 2,000 feet and the 190 became enveloped in black smoke. I turned to starboard and watched it continue the dive into the sea. Paddy undoubtedly gave me two opportunities to make a kill.'[50]

Finucane did not claim for either of these 190s and Thorne was credited with the first as damaged and the second as destroyed. Arthur Strudwick, following hard behind Finucane and Thorne, added a description to Thorne's combat report confirming the effect of Finucane's and Thorne's fire and seeing the 190 go into the Channel.

Interviewed by Leigh-Mallory for his commission Thorne slammed the sweeps and told L-M they were wasteful in terms of RAF pilots, but the AOC was prepared to accept critical comments because Thorne still got his commission, recommended by Finucane. Thorne later became an experimental test pilot at AFDU, Wittering, and considered a captured Fw 190A one of the three best aircraft he had ever flown.[51]

---

[50] This was Circus 138 to St Omer railway station; letter to the author vis-à-vis Thorne's combat report for 26 April.

[51] Telephone conversation with the author.

14

Smoke Trails Like Spaghetti

John Niven was promoted to acting flight lieutenant and appointed by Finucane to command A Flight:

'On one occasion when I was acting flight commander I had to interview one of the boys on a compassionate matter. I was sitting on the windowsill with my feet on a chair in the dispersal office hearing the case when the Boss looked in around the door, excused himself and disappeared. When the interview was finished I was treated to a precise pointed lecture on how to conduct an interview – hat on, sitting erect, interviewee seating or standing as appropriate. When I got my flight in April I was told very quickly that I was no longer "Johnny" to the sergeant pilots but "sir" and I had to tell them myself. Paddy said quite politely that he could tell them himself but that he felt it was my responsibility – the crafty bastard sat outside and killed himself laughing while I grew up in two minutes flat! The boys took it without a murmur.

'This was not just bull. He ran the squadron in the good old- fashioned way and everyone knew exactly where they stood. If anyone wanted a rocket, they got it right in the neck from auld Ireland and then it was past and forgotten. He was always "the Boss", "Boss" or "sir" and I never recall hearing any of the boys trying to be familiar. He was very conscious of proper procedure and protocol on duty and made it clear with "his boys".'

'There was a hidden strength about him which one felt rather than observed. He was physically very strong and wiry and fast on his feet. When he got engaged we pulled his leg and I got punched halfway around Kenley for it, Queensberry rules, but he had four pairs of fists! He didn't like a lot of drink and I think this was because he disliked the idea of having his senses impaired. His language was precise and he had no need to fill in with the crude stuff. He could bloody and hell with the rest of us but he didn't use the copulatory adjectives unless really under stress.

'His friendship was genuine and accepted with great pleasure by all who really knew him and he was one of the few I was pleased to have as a friend. We both had steady girlfriends and his ambition matched mine – get the war over and settle down. We talked a great deal about taking leave to visit my home in Edinburgh but we never made it and I regret it deeply. I wanted my folks to meet him, not just because he was the great ace Paddy Finucane but because he was a nice bloke whose ideas were similar to mine.

'Practically every mess I was ever in had a radiogram and a selection of records. There was always a proportion of swing which received more playing than the rest put together and hearing some of the records again brings back vivid memories of ante rooms and dispersals all over the place. My passion for jazz and swing brought me into contact with 485 Squadron at Kenley and I used to hog the records a bit. The Kiwis had the same taste probably because at home they could receive the United States on their radios and knew the bands, just names on records to a select few in the UK. Kenley had Jimmy Dorsey's

"Contrasts" and "Dolomite", Ella Fitzgerald's "Sugar Blues" and "Imagination", Jimmy Dorsey's "Blue" and "When the sun comes out", the inevitable Andrews Sisters' "Well, all right", "Boogie Woogie Bugle Boy", Duke Ellington and so on. The one flogged to death was 485's favourite Dinah Shore's "Mocking Bird Lament" and "Honeysuckle Rose".

'The record to end them all was Bing Crosby's "Sweet Potato Piper" with a passage in the middle played by occarinos. We had a hell of a party one night at Redhill and late in the evening, I think it was Max Charlesworth, took a red hot poker and put another hole about one inch off the centre and played it. Stone-cold sober it sounds damn funny but half cut the result was hysterical and it was the highlight of many a party.'[52]

The Kenley squadrons flew as escort wing to six Bostons of 88 Squadron, 2 Group, on Circus 144 on Tuesday 28 April to St Omer. It was a fairly big show, sixteen squadrons from six wings. Kenley's squadrons were stepped up from 12,000 feet to 15,000 feet around the Bostons. Above them was the Northolt Wing as escort cover shadowed above by the Hornchurch Wing flying high cover. The forward support wings were from Debden and North Weald, and Biggin Hill was rear support wing. Cloud at 20,000 feet forced the escort cover and high cover wings to fly below their scheduled height and visibility was poor, but the Bostons hit the target. The fighter action started while they were bombing St Omer railway station and 317 Squadron got three destroyed and two damaged. The top squadron of the forward support, 121 Squadron, was attacked by about thirty Fw 190s and in a running fight to the coast destroyed two and damaged one for the loss of three pilots. 401 Squadron of the rear support wing between Calais and Gravelines got two probables and one damaged, but the wing lost three pilots.

On the way back nearing the coast, at Audruick, the escort wing met the Fw 190s, causing Finucane to put in one of his shortest combat reports:

> I was Red 1 leading 602 Squadron … I saw two Fw 190s approaching head-on and about twenty to fifty feet above me. I opened fire on the left hand one at about 350 yards and gave a short burst.
>
> I opened fire with cannons and saw strikes about 7 o'clock on his engine and on his starboard wing root. Enemy aircraft passed over my head and was lost to my view.

A head-on attack was over in seconds at closing speeds of about 700mph. Finucane did not like this type of duel but he was a better shot than the German pilot who missed. Finucane often said the only sure way to get your man is from dead astern – 'Get on his tail.' Dennehey, flying as Finucane's wingman, noted in his logbook, 'CO and self attacked head-on, saw strikes on engine cowling and fuselage near wing root.' They both claimed 109s as damaged; Dennehey had tackled the second one.

The next day, Wednesday 29 April, Finucane left 'Bo' Bocock in command of the squadron and went home to Richmond for a very important date – Jean Woolford's twentieth birthday and the announcement to both families in Castlegate of their

[52] Letter to author.

engagement. This was the day that King George VI toured Kenley with Sholto Douglas and Leigh-Mallory, and chatted with 602's pilots at dispersal, but Finucane missed the VIP visit. Bocock introduced the King to 602 on returning from Circus 145.

Jean and Brendan's engagement party was a family affair, dinner at Oddenino's. They had known each other for four years and for a few hours he was happy and relaxed in their favourite restaurant, with the music of the Tommy Rogan Orchestra in the grill room on the first floor where they still managed an air of opulence in wartime with crystal chandeliers. Rogan knew them as 'Paddy' and 'Jean'. He knew who Finucane was and was always pleased to play a request, proud to know that Finucane liked his music. But even as they danced, the teleprinters at 11 Group HQ were sending out the Form D, chattering insistently in the orderly rooms at Tangmere, Northolt, Biggin Hill and Kenley with the operational instructions of courses to fly, heights, rendezvous, wing roles and target for Circus 148 to be flown tomorrow morning, 30 April. At Oddies the music played on … at Kenley the orchestration of war was a briefing by the wing leader at 10am, take-off at 11 am: Target Le Havre.

Finucane opened fire from 100 yards on the left of an Fw 190 at 18,000 feet fifteen miles north west of Le Havre at about ten minutes to midday. The square wingtips were framed fractionally in the circle of his reflector gunsight and he noted the German aircraft had a speckled light grey camouflage and no cannons. Seconds before, the Fw 190 and another one flying as a pair had fired at him and his wingman Len Thorne but had overshot and passed to their right and were now about fifty feet below and in a turn to port. Finucane saw his fire striking in and around the cockpit area and after a few seconds the propeller stopped; then his own engine started running badly and he broke off the combat.

There was no cloud and visibility was excellent with only a slight haze. The six Bostons of 226 Squadron bombed from 12,500 feet but all six were hit by flak, two belly-landed at Thorney Isle and another two, badly shot up, landed on one engine. Kenley was target support wing with the Biggin Hill squadrons, whose wing leader James Rankin claimed one destroyed and one damaged by 124 Squadron. Escort wing was from Tangmere, and Northolt provided escort cover. The 11 Group report on Circus 148 noted: 'The enemy aircraft appeared very keen to engage.'

Len Thorne:

'This was a big show. The target area over the Le Havre docks was very congested – Spitfires, Me 109s and Fw 190s all over the place making smoke trails looking like spaghetti high above. I flew as No 2 to Paddy and we orbited two miles off Le Havre. I attacked a 190 heading inland, broke off and returned to orbit. We attacked two e/a which came below us and I had to dive almost vertically to get the sights on with considerable deflection.

Saw strikes on engine and it went straight down pouring black smoke and apparently out of control. Could not wait to see it crash and only claimed it as probable. While this was going on Paddy shot another one off my tail and undoubtedly saved my neck. Unfortunately I could not confirm that it crashed.'[53]

Finucane claimed his Fw 190 as probably destroyed. Eric Bocock destroyed one with a

[53] Letter to author.

full deflection attack from 200 to 250 yards from above with a two-second burst, closing from astern 250 to 400 yards finishing it off with a five-second burst and saw it crash into the sea. Gwyllim Willis got a probable and Dennehey damaged one.

This was a day of intensive operations for Fighter Command and the squadrons flew a total of 730 sorties on two circuses, two rodeos and a fighter ramrod. Kenley were off again at mid-afternoon on Rodeo 7 and Finucane noted in his logbook, 'Up and down French coast 14,000 feet.' He had now flown on 85 sweeps and operational flying time totalled 262·20 hours and he entered his victories as 28 (confirmed) 7 probably destroyed and 9 damaged.

His engagement to Jean was widely publicised in 'Paddy to Wed Girl Next Door' stories by the BBC and newspapers on 1 May. Truscott also had an English girlfriend, Margaret Rees, aged twenty-two, of Tolworth, Surrey, a typist at the Food Ministry, London, it was disclosed. He went into hiding under an assumed name to avoid a hero's welcome in Australia. An RAAF press bulletin of 25 May said:

'All he asks for is quiet, seclusion, freedom from public attention and "a fair go".'

Finucane and 602 Squadron were on Circus 150 to Marquise on 1 May; Bocock and Bill Loud both got Fw 190s probably destroyed and Thorne claimed one probably destroyed and one damaged. The weather was too overcast for flying on the 2nd but on the 3rd they were out again on Circus 145 to Desvres and a fighter rodeo to Hardelot; on the way back Finucane climbed the squadron to 33,000 feet to intercept Me 109s but there were no claims or casualties. On 4 May 'Doc' Hands noted in 602's medical diary that the CO was 'Very tired, needs a rest' and Finucane went home to Castlegate on a week's leave the next day.

On 14 May 602 Squadron moved back to Redhill. John Niven:

'Redhill[54] was a cosy mess. The great asset at Redhill was the chef, the envy of Fighter Command. He was a Czech who could hardly speak English who made red soup for us on several occasions without using tomatoes, deep crimson and delicious. What that bloke could do with RAF rations was nobody's business and there was a constant fifth column attempt to get him to (a) Kenley (b) 11 Group (c) Fighter Command.'[55]

The chef was Frank Decmar, aged twenty-nine, from Prague, and the soup was borscht, a Russian beetroot soup which he served with cream on top with wine to add piquancy. Decmar was a maitre d'hotel and chef of international repute who had trained at Lausanne and had worked in France, Germany, Austria and Switzerland. A notice was later posted in the mess of a Canadian Spitfire squadron:

All operational pilots are being informed by the catering officer that there is a premium in this mess. For every Hun destroyed a special cake is awaiting the pilot concerned. Good luck. The notice is from a Czech who has already improved the quality of the coffee. He is making it Canadian style, and that is something!

[54] Barnridge

[55] Letter to author

The victory cake idea originated with Decmar at Redhill. Kenley operations would phone through to Barnridge with news that a pilot had just got a Hun and Decmar would have the cake ready and waiting. One of his best cake customers had been Truscott when 452 were at Redhill:

> 'Nothing was too good for them. My country had been overrun and these young officers were fighting for me. I would have done anything for them and scrounged to get the ingredients on the black market in London.
>
> 'Paddy was very friendly towards me but only once spoke about his combats. He had just come back from a sweep and said, "I saw the bastards first, Decmar, or I wouldn't be here now." I replied, "Good luck to you, sir."[56]

Decmar improved the quality of life for 602 at Barnridge and helped along the social life by doing the catering for the dances and garden parties which were a feature of the parkland setting at the mess. The parties were a necessary adjunct and therapy to the fighter pilot's life and there were some lively personalities on 602; the old house Barnridge was ideal as a fighter mess. Amusing incidents are recalled. Finucane went to bed early leaving one party going full bore, to be woken later by Eric Bocock blundering in thinking he was in the urinal, and making appropriate use of the radiator in Finucane's room. The CO's sense of humour was equal to the occasion. As well as the swing music recalled by Niven and Charlesworth's fun with the Bing Crosby record, there was the famous incident of Roland de la Poype, resplendent in Free French Air Force uniform, swaying slightly across the crowded noisy room and approaching a well-built girl at one of the parties. Local girls from Nutfield village, Waafs and nurses were usually among those invited, delightful company on a warm summer evening in the wide oak panelled room overlooking the scenic grounds – and de la Poype got a mention in 602's linebook:

> Popeye asked, 'What ees eet zat you call what a girl 'as 'ere and 'ere?' One of the types said, 'Oh, you mean tits,' and Popeye pranced off and jabbed his index finger into her ample bosom and gleefully proclaimed, 'Teets, very nice!'

Dawn Readiness. Finucane was in the cockpit of LO-W ready to start up. Mist was rising from the airfield and breath vaporised in the cold air. His groundcrew, Alan Wilson, fitter, and Joe Pollard, the rigger, hovered around. Wilson, the 'whelp' of the groundcrews, was six months older than Finucane who had yesterday turned down his application for aircrew and told him: 'You are more useful here as a mechanic.' Now, on this readiness state, he opened up slightly. Wilson: 'Paddy said, "It's not all beer and skittles" and then went on to say he was uneasy at the thought of having to ditch a Spitfire in the Channel. This was the only time he mentioned it, he was usually very formal and correct with us providing his Spitfire was on the top line, but very friendly.'[57] Finucane's concern for the welfare of the groundcrews was appreciated. George Outch was another Glaswegian fitter who worked for a time on LO-W:

[56] Interview with author.

[57] Interview with the author. Wilson ignored the advice, remustered to aircrew and flew as a Lancaster flight engineer with 9 and 83 Squadrons in Bomber Command's pathfinder force, completing 54 trips and winning the DFM. He was on the raid in which Guy Gibson was lost. Gibson's flares refused to release and he was never seen again after his third attempt to mark the target. Wilson's 83 Squadron crew from Coningsby went in and did the job.

'At Redhill we picketed the aircraft for the night among a clump of trees behind dispersal and unofficially taxied them outside the dispersal huts early morning for the pilots. Oil streaks on the cowlings were washed clean with a mixture of oil and 100 octane, Paddy was particular about this.

'I was on the messing committee and was helping him on with his parachute on an early morning show when he said, "You are looking a bit miserable this morning, Outch." I said, "Yes sir, they have been binding to me about the food." He said, "I will see you when I get back and we will look into the matter." Returning, I helped him down from the aircraft and took his parachute and he said, "Have you had breakfast yet?" I said, "No sir, we're just off." He replied, "Right, I will go with you." The airmen's mess was in an old house at Nutfield a short distance from the airfield and Paddy, unannounced, got into the queue. There was an untidy Waaf serving and Paddy said to me, "Is this what you usually get?" I said, "No sir, but it's never much better." He said, "Very well, Outch, I will be looking into this for you!" '[58]

The sight of the highly decorated young squadron leader queuing up with armourers, fitters and riggers on the early shift caused some consternation among the catering staff, and the food improved after he took appropriate action. Not many squadron commanders would have acted so promptly or unorthodoxly.

Finucane's armourer was Jack Clements, the only 'sassenach' in the armoury, which was a small wooden hut among the trees.

Clements always carried a piece of chalk in his overalls to draw the outline of the shamrock on any Spitfire that Finucane flew when LO-W was in for servicing and he had to fly a spare aircraft. 'We knew he was never happy flying without the emblem and had great faith in the letter W and if the chalk outline came back smudged with oil or glycol fumes I cleaned it up and re-drew it before the next sortie.

'Returning from one sortie the CO was angry because his cannon had packed up and he had to break off the chase. Cannon stoppages were common in those days and the corporal in charge of the armoury hissed in my ear as I rushed out with a screwdriver, "He will have your guts, wee Jackie, if you're at fault." Happily I wasn't, but Paddy questioned me closely on the technicalities and a few days later when a stoppage occurred on another kite, not one of mine, he said, "Send for young Clements, he has the griff." From then on I graduated to looking solely after Paddy's guns although the armourers, unlike the riggers and fitters, worked three aircraft each.

'Serviceability was extremely high on the squadron – Paddy's aircraft was very highly maintained by some of the best technicians on the unit; people like Alan Wilson and Georgie Outch, they were good!

'Incorrect loading could cause a cannon stoppage. Each magazine held sixty 20mm shells which were loaded in the armoury, great care being taken that the ammo links were properly aligned by means of a zinc coat shaft down which the armourer fed the shells while his assistant wound up the magazine with a special spanner.'[59]

[58] Interview with author.

[59] Letter to author.

Bill Lathey became senior NCO i/c B Flight at Redhill in May:

'There was a tolerance on flying times so that an extension could be granted for a few hours. Paddy always insisted on having this extension but when it was exhausted and he had to do without LO- W for a few days he filled in the Form 700 aircraft serviceability log with any number of defects he had noticed while flying but which did not make the aircraft unserviceable. After one extension W developed a savage oil leak caused by a holding down stud which came adrift from the crankcase and could have led to engine failure.'[60]

At the end of the day's flying Finucane got his chaps together as his Waaf driver LACW Trixie Kay – or her oppo Cecily Wilkinson, a small gritty blonde who could hold her own with leg-pulling pilots, working a 24-hour shift – pulled up in the 10 cwt canvas topped Standard truck by the parked Spitfires at dispersal. They piled into the back over the tailboard and on to Barnridge, the evening sun ploughing a golden furrow through the treetops, dappling the winding country road and the bonnet of the truck with light and shade.

As well as The Chequers, there was The Wagon Wheel at Horley among 602's favourite evening pubs, or The Whyte Hart at Bletchingly. At Kenley it had been The Greyhound, Croydon, or The Tudor Rose, Old Coulsdon, a favourite with the Australians.

Sometimes it was the cinema or up to the West End to Oddenino's to see Jean. They usually kept together as a crowd, Finucane and his pilots completely identifying as 602 Squadron. 'Doc' Hands, the MO, was often invited and they were enjoyable times.

---

[60] Letter to author.

15

Thirty-two Victories

On 17 May 602 Squadron was airborne at 10·33am on Ramrod 33 escorting twelve Bostons to attack the Boulogne docks. Finucane, leading 602 with 485 Squadron, rendezvoused at 11am with the Bostons at low level (500 feet) at Beachy Head and then headed out over the Channel; 602 gained operational height of 25,000 feet above 485, led by Hawkeye Wells, who had been promoted to wing leader on 6 May. They were providing high cover to the Bostons and their close escort. The bombers hit a ship in the basin and the railway yards, leaving a pall of smoke over the target. The Kenley controller reported fifteen bandits near Le Touquet.

Finucane led 602 inland to Guines:

> 'Yellow 1 reported two e/a below and went in to attack. I saw a further eight or ten e/a behind yellow 1. We went down to attack and I took a short squirt at 1 e/a about 400 yards ahead of me. He did a steep right hand turn and dived away. By this time I was at 15,000 feet. I picked on another Fw 190 with dark brown camouflage on wing tips and closed to 350 yards. I opened fire with cannon and machine guns and fired a three-second burst. We were diving at an angle of 45°. E/a went on in the dive and hit the ground at cross roads near Guines. Before it hit the ground it did a slight right hand turn. I observed no strikes or smoke from e/a.'

Finucane crossed the coast about four miles east of Gris Nez and saw a Spitfire go into the Channel with two 190s circling it. He went down to direct two rescue launches with three bursts of machine gun fire. The pilot was Flight Lieutenant Tony Majors, yellow 1. John Dennehey threw out his dinghy but Majors was already dead. Flight Sergeant Willis was also missing. Colin Tait claimed a probable.

The Fw 190 destroyed was Finucane's thirty-second kill and he got one of Decmar's victory cakes at Barnridge that night. But on Fighter Command's ace list he was still credited with only 29. The explanation is that his two combats of 28 March, which were amended to probables, were included as destroyed on the list for April and two of his subsequent victories on 26 April and this one on 17 May were not included on the later lists to redress the official balance. The news, however, had apparently not filtered through to the Air Ministry public relations men who issued a bulletin on 26 April 'bringing his score of confirmed destroyed to 31' although Finucane had not even put in a combat report and allowed Len Thorne to claim the kill, and 602's operational log recorded that he shared it with Thorne.

The bulletin describing the action of 17 May is even more bizarre, indicating that perhaps the publicists were being warned off. If they were, Finucane would have been happy about it. Air Ministry Bulletin No 7011 was a lengthy press release ending as an afterthought with the paragraph: 'Squadron Leader Finucane DSO DFC and Bars, flying with another wing in the second operation, destroyed an Fw 190 which brings his total of destruction to 32', resulting in predictable headlines. The publicity would have been difficult to counter at this time because John Wren a Melbourne businessman presented a £1,000 cheque to be divided between Finucane and Truscott and this was widely publicised in May 1942. Mrs Finucane cabled her thanks and acceptance of £400 to Mr Wren.

On 26 May Group Captain Atcherley, chased by three Fw 190s on one of his lone flights, baled out near Dover and was picked up by a fishing trawler. There were more changes on the Kenley Wing. 457 Squadron commanded by Peter Brothers DFC, the second Australian fighter squadron which replaced 452, was posted from Redhill to be replaced by 402 (Canadian) Squadron which had been flying from Kenley since 17 May, and now joined 602 at Redhill on 1 June.

June 1942 was a month of blazing hot weather with clear blue skies, a brassy sun and limitless visibility ideal for the circus operations. On 8 June Finucane led the Kenley Wing, 602, 611 and 402 Squadrons on a diversionary sweep for Circus 191 against Bruges docks and flew along the French coast from Ambleteuse and then inland to St Omer to draw German fighters away from the main attack. He was leading with 611 Squadron with Bocock leading 602. Warned by John Niven of Fw 190s crossing the wing's track below – 'I ordered the wing to attack making sure that the wing above were in a position to cover us.' Once he'd committed the wing to the attack Finucane went down to 10,000 feet, swung in behind an Fw 190 which had just shot the tail from a Spitfire, got to 350 yards unseen by the German pilot and opened fire and cannon from astern, seeing two strikes on the port wingtip and three more close to the wing root. Finucane broke off the attack when another Spitfire got into his line of fire, but then went in again with machine guns scoring hits on the side of the cockpit... 'e/a rolled over slowly onto its back, a great puff of smoke came from its engine and the e/a started to spin slowly.' He lost sight of it in cloud at 8,000 feet, reckoned he had killed the pilot but only claimed it as damaged. It went down through a cloud gap near the parachute of the baled-out Spitfire pilot.

Bocock and Bill Loud each damaged one and Niven got a probable. Loud's tailplane was practically shot to pieces by cannon but he still made a successful landing at Redhill. Loud counted 59 bullet holes in his Spitfire. Colin Tait was missing.

On 9 June Pilot Officer Ralph Sampson arrived from 57 OTU. He had transferred to the RAF from the army and had a chance meeting with Finucane and Truscott in a London pub in 1941 when he was still in the Cameron Highlanders:

> 'I was all set to remind Paddy of the meeting but his opening remark was, "I hope you've brought your kilt with you." This did my ego no end of good as did his next remark, "You must have done bloody well to be posted here." Another time I entered the bar and Paddy was having a drink with Johnny Niven. Other members of 602 were in a separate school, so to speak, and I was on the point of joining them when Paddy said, "Come and join the rebels, leave the English alone!"'[61]

Sampson, who later commanded a fighter wing in 2nd Tactical Air Force, completing more than 200 operational flying hours and promotion to wing commander, twice winning the DFC, says Finucane was the most brilliant leader he served under. 'He had a natural flair for leadership and as a fighter pilot but was not always an immaculate aviator. Eric Bocock teased him about a bouncy landing and Paddy replied, "Hamfisted flyers make the best fighter pilots, not your Rate 1 turn experts." I could not reconcile his age as twenty-one. To me he seemed more like twenty-five and certainly more

[61] Letter to author.

mature than his contemporaries whose excessive youth frequently showed through while his rarely did.'

Despite the fine weather Fighter Command eased off on the circus operations during June and Finucane flew his last sweep with 602 on 20 June. This was Circus 193 to Le Havre.

Ralph Sampson:

'Wing Commander Wells came over to Redhill to brief us. 602 were to be target support and would take off five minutes before the other two squadrons, flying towards the south of Le Havre at nought feet – climbing fast to arrive over the target area at 3.25pm at 30,000 feet and then following the rest out after the bombing scheduled for 3.30pm. 611 Squadron, led by the wing leader, would be close escort and above and to one side, radio silence until after the bombing or until menaced. Paddy's briefing was similar but he added that 602 was both the bait for high patrolling Huns and interceptors of Huns stalking the beehive below. All were to rendezvous with the Bostons at nought feet over Beachy Head climbing and crossing the French coast near Fecamp at 15,000 feet.

'I was Yellow 4 at the back of the squadron. Not long after being airborne on a lovely cloudless day and still low down we heard the various controllers on the same frequency report enemy reaction in several different areas. Soon after we started climbing there was a report of 20-plus climbing southwards from Abbeville and I thought, "Those are for us". About fifteen minutes to bombing time we were climbing above the Seine estuary at 22,000 feet. This was the point of no return and bandits were now waiting for us over Rouen at 30,000 feet.

'We turned north leaving the harbour on our left and I heard the wing leader say, "Eggs gone". My watch showed 3.25pm – so they were early. We were at 27,000 feet and Paddy started levelling off and cutting the corner to the left and on to a north-westerly course which took us right over Le Havre and heavy flak which was pouring upwards -1 must say, I cursed Paddy for taking us over the flak – but I soon forgot this when the controller came on again with, "Bandits in your vicinity at 26,000 feet.' Simultaneously as necks were straining to look around Paddy calmly announced, "Twenty 190s 3 o'clock, parallel course and height." The way they were weaving they had obviously seen 602 and were stalking us. They had apparently not seen the beehive below and ahead of us at 10,000 feet.

'The Huns it seemed were waiting for us to make the first move. Paddy called the wing leader and said he was going to take us down in a fast S dive which should place the Huns in front of 611 Squadron which Paddy said he could see and which might pick off a straggler or so. He then said, "Let's go". We followed him down in a screaming dive to the right followed by a turn to the left, at the same time getting a running commentary from Paddy on the Huns and the fact that they were after us. We had the initial advantage of surprise in the manoeuvre but we all knew that the 190 could out-dive us and would eventually catch up. Being Yellow 4 I had great difficulty in following the No 3 ahead of me and at the same time looking behind at the following Huns.

'Suddenly I saw two 190s on either beam about 600 yards. One started firing and I over-tightened my turn and went into a high speed spin. I caught sight of one 190 still above and went on spinning, pulling out at sea level before shaking them off. I heard the wing leader say he had got one and Paddy's reply a moment later, "I can see the splash. Two splashes now."[62]

'I landed back at Redhill some minutes after the squadron and received two raspberries – one from Paddy for losing the formation (although I was not alone in this, there were three of us – red, blue and yellow 4s) – the second from the engineering officer for having pushed the throttle through the override boost and kept it there for eighteen minutes. Rolls-Royce only guarantee five minutes after which the engine is liable to blow up. To Paddy I explained my predicament and to the engineering officer I said, "You try sitting in a Spitfire with Huns on your tail, overhauling you and then looking at the temperature gauge so as to pull back the throttle after five minutes.'

'The tactical plan produced by Paddy on the spur of the moment had succeeded and we lost no fighters or bombers. I told Paddy I had spun because of over-tightening my turn and he replied the Huns were still out of distance and the way we were turning they couldn't get deflection either.

'On another show Sergeant Francis had called Paddy: "One of them is firing at blue 4" and Paddy replied, "I see it but he can't get the deflection." Not much comfort to the man being fired at! One other remark of Paddy's was, I thought, tempting the fates. We did an early morning squadron recco at nought feet near Calais and Boulogne harbours to check shipping rumoured to be creeping along the coast. As we left Boulogne we had plenty of flak – ahead, behind, between and on the far side. We could see the splashes and Sergeant Strudwick called up to report Flak to which Paddy replied, "Bloody awful shooting, isn't it?"'

Circus 193 was Finucane's last show with 602. On the same day, 20 June, he was promoted to Wing Commander and appointed to command the Hornchurch Wing, Essex. He was the youngest Wing Commander in Fighter Command. Arthur Wilson, a press officer at command HQ, said: 'This was checked at the time.'[63] Finucane regretted leaving 602 and the Canadians of 402 Squadron; he got on particularly well with the Canadians and their CO, Bob Morrow from Toronto, although he ticked off 402 pilot Bud Malloy for beating-up the dispersal on his last day at Redhill. Malloy, also from Toronto, did a roll from the top of a loop then hit two high speed stalls and came down to within two feet of the dispersal hut roof and over two parked Spitfires with groundcrews running in all directions. The Canadians loved aerobatics and Morrow had asked Malloy to put on a show for some visitors but Finucane was unaware of this.

In the evening the Canadians joined 602 for a farewell party for Finucane at the White Hart, Reigate. 602's new CO was Peter Brothers. The next day, 21 June 1942, Finucane left for Hornchurch.

Paddy Finucane seen as a Squadron Ldr probably when commanding 602 Squadron in 1942.

[62] Wells claimed a probable. Pilot Officer Graham, 611 Squadron destroyed another one and saw the pilot bale out.

[63] Interview with author.

16

Wing Leader

The station commander at Hornchurch was George Lott DSO DFC who, introducing Finucane, said: 'This is Paddy Finucane, our new wing leader', and adding jokingly, 'Watch this type, Paddy – he'll get you swept under the carpet at Shepherd's' – a favourite London bar with Hornchurch pilots. The 'type' was Duncan Smith DFC and Bar, aged twenty-six, the commander of 64 Squadron which was now converting to the new Spitfire Mk IXs – they were the first squadron to get them, an indication of their high standing in Fighter Command – and Finucane, keen to try one, took Duncan Smith's personal aircraft for a test.

Duncan Smith joked:

'This is rather a special aircraft. I hope you are good enough to bring it back in one piece.'

Finucane grinned back as he tightened up the straps:

'I hope it's been properly serviced or there will be trouble.'

Wearing the rank of Wg Cdr, this photo must have been taken just as he took command of the Hornchurch Wing on 27 June 1942; in the background is a 602 Squadron Spitfire which would indicate the photo was taken at Redhill or Kenley.

Finucane noted in his logbook that this was on 26 June. He flew the Mk IX for forty minutes and went to 36,000 feet.

The Spitfire IX had a new Merlin 61 1600 hp engine developed for high altitude performance with a two-stage supercharger which cut in at 15,000 feet, climbed at 4,000 feet a minute, had a ceiling of 43,000feet in a complete range of power from ground level to 40,000 feet and a four-bladed Rotol constant speed propeller to absorb the extra thrust. 'We would have all been dead ducks if we'd been stuck with the old VBs to cope with the Fw 190s,' commented Duncan Smith.[64]

Finucane's appointment to Hornchurch was a remarkable achievement. In less than a year he had become a nationally known fighter pilot with a reputation on the squadrons for getting among the stuff and shooting it down, and with a highly individualistic style of leadership and command which they had heard about at Hornchurch.

He was still the top scoring and highest decorated sweep pilot operational in Fighter Command, with the experience to lead, and noted in his logbook at the end of June that he had done 108 sweeps. Wing leader, officially Wing Commander Flying, was a senior and responsible appointment with authority on fighter airfields second only to the station commander, and the wing leader was answerable to him for the operational efficiency of squadrons, deciding tactics and leading in the air. They were hand-picked by Leigh-Mallory and approved by Sholto Douglas.

The other difference between Finucane and wing leaders at this time was that he was younger by several years than other officers who held this important post – giving him the triple distinction at Hornchurch of being the youngest wing leader with the highest score and more combat awards than any other wing leader.

By the time they were judged to have the right amount of combat time and leadership the average age of wing leaders in Fighter Command was twenty-four to twenty-six, with a proven combat record to match. Malan and Bader, the first two wing leaders of the previous year, were both thirty at the time and were exemplars of men who led their wings by sheer strength of personality and character with air victories to inspire the younger inexperienced pilots and command the respect of the veterans. In the same mould was Harry Broadhurst DSO DFC, who formed the Wittering Wing in the summer 1940 at the same time as Bader formed the Duxford Wing, and moved south to command Hornchurch at the same time that Bader went to Tangmere and Malan to Biggin Hill to lead the new big wings to start Fighter Command's 1941 sweep offensive over Northern France.

Broadhurst led his wing in the air at Hornchurch, although there was no call for him to do so as station commander, because there was a shortage of men of the right experience: 'I would not have done so if we'd had people of the right experience,' he told me. Broadhurst got on well with Leigh-Mallory who was known for having favourites – he was one of L-M's three Bs, Bader, Beamish and Broadie – and was at the time of Finucane's appointment the deputy senior air staff officer at 11 Group where Leigh-Mallory could keep an eye on him and stop him from flying operationally, with the first two Bs now out of the air war.

Sir Harry spoke to me about some of his conversations with Leigh-Mallory and commented on the ability of Australian fighter pilots, though not related to 452's success of 1941:

[64] Interview with author.

'My experience of Australians is that they were quick at seeing the enemy and getting at him and provided some of the best fighter pilots. The average of British fighter pilots on a squadron who could score kills was ten per cent; on an Australian squadron – and I met a lot of Aussies when commanding the Desert Air Force – it was twenty per cent. They were strong individualists with a feel for air fighting.

'Leigh-Mallory was a bit shy which gave the impression of being pompous but he would always listen to what his fighter leaders were saying, and was a good judge of character with the ability to pick the right men for the job.'

It is in the context of Leigh-Mallory's ability to pick the right men for the job that Finucane's appointment to Hornchurch must be seen.

He met with reserve and caution from some at Hornchurch where the squadron and flight commanders were mostly several years older, and even allowing for rivalry between squadrons and fighter stations those on the Kenley Wing were not amateurs despite what some at Hornchurch appeared to think about the publicity and high scoring.

But Broadhurst had trained and led the wing to a high standard and left a tradition at Hornchurch which the veterans still there when Finucane arrived as wing leader properly respected and were keen to live up to.

Duncan Smith told me:[65]

'I had nearly always flown as wingman to Broadie who was an exceptional pilot and leader and I was very biased as regards wing leading. Before Paddy's arrival I had led the wing as senior squadron commander at Hornchurch.

'I liked Paddy but I resented his posting to Hornchurch because I did not consider he was more qualified to lead the wing than I was. I believe he appreciated this. But our relationship was always cordial and we had several discussions about tactics and personal combat experiences. He was forthright but rather quiet and a moderate drinker.

'His reputation had gone on ahead of him through the terrific publicity and a lot of people felt the press was attributing more to him than was justified.'

Finucane may well have agreed with Duncan Smith. There had been a recent rash of 'Paddy to command RAF wing at 21' and 'Finucane promoted Wing Commander at 21' headlines following his appointment on 21 June. Another Hornchurch ace of this time who was also much publicised was Don Kingaby, a 64 Squadron flight commander, who, like Ginger Lacey, had been an individualistic and top-scoring sergeant pilot. In July 1942 Kingaby DFM and two Bars, aged twenty-two, was seventeenth on the Fighter Command list with eighteen victories; a former insurance clerk and VR entrant, the son of a country vicar, he was usually billed in the press as 'the 109 specialist.'

Leon Prevot, aged twenty-six, the Belgian commander of 122 Squadron, was another Hornchurch pilot to be publicised, billed in an Air Ministry communique to

[65] Personal interview and letter.

the press as 'one of the finest aerobatic pilots in Fighter Command' on his appointment as 122's CO.

Finucane had some good flyers under his command at Hornchurch in the three squadrons at the home airfield, 64, 81 and 154, and 122 at the Fairlop satellite, which comprised the wing. Two of his squadron commanders were aged twenty-six, 'Razz' Berry, 81's CO was in his mid-twenties, and Gus Carlson, the New Zealand CO of 154 Squadron was nearer thirty. Some got publicity, some didn't. Most of those who did, like Finucane, agreed they could have done without it.

The truest press comment ever made about Finucane was in *The Bulletin and Scots Pictorial* on his appointment as CO of 602 Squadron: 'He is regarded as a brilliant tactician and leader and is noted for his robust fighting methods.' The robustness was particularly apt. He was judged on these qualities at Hornchurch and Duncan Smith, candidly admitting he felt he should have got the job of wing leader, did not prejudge on hearsay. Duncan Smith became a distinguished Group Captain, with a double DSO and triple DFC. Berry DSO DFC, from Hull, had flown from Hornchurch in 1940 on 603 Squadron with Richard Hillary, author of the Battle of Britain memoir *The Last Enemy*. Alan Eckford, another 1940 veteran, was a 154 Squadron flight commander. Mike Donnet, Belgian military, naval and air attaché in London in the 1970s as Lieutenant- General Aviation Baron M. Donnet CVO DFC, was an experienced pilot on 64 Squadron.

Finucane quickly made his presence felt at Hornchurch. He picked as his personal Spitfire BM308 from the station flight, had the shamrock painted on – this was done by Bill Hooper whose cartoon character Pilot Officer Prune was known throughout the RAF in Tee Emm (training memoranda) – and followed the custom of wing leaders by having his initials on the fuselage as identification letters. Much had changed since he had last flown operationally from Hornchurch in 1940 as a pilot officer and he quickly met the men of his new command, and was popular in particular at 81 Squadron's dispersal where they noticed he was usually followed around by a dog.[66]

Finucane kept a firm grip on what was going on with his usual self assurance. After two 154 Squadron Spitfires collided on landing he got the wing together and lectured on flying discipline. 81 Squadron's log noted for 7 July 'Pilots assembled for blitz talk by G/Capt Lott on R/T discipline followed by W/Cdr Finucane tearing off a strip on the same subject and also on the general conduct of pilots.' A few days later Finucane assembled the wing in the briefing room and lectured on ground strafing.

Donnet recalls, 'We did a four squadron formation exercise with Finucane leading and after the exercise he tore us off a strip because our formation was not what he expected. He had fixed ideas as to what he wanted and how the squadrons should fly. In the evening he would join us for a drink on the lawn outside the officer's mess and discuss tactics. It was a pleasant atmosphere.'

Finucane, in fact, ordered Hornchurch to fly a looser formation. They were in the usual Fighter Command battle formation of fours line-astern but tighter than he was used to on the Kenley Wing and he made it clear they had to open out.

Sidney Moston, a young sergeant pilot on 81 Squadron, recalls:

[66] He did not own the dog. It was possibly one of 54 Squadron's dogs of 1940 which recognised him and adopted him rather than the other way round.

'He was very popular with our blokes and absolutely dedicated to getting at the enemy. Group objected to a number of unofficial sorties Paddy led into Europe so he organised wing formation training exercises which somehow due to "navigation error" found their way across to France.'

For those who had been through it before, as well as the newcomers, a wing take-off was always a time of tension. Charlton Haw DFM, 81 Squadron: 'When Paddy said at briefing it was low level there were groans all around – when he said low he meant really low. A green light from control was the signal to start up and move out of dispersal. There was silence all around the airfield as we sat in our cockpits before the start-up. Then the green flare arcing out – moving out was an intricate business – if you were out of line you could end up in the wrong squadron. It was the wing leader's job to sort this out at briefing.'

Haw, aged twenty-two, a Yorkshireman with, 504 Squadron in the Battle of Britain, played the piano in the mess for relaxation and squash in the gym with Finucane recalls, 'He was always approachable and relaxed at briefings, on and off duty, and often at our dispersal.'

It was not Finucane's low flying that bothered Haw as much as a previous eccentric wing leader who climbed them to 20,000 feet over Cap Gris Nez and then broke radio silence with, 'Here we are, come and get us', which put the fear of God into thirty-five Hornchurch pilots who broke left, right and centre in all directions.

Ken Waud, aged twenty-three, a senior NCO pilot on 81 Squadron, sometimes flew as Finucane's No 2. Hornchurch was an all grass airfield and squadrons could take-off near enough in line abreast.

Waud:

'A wing take-off was a dramatic and stirring sight. The whole airfield went silent, groundcrews stopped chatting and you could hear the birds twittering in the trees around dispersal. In summer you sat in the cockpit in full flying gear sweating from the heat and nervousness. Aircraft were plugged into the trolly-accs and your finger hovered over the starting button as you waited for the green flare. Then a shattering roar as Spitfires started up all around the airfield. The blast from your own prop wash was a relief and cooled you down.

'Low flying in formation presented problems and the worst was from turbulence from the aircraft in front of you. The slipstream could turn you over onto your back and into the drink or ploughing a hundred yard furrow through farmland or demolishing a row of houses. You had to keep slightly below the one in front of you and if the wingco was already as low as possible you had a problem.

'Often with Paddy we were right on the deck until the rendezvous on the coast and then climb like hell over the Channel. In sweltering summer conditions it was tricky, you were hazy with the heat and aircraft all around you all going at 300 knots at nought feet. Once I got to 20,000 feet I wasn't bothered about the enemy, it was such a relief to get there and cool off. Halfway across the Channel and climbing you could put your feet on the top deck of the rudder bars and think, "Thank Christ, now I'm in control."

'If I recall correctly, once we were in take-off positions facing into wind the wing leader put his hand in front of his face and then forward – real world war one stuff – to his wingman and No 3 and the rest followed when they saw his section moving.'

'A slight mistake in flying at low level,' said Haw, 'would put you in the drink. We were often at 100 feet over town and country and then right on the deck at the English coast.'

From 21 to 29 June Finucane led the wing on two practice sweeps, two fighter ramrods and two rodeos, and on Circus 195 when Hornchurch were close escort to twelve Bostons raiding Hazebrouck. There was a welcome break on 27 June when he took a few hours off to fly up to Bourn to see Ray and they had dinner in Cambridge.

The weather clamped down in the first week of July, cloud alternating with stray sunshine, and there were no operations. Captain John McLaren, of the Duke of Cornwall's Light Infantry, and other visiting army officers at Hornchurch were keen to get the views of fighter pilots on the effectiveness of small arms fire against low flying aircraft. Finucane and most of them thought the chances of being hit were negligible, recalls McLaren. Finucane had to cope with being a celebrity and the Women's Land Army asked him to accept a £5,000 cheque for the Minister of Aircraft Production. On Saturday evening, 11 July, Finucane accepted an invitation to dinner from the Lord Lieutenant of Essex, Francis Whitmore, and, walking in the grounds afterwards, commented on the rose garden, 'Is this not well worth fighting for,' showing an appreciation perhaps for what we today call the quality of life.

While they completed the conversion to Spitfire IXs 64 Squadron became non-operational and on Sunday morning, 12 July, Finucane left mass in the Catholic chapel early at 10·45 am to brief the other three squadrons for a fighter rodeo along the French coast from Le Treport to Ambleteuse, climbing out over Beachy Head at nought feet. In the afternoon they were off again on Circus 198 to Abbeville. Circus 199 to the marshalling yards at Boulogne was flown on 13 July and on the 14th a low level fighter roadstead to Ostend where they got through a lot of flak to beat up three minesweepers.

Finucane was in his usual good form when he gave the briefing on 15 July for a fighter Ramrod (cannon and machine gun attack by fighters) on a German army camp at Etaples a few miles inland from Le Touquet. Berry returned from Northolt with the target photographs at 10·45 am and Finucane held the wing briefing at 11·30 am. Group Captain Lott was to take off five minutes after the rest and fly at 20,000 feet as R/T linkman between the wing and Hornchurch control. The wing intelligence officer gave details of the hutted camp and said they could expect some light flak. The meteorological officer said they could expect scattered cloud at 2,000 to 3,000 feet and it was ideal for a low-level op.

Finucane gave the take-off time as 11·50 for 81 and 154 squadrons with 122 Squadron at Fairlop ten minutes earlier to join up over Hornchurch. The route was east to the Thames Estuary to get around the London balloon barrage to Pevensey Bay and heading out over the Channel at nought feet. Right on the deck, chaps! He was leading with 154 in place of Gus Carlson who had flu. Berry would take six aircraft of 81 Squadron and Prevot with twelve from 122 Squadron would be on the left of the formation with 81 in the centre and 154 on the starboard. The North Weald Wing was to give air support behind at 4-5,000 feet. The raid was timed to arrive over the target when the German troops would be queuing for their midday meal.

Easing the tension which everyone felt before flying he got some well received laughter by indicating the German officers' mess on the target map and threatening dire consequences to anyone attacking it as he was reserving that building for himself.

Finally – 'Butch, you're my No 2.'

Alan 'Butch' Aikman, aged twenty-three, from Toronto, always flew as Finucane's No 2 — 'wingman to the wingco' – when he was with 154 Squadron. The only thing Aikman had against the wingco was that he was hot on saluting. Aikman, a nonconformist with a total contempt for bull in any shape or form, had survived the shock of hearing that he put two airmen on a charge for not saluting the flag outside station HQ – 'Well, godammit, you don't say, no kidding!' – was as usual pleased to be chosen.

Aikman formated to the right of Finucane's Spitfire as they crossed the Sussex coast at Pevensey Bay at 12.10pm, the beach passing below the fleeting Spitfires in an instant. Finucane set course for the French landfall at Le Touquet. From now on everyone keep a good lookout. Aikman reckoned he was picked as wingman because he was such a sterling chap but it was more likely to have been insistence on 'eyeballing around' all the time.

Over Dungeness Lott in a lone Spitfire tuned in to the wing frequency and maintained a listening watch. Twenty thousand feet below as the wing neared the French coast Sergeant Moston, 81 Squadron, had listened to Tangerine on the wind-up gramophone at dispersal, the usual ceremony before an op, and this morning for the first time the wingco had failed to come in and hear it.

At 12.22pm as they crossed the beach at Le Touquet a burst of ground machine gun fire hit Finucane's starboard wing and immediately a wisp of white vapour streamed back from the damaged radiator. It was an extraordinary shot because the chances of a small calibre machine gun hitting a low flying Spitfire going at over 300 knots were minimal, an almost impossible target for the two German gunners faced with a whole wing of Spitfires heading straight at them, looming out of the Channel mist at wave-top height. Aikman had not seen them – the first he knew of their presence was when he saw fire hosing into the starboard wing – and he was convinced that Finucane did not see them either.

Aikman immediately broke R/T silence with Finucane's callsign and said, 'You've had it, sir, in your radiator.' There were no more dramatic R/T conversations. Finucane acknowledged with a thumbs-up to Aikman and went hard over in a tight vertical turn to the right, back over the beach and over the Channel again. There was no need for further chat to alert the German monitoring service that someone important was hit. It was understood at briefings that if the leader went down the attack would continue, and 81, 154 and 122 Squadrons swept in behind Le Touquet to Étaples as planned while Aikman turned back with Finucane.

Aikman made a slightly later turn which brought him further back over the beach; Finucane had passed to the left of the gunners and he roughly where they were from the line of fire. As he completed the turn he saw them with a tripod machine gun on an unprotected ridge of sand about 20 feet above the dunes. He depressed the nose slightly and opened fire seeing the whole lot disappear in a sandstorm effect.

Low level over Étaples 81 and 154 squadrons were strafing the camp covered above by 122 Squadron which made a large sweep inland to come in behind the other two squadrons. Leon Prevot fired at three tents and German officers, seeing his shells find the target. 81 Squadron ran into heavy flak and three aircraft were hit.

Finucane ditched his Spitfire into the Channel about ten miles out from Le Touquet at 12.28pm. Aikman, about two wing spans away on his right and throttled back to say with him, his landing gear and flaps down, to maintain a slow speed and stay in the air, heard Finucane's R/T comment, distorted by the low altitude, that the engine was overheating. The temperature gauge must by now have been well into the red and Finucane had throttled back, flying very slowly to save the engine. He jettisoned the cockpit canopy and just before removing his helmet radioed, 'This is it, Butch.'

The engine had not seized. The propeller was still turning and the long white plume of escaping coolant trailed 100 feet behind as Finucane looked across at Aikman with a 'here we go' thumbs up signal and eased back on the stick.

Aikman recalls it was a classically correct ditching, but the Spitfire disappeared in a 'wall of water', nosed down and sank instantly. Just before this Aikman had seen Finucane releasing what he thought was the parachute harness; he was not near enough to be sure of the detail, but what Finucane could have been doing was tightening his Sutton harness. Since early days at Kenley he flew with the harness loose to give greater freedom in looking around from the cockpit but tightened it up before going into combat. This is confirmed by Keith Chisholm of 452 Squadron and Ralph Sampson of 602 Squadron. He may have left it late to tighten the harness fully this time before

Official telegram informing Paddy Finucane's mother that he was missing in action 15 July 1942.

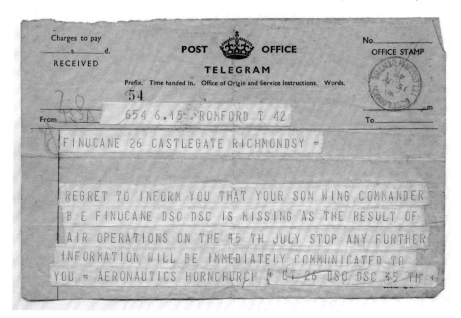

hitting the water. If so he would have been thrown forward on to the gunsight and was unconscious as the aircraft went down. The question must remain unanswered.

The Spitfire was difficult to ditch on water and usually stayed afloat at the most a few seconds, long enough for a pilot to get out or disentangle himself sufficiently if he went down with it to float to the surface with the buoyancy of the inflatable dinghy. Finucane could have gained height and baled out but as he was too near the French coast and captivity, had obviously decided against this.

Letter to Paddy Finucane's mother written by Gp Capt George Lott, Station Commander RAF Hornchurch after he was reported missing.

to say he will be missed by the RAF as
a whole, but it is a fact which cannot be
denied. It is given to very few to make
such a name and such progress as
Paddy made, in such a short time, and
you must be very proud of him. He was a
fine fellow.

I offer you my sympathy and that
of all the pilots of this wing who looked up
to your son as a leader in all things, as
a very small palliative to the grief you must
feel. Please believe that it is sincere.

Yours Sincerely

C. Y. ___ S/Capt.

Aikman orbiting at a few hundred feet noted that once the water settled there was no oil or debris to mark the spot. He circled higher and transmitted a mayday ditching signal. Leon Prevot coming out of France ordered his sections to reform in fours line abreast to search a wide area looking for stragglers, and was in time to see the ditching. The squadron circled for ten minutes but short of fuel returned to Hornchurch. Aikman stayed another ten minutes before he had to get back.

At the Barnridge officers' mess, Redhill, Bob Morrow and the Canadians of 402 Squadron were off duty when ops ran with the news at 2.30pm. Morrow immediately got permission for 402 to take off and search the Channel. Without waiting to form into flights Morrow got together all available pilots and they poured off from Redhill and went out at deck level all the way, arriving at 3.05pm to find evidence of some action; three motor gun boats were in the area, one on fire and apparently abandoned. Morrow formed 402 into a defensive circle at 500ft above the other two and for twenty- five minutes fought off fifteen Fw 190s which came at them in pairs. Morrow and Bud Malloy both fired and saw one Fw 190 go into the sea. They did not get away unscathed. One 402 pilot baled out and was picked up by an MGB and another crash landed at Manston.

Telegram from the Australian High Commissioner S M Bruce to Paddy Finucane's mother expressing sympathy as to his loss.

Among the hundreds of tributes arriving at the Finucane family's Richmond home were:
Sholto Douglas:

> Your son's courage, skill and powers of leadership were a great inspiration to the Fighter Command, including myself. His influence among his fellow pilots was remarkable for one of his age. We shall all miss him greatly. He was the beau ideal of the 'fighter boy'.

Leigh-Mallory:

> I admired his work tremendously and on the few occasions when I had talks with him found him most hard-headed and thoughtful over all that he was doing. As well as being a brilliant fighter pilot I felt that he had the true spirit of a crusader and a high purpose in all that he did. As a Wing Commander I anticipated he would turn out to be one of the greatest leaders we have ever had … he is a very great loss not only to the Royal Air Force but also to our country.

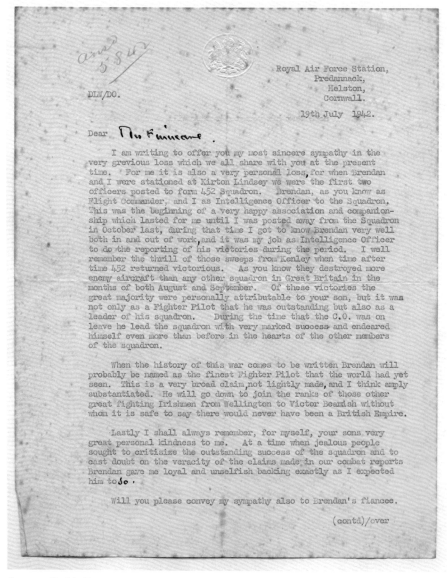

Letter to Paddy Finucane's mother from Fg Off Denys Lane Walters, former Intelligence Officer of 452 Squadron. It shows clearly what many thought of Paddy.

McNamara, RAAF Overseas HQ:

> His name will be for ever closely associated with Australia because of the splendid qualities of courage, skill, leadership and comradeship which he displayed while serving in 453 Squadron, Royal Australian Air Force. The Royal Australian Air Force recognises the tremendous debt 452 Squadron owed to the fine example and inspiration which your son was to that squadron.

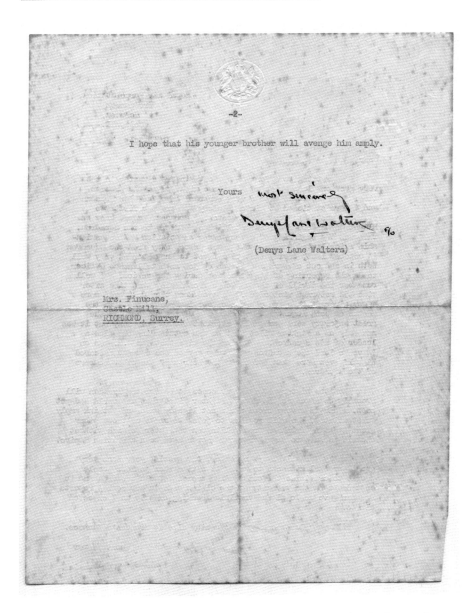

-2-

I hope that his younger brother will avenge him amply.

Yours most sincerely

Denys Lane Walters

(Denys Lane Walters)

Mrs. Finucane,
Castle Hill,
RICHMOND, Surrey.

On 28 March 1943 Truscott, commanding 76 Squadron operating in the south-west Pacific, misjudged his height in hazy conditions off the west Australian coast and was killed flying his Kitty Hawk into the sea practising a mock attack on a Catalina flying boat within sight of the US Naval Air Station Exmouth Gulf.

Finucane was one of the RAF's most accomplished fighter pilots. He was a complete man of his time, the only rightful place on a fighter squadron; there was a resolution about him which few could fail to notice, and a determination to be among the best once he got there. At Kenley the dramatic events of those days seem imprinted on their surroundings like a photographic negative, trapped by a time capsule in the eroded runways and brick walled dispersal bays which once clamoured to the volley of Spitfire engines. All is now peaceful and quiet by the long grass at the unkempt dispersal site but it does not take much mental effort to tune in to R/T voices distorted by time and distance… 'About three o'clock, Blue, slightly above, about eight of them going to pass above and behind'… 'OK Paddy, I got them'… an occasional brassed off New Zealander 'For Christ's sake shut up and give the rest of us a chance.' Returning from a successful fighter sortie over Northern France, the wind whistling in the open gun ports, perhaps youthful exuberance for a moment overcame the discipline and a Spitfire is cracking along just above the grass and then upwards into fast climbing rolls, the letters on the fuselage UD-W: Finucane flying with all his old skill and precision. *Magni Nominis Umbra.*

Memorial poster for Paddy Finucane.
The Wings For Victory campaign using Paddy Finucane's image.

APPENDIX A

Promotions, postings, citations
Wing Commander B E Finucane DSO DFC (41276)

Acting pilot officer on probation (from 29 August 1938) short service commission GD branch	29 October 1938
Pilot officer on probation	29 August 1939
Confirmed in appointment	29 February 1940
Flying officer	3 September 1940
Acting flight lieutenant	14 April 1941
Flight lieutenant (war substantive)	3 September 1941
Acting squadron leader	26 January 1942
Acting wing commander	21 June 1942
Elementary and Reserve Flying Training School, Sywell	29 August 1938
1 RAF Depot, Uxbridge	29 October 1938
8 Flying Training School, Montrose	12 November 1938
13 Maintenance Unit, Henlow (pilotless aircraft section; 21 August 1938 practice and parachute test flight)	26 June 1939
7 Operational Training Unit, Hawarden	28 June 1940
65 Squadron	13 July 1940
452 Squadron, flight commander (13 October 1941 Sutton emergency services hospital; 14 October Epsom ESH; 14 November RAF Hospital, Halton; 21 November RAF Hospital, Torquay)	14 April 1941
452 Squadron, supernumerary	19 January 1942
602 Squadron, squadron commander	26 January 1942
Wing Commander Flying, Hornchurch	21 June 1942

Dates given below are those when published in the London Gazette:

Distinguished Flying Cross – 13 May 1941: This officer has shown great keenness in his efforts to engage the enemy and he has destroyed at least five of their aircraft. His courage and enthusiasm have been a source of encouragement to other pilots of the squadron.

Bar to the DFC – 9 September 1941: This officer has led his flight with great dash, determination and courage in the face of the enemy. Since July 1941 he has destroyed three enemy aircraft and assisted in the destruction of a further two. Flight Lieutenant Finucane has been largely responsible for the fine fighting spirit of the unit.

Second Bar to the DFC – 26 September 1941: This officer has fought with marked success during recent operations over Northern France and has destroyed a further six enemy aircraft. Of these three were destroyed in one day and two in a single sortie on another occasion. His ability and courage have been reflected in the high standard of morale and fighting spirit of his unit. Flight Lieutenant Finucane has personally destroyed 15 hostile aircraft.

Distinguished Service Order – 21 October 1941: Recently during two sorties on consecutive days Flight Lieutenant Finucane destroyed five Messerschmitt 109s bringing his total victories to at least 20. He has flown with this squadron since June 1941 (sic) during which time the squadron has destroyed 42 enemy aircraft of which Flight Lieutenant Finucane has personally destroyed 15. The successes achieved are undoubtedly due to this officer's brilliant leadership and example.

Mentioned in Despatches – 1 January 1942.

APPENDIX B

Combat summary of the 49 engagements
in which Finucane got results
from 12 August 1940 – 8 June 1942

Me 109 destroyed	August 1940, 11.30am, 20,000ft off Deal, 250-50 yards, smoking and diving, independendy seen to crash into Channel.
Me 109 probably destroyed	12 August 1940, 12.45pm, 3,000-1,000ft off Margate, smoking and diving after two bursts 200ft above the Channel.
Me 109 damaged	August 1940, 12.45pm, short burst, strikes seen but lost in cloud.
Me 109 destroyed	August 1940, 4pm, 19,000ft off Dover, long bursts 300-75 yards, in flames.
Me 109 probably destroyed	13 August 1940, 4pm, one burst 200 yards, smoking and spinning.
Me 110 destroyed	January 1941, 9.50am, 7,000ft S of Selsey Bill 15 miles, four attacks – one from 25 yards, 4-second burst, in flames, crashed in Channel.
Ju 88 destroyed (shared)	19 January 1941, 2-2.10pm, 120-50ft sea level chase from St Catherine's Point, IOW, to five miles off Cherbourg, both engines in flames.
Me 109 destroyed	February 1941, 1pm, 12,000ft ten miles E of Cap D'Alprech, two short bursts 250-50 yards, crashed in a wood.
Me 109 destroyed	15 April 1941 5.30pm, 14,000ft S of Dover 15 miles, 5-second burst 250 yards, 4-second burst 200 yards, crashed in Channel.
Me 109 destroyed	11 July 1941, 3pm, 18,000ft W of Lille five miles, 3-second burst 150 yards, pilot baled out.
Me 109 destroyed	3 August 1941, 7.25-30am, 14,000ft W of St Omer five miles, 3-second burst 200 yards, in flames.
Me 109 probably destroyed	3 August 1941, 7.25-30am, 2-second burst 100 yards, tail unit hit, in vertical dive.
Me 109 destroyed	9 August 1941, 11.25am, 20,000ft above cloud Gosnay-Béthune area, 4-second burst 100 yards, in flames.
Me 109 destroyed (shared)	9 August 1941, 11.25am, 3-second burst 25 yards, tail unit hit, vertical dive.

Me 109 destroyed (shared)	9 August 1941,11.25am, 5-second burst 100 yards, in flames.
Me 109E destroyed	16 August 1941, 8.40am, 9,000-5,000ft, off Gravelines, 2-second burst 100 yards, spinning below 1,000ft.
Me 109F destroyed	16 August 1941, 6.30pm, 14,000ft NE of Boulogne 15 miles, 3-second burst 75 yards, in flames.
Me 109 destroyed	16 August 1941, 6.30pm, closes to ten yards when gunsight fails 3-second burst, tail unit shot off.
Me 109 destroyed	19 August 1941, 11.10am, 18,000-4,000ft Gosnay area, three bursts 2-seconds, 3-seconds, 1-second 200 yards, pouring black smoke skidding out of control.
Me 109 probably destroyed	19 August 1941, 11.10am, off Calais, 4-second burst 600-150 yards, smoking, 500ft above the Channel.
Me 109E destroyed	27 August 1941, 7.20am, 300ft NW of Gravelines three miles, cannon 100 yards, crashed in Channel.
Me 109E destroyed	27 August 1941, 7.20am, sea level Calais-Gris Nez, cannon bursts 180-200 yards, independendy witnessed 30ft above the Channel on its back.
Me 109F destroyed	20 September 1941, 3.35pm, 20,000ft NW of Abbeville five miles, 1-second burst cannon 50-75 yards – 'Me 109 went to pieces'.
Me 109F destroyed	20 September 1941, 3.35pm, 1V6-seconds cannon 120 yards, diving in flames.
Me 109 destroyed	20 September 1941, 3.35pm, cannon and mg 150 yards, strikes near wing root and engine, debris, white smoke in vertical dive.
Me 109F destroyed	21 September 1941 3.25pm, 21,000ft E of Hardelot 20 miles, 2-second burst cannon 100 yards, black smoke and diving – wingman sees one explode in dive.
Me 109 destroyed	21 September 1941, 3.25pm, $1\frac{1}{2}$-second burst 200 yards, strikes on engine and tail unit, in flames.
Me 109F destroyed	2 October 1941,5.40pm, 22,000ft E of Boulogne 10-15 miles, 5-second burst 200-50 yards, port wing breaks off.
Me 109F damaged	2 October 1941, 5.40pm, 4-second burst 250-100 yards, spinning.

Me 109F destroyed	12 October 1941, shortly after midday, 20,000ft SW of Le Touquet, 3-second burst cannon and mg 350-120 yards, strikes on engine, cockpit and tail unit in flames.
Me 109F destroyed	13 October 1941, 1.18pm, 16,000ft inland St Omer/ Boulogne, 3-second burst cannon 150-70 yards, tail unit shot up.
Me 109 destroyed	13 October 1941, 1.18pm, 8,000ft, 3-second burst cannon 200-100 yards, crashes in Channel about three miles off Boulogne.
Me 109F damaged	13 October 1941, 1.18pm, 4½-second burst mg 250-150 yards, strikes on starboard wingtip.
Fw 190 damaged	20 February 1942, 11.20-30am, 500ft mid-Channel off Calais-Gris Nez, strikes seen, debris.
Fw 190 destroyed	13 March 1942, 3.12pm, 23,000-8,000ft E of Cap Gris Nez 20-25 miles, 2-second burst cannon and mg, crashed, independently witnessed.
Fw 190 destroyed (shared)	13 March 1942, 3.12pm, 20,000ft, 1½-second burst and two shorter bursts, crashed.
Ju 88 probably destroyed (one-third shared)	14 March 1942, 5.17pm, 4,000ft to sea level, NNW of Le Havre 25 miles, 400-350 yards mg, port engine in flames.
Fw 190 destroyed	26 March 1942, 4pm, 12,000ft N of Le Havre 8-12 miles, 1-second burst and 2-second burst at long range, smoke from engine, crashed in Channel, independently witnessed.
Me 109 destroyed	28 March 1942, 5.35pm, 20,000ft Gris Nez-Gravelines from 200 yards, strikes on port wing root and engine, debris and in flames, independently witnessed spinning at 1,000ft.
Fw 190 destroyed	28 March 1942, 5.35pm, 150 yards cannon and mg strikes on starboard wing, hits on tail unit, in vertical dive and spinning.
Me 109 destroyed (shared)	28 March 1942, 5.35pm, 200 yards short bursts, second attack 75 yards, in flames.
Fw 190 damaged	2 April 1942, 2.35pm, 17,000ft St Valéry/Gris Nez, two 4-second bursts 240-125 yards.
Fw 190 damaged	10 April 1942, 5.39pm, 20,000ft SE of Mardyck five miles, 270 yards, cannon strikes on engine, confirmed by wingman.

Fw 190 damaged	16 April 1942, 7.45am, 26,000-27,000ft S of Mardyck, 2-second burst cannon and mg 230-260 yards, debris, smoking, diving.
Fw 190 destroyed (shared)	26 April 1942, 10.37am, 22,000-23,000ft Mardyck/Gravelines, smoke, diving, crashed in Channel, in-dependently witnessed. Finucane did not claim.
Fw 190 damaged	28 April 1942, 11.30am, 13,000ft Audruicq, cannon 35 yards, second burst strikes on engine and starboard wing root.
Fw 190 probably destroyed	30 April 1942, 11.55am, 18,000ft NW of Le Havre 15 miles, $3^{1}/_{2}$-second burst 100-200 yards, strikes on cockpit area, propeller stops.
Fw 190 destroyed	17 May 1942, 11.40am, 15,000ft Guiñes, 3-second burst cannon and mg, crashed.
Fw 190 probably destroyed	8 June 1942, 1.50pm, 10,000ft St Omer, long burst cannon and mg 350-300 yards, strikes, smoking and spinning.

Note: Where the same time is given for more than one combat on the same sortie it can be taken as the time when the action started)

APPENDIX C

Fighter Command Operational Instruction 93
22 November 1941

Fighter Command Operational Instruction 93 of 22 November 1941, under the heading enemy casualties gives the following definitions:

Destroyed: This category will cover cases when:

The aircraft is clearly seen to hit the ground or sea.

The aircraft is seen to break up in the air or to descend in flames whether or not confirmation from a second source is available.

The enemy aircraft is forced to descend and is captured. The pilot of a single-seater aircraft is seen to bale out.

Probably destroyed (ie believed to have been destroyed): This category will cover cases in which the enemy aircraft is seen to break off combat in circumstances which lead to the conclusion that it must be a loss though it is not actually seen to crash.

Damaged: This category will cover cases in which the enemy aircraft is obviously considered damaged as a result of the attack of our aircraft, eg cases in which the undercarriage is dropped or engine or aircraft parts are shot away.

Notes on assessment of categories: Complete disintegration is not necessary for the acceptance of a claim of destroyed. If a main plane drops off or elevators are shot away the enemy aircraft may be admitted destroyed. A Me 109 which would otherwise have been claimed as probably destroyed in a vertical dive at less than 2000ft may also be admitted destroyed as below this height the Me 109 cannot pull out of a steep dive before crashing.

Smoke by itself is not an indication that an enemy aircraft is on fire. If black it may be the result of using extra boost to escape. If white it may be escaping glycol and indicate no more than damage to the enemy aircraft. If a smoking aircraft is seen going down but not seen to crash it may be claimed as probably destroyed if its motion suggests lack of control.

Damage may be claimed if de Wilde ammunition is seen to enter the enemy aircraft even though no parts appear to shot away. Even if spinning down completely out of control an enemy aircraft may only be claimed as probably destroyed unless it is seen to hit the ground or sea.

Damage will also be admitted if cannon strikes are seen even though there is no other evidence than that of the strikes. It is considered most unlikely that a cannon shell exploding inside an aircraft can fail to do damage.

Where the pilot or his intelligence officer feels that the special circumstances of the case merit the stepping up of a claim it should be entered in the lower category with a request that it may be submitted to command through group for re-assessment in the high category.

These definitions were repeated in Operational Instruction 4/1942 for the spring and early summer of 1942. But Fighter Command Intelligence Instruction 5/1942, of 27

June 1942, while covering exactly the same ground in the same words, omits section (d).

The three categories of destroyed, probably destroyed and damaged date from 12 August 1940. It is an extraordinary fact that before this for one whole month, April 1940, the Air Ministry ruled that a combat had to be independently witnessed before a claim for destroyed would be admitted. Fighter Command soon convinced them of the impracticality of that idea and from May until mid-August the categories were destroyed (confirmed) and the equivocal destroyed (unconfirmed): in the latter they were prepared to take the attacking pilot's word for it.

But this was an unsatisfactory compromise which needed clarification and it came at a group commanders' conference at Fighter Command headquarters, Bendey Priory, on 10 August while the Battle of Britain was in progress. The notes on this meeting are:

Method of assessing enemy casualties
9. Air Ministry and 11 Group proposals on this point were discussed.
10. In summarising the discussion SASO said that the reasons for asking for some alteration in the present method of assessing enemy casualties are that, firstly, from the group point of view it is considered desirable to keep category 1 divided between those that are witnessed and those that are not witnessed as this distinction is useful as a deterrent to over-optimism. Secondly, the reason for the proposal that the first two categories (in 11 Group's proposals) should be logged together for Air Ministry purposes under the heading of 'destroyed' is to simplify the sorting within the Air Ministry of results into two categories as used at present but under titles that are more appropriate to their exact meaning. This has the further advantage of enabling group commanders, in making recommendations for awards, to put all successes logged within the group under 1A and IB under the general heading of 'aircraft destroyed'. Finally, we do see some advantage in keeping the third category 'damaged'.
11. The term 'destroyed' was defined as:
Aircraft seen to hit the ground or sea.
Seen to break up in the air.
Seen to be generally on fire (ie not merely with flames coming from engine).
Confirmed from other sources as coming within (i) to (iii) above.

The three categories 'destroyed', 'probable' and 'damaged' were ratified by the C-in-C Sir Hugh Dowding, who left the meeting early before they were discussed, and at Air Ministry two days later to become the law in Fighter Command. Neither the 11 Group commander Keith Park, who sensibly asked for the alterations, nor Leigh-Mallory (then commanding 12 Group) were at the conference.

The changes in rules led to some acrimonious correspondence a year later between 74 Squadron (Latterly commanded by Sailor Malan) and Fighter Command, resulting in the squadron's score being downgraded from 187½ destroyed to 122. In an aggrieved letter of 24 July 1941 the squadron said according to command's assessment it was credited with 116½ to 1 June, and for 187½ up to 7July, listed the pilots' names and types of aircraft destroyed requesting a search in the records to breach 'the large discrepancy.'

Command replied on 29 July that up to 7 July the score was 122:

The discrepancy is admittedly large and it is suggested that prior to August 1940 when the present assessment of enemy casualties in the three categories destroyed, probably destroyed and damaged was introduced the enemy aircraft admitted under the former category 'unconfirmed destroyed' have been assessed by the squadron as destroyed, whereas this command only admitted enemy aircraft claimed as confirmed destroyed. The former category 'unconfirmed destroyed' is the equivalent of the present category 'probably destroyed' established with the approval of Air Ministry in August 1940.

The commanding officer wrote back on 14 September:

... you state that the former category unconfirmed destroyed is the equivalent of the new category probably destroyed. In my opinion this is unjust for under the old classification rules a confirmed destroyed . ... had to be seen by two independent witnesses; and an unconfirmed was not, as with the present probably destroyed, merely an enemy aircraft considered by the attacking pilot to have been destroyed but not actually seen to disintegrate or crash, but an enemy aircraft definitely destroyed by the attacking aircraft but not seen to crash by two independent witnesses.

Informatively, Fighter Command replied on 21 September:

2. On 29 August 1939 the Director of Intelligence issued War Instruction No 1 which established the following:
Category (a) 'conclusive' which was identified with the present category destroyed.
Category (b) 'inconclusive' under which the enemy breaks off the engagement in circumstances which suggest he has been damaged.

3. Air Ministry letter to commands, dated 30 March 1940, stated: 'Claims that enemy aircraft have been brought down will only be accepted as confirmed when supported by the evidence of independent sources. Claims by a single pilot will be assessed as unconfirmed unless the loss is confirmed by other sources.'

4. The above ruling was immediately contested by this command and Air Ministry letter dated 7 May 1940 stated: 'The claim of a pilot of a single seater aircraft to bringing down an enemy over the sea where corroboration by eye witnesses is impossible allows the station commander to express his opinion of the value of the pilot's claim.

5. Air Ministry letter to commands dated 28 May 1940 put the onus of the decision whether losses should be accepted as confirmed or otherwise on to commands. For their guidance the following principles were set out:
To be reported as confirmed losses as a result of air combat.
The aircraft must be seen on the ground or in the sea by a member of the crew or formation or confirmed as destroyed from other sources, eg ships at sea, local authorities etc.
The aircraft must be seen to descend with flames issuing. It is not

sufficient if only smoke is seen.

The aircraft must have been seen to break up in the air.

To be reported as an unconfirmed loss as a result of air combat.

The aircraft must have been seen to break off the combat in circumstances which lead our pilot or crew to believe it will be a loss.

6. From paragraphs 3 and 4 above it will be seen that the independent confirmation of a single pilot's claim was required only during the month of April 1940, while paragraph 5 (ii) shows that the definition of the category 'destroyed unconfirmed' laid down in May 1940 is identical with the present category 'probably destroyed' laid down by the Air Ministry on 12 August 1940 which reads: 'Probable (ie believed to have been destroyed). This category will cover cases in which the enemy aircraft is seen to break off combat in circumstances that lead to the conclusion that it must be a loss but was not actually seen to crash.

The letter concluded:

... there would appear to be no purpose in attempting to re-assess the squadron's claims on a basis which does not give as accurate a picture of enemy losses as has hitherto been the case. Air Ministry is in a position to assess from other sources enemy losses claimed by this command, and has stated that over a reasonable period the present method of assessment attains a satisfactory degree of accuracy.[67]

As can be seen, Finucane was not the only one having trouble over his score. More than a third of 74 Squadron's claims were downgraded by Fighter Command. There is no suggestion in this that any of the squadron's claims after 12 August were under scrutiny but the last part of the 74 commander's letter indicates that in 1941 there was still confusion over claims in the minds of some squadron commanders, and if so, also in the minds of the men under their command, unsure whether to claim a destroyed or a probable. The command's own files show that other squadrons and individual pilots were having much the same problem and many combat results, under the new classifications, were revised in 1941 and 1942 from destroyed to probable.

In support of this it is interesting to note that the 74 Squadron letter states: '... our intelligence officer was told by the senior and second- senior intelligence officers at 11 Group that claims rendered as unconfirmed destroyed could definitely be considered as destroyed under the new classification.'

So when Finucane was questioning the efficacy and reliability of the system so were others. The more stringent ruling sought to be more definitive and stricter without cramping the fighter pilot's style; trying to get the best of both worlds in an honest attempt to simplify the problem from the fighter pilot's view by paradoxically – but realistically – giving him more leeway in claiming an aircraft as destroyed. Small wonder that squadron intelligence officers, from their lowly rank

[67] In a Fighter Command list of the top twelve squadrons on 2 March 1942, 74 Squadron was credited with 123 destroyed.

and total lack of experience on air operations, sometimes had trouble interpreting the rules. Finucane himself never had any such doubts about his claims but he had a good many about how they were sifted and interpreted.

There are other flaws and imponderables in the rules to be considered. In Operational Instructions 73, 93 and 4/1942, section (d) notes on assessment of categories, no distinction is made between black smoke caused by boosting an engine and that caused by battle damage. Yet the distinction was obvious to Finucane and any other combat experienced pilot: a vast difference in the thin streams from high-revving engine exhausts and the clouds of effluent from a seriously battle damaged aircraft. This was why seven of Finucane's thirty-one combat reports state black (or grey) smoke from his victims.

Similarly, the ruling about white smoke is questionable. Fighter Command's experience in the Battle of Britain proved that an aircraft couldn't get far with escaping glycol but the argument against it has less validity in 1941, when German aircraft had scores of captured French bases within gliding distance, than in 1940 over Southern England. Finucane claimed one streaming white smoke (20 September 1941) but this was also in a vertical dive and he had hammered it with cannon and machine gun fire at the wing root and engine.

Section (d) admits that 'complete disintegration' was not necessary to claim a destroyed or if a main plane dropped off. (No aircraft would get far on one wing!). The statement on elevators being shot away has great validity in assessing the result of combats as has that stating a Me 109 could not pull out of a steep dive below 2,000 feet. There was usually only one end to an aircraft deprived of fore and aft control from the elevators, it went straight in. Seven of Finucane's combat reports state 'tail unit hit' (three followed by a vertical dive), including 'shot away tail unit' from ten yards (16 August) and 'tail unit practically destroyed' (13 October). Four of Finucane's combat reports record aircraft spinning, including 'spinning in' (28 March). No pilot went into a voluntary spin which presented an easy target and spins could indicate that the pilot had temporarily lost control, but this has to be read in conjunction with other damage reported by Finucane.

The group commanders' conference at Fighter Command on 10 August 1940 on the question of burning aircraft (seen to be generally on fire, not merely with flames from engine) was sensibly modified in the command's later operational instructions to seen 'to descend in flames', confirmed in the letter to 74 Squadron. The pilot of a single engine aircraft on fire would be in a lot of trouble. Me 109 pilots were sitting on top of a petrol tank under the seat. Spitfire pilots had two tanks full of 100 octane direcdy in front of them behind the instrument panel. There were instances of exceptionally courageous men on both sides staying at the controls of a burning single seater fighter and continuing the battle (Fighter Command's only VC was won that way) but most baled out rapidly. The command conference decision on an 'engine on fire only' ruling was clearly erring too far on the side of caution, and righdy amended.

Billowing smoke (as distinct from boost smoke trails) indicated fire somewhere (probably in the engine) and the ruling that smoke was 'inconclusive' appears to be a contradiction at variance with the command's operational instructions on claiming an aircraft as destroyed if it was seen going down in flames. A pilot under pressure in a dogfight was not going to hang around too long to see if flames emerged from the smoking wreck; if smoke didn't indicate fire, what did it indicate? In the fighter pilot's jargon they were 'flamers'.

Ten of Finucane's victories were flamers. Only three were twin engine aircraft (Ju 88, 19 January 1941) and another Ju 88 shared with two other pilots on 14 March 1942, and the Me 110 on 4 January 1941. The other seven were Me 109s, including his second confirmed victory in the Battle of Britain; the rest were all claimed on the sweeps later. With his sort of experience Finucane could lay great claim to knowing what he was talking about.

Two further points need to be noted here about section (d) in the operational instructions which were guidelines for the greater part of the sweep period up to the end of June 1942. Section (d) states damage may be claimed if de Wilde ammunition is seen to strike the enemy aircraft; fair enough, because this ammo made a flash on impact and like tracer ammunition was an indication of accuracy of aim. But the statement 'It is considered most unlikely that a cannon shell exploding inside an aircraft can fail to do damage' is inexplicable. The operations staff at headquarters Fighter Command had obviously not read the Air Fighting Development Unit file on the subject: 'The penetration of a 20mm cannon shell is sufficient to go through both sheets of armour plate, the petrol tank and the pilot of a Me 109, so it can be seen that a short well aimed burst of two three seconds in a vital part is enough to put any enemy aircraft out of action irrespective of the amount of armour plating carried.' Perhaps this was why the responsibility for defining combat claims was transferred from the operations staff to the intelligence staff, who promptly dropped section (d) as misleading to the new generation of fighter pilots coming onto squadrons after the Battle of Britain and now employed on the sweeps. The veterans knew better, if the ops staff didn't, and briefed their protegees accordingly.

Finucane himself knew the devastating effect of a well aimed cannon burst. On 20 September 1941, using cannon only from 50 to 75 yards, he got in an accurate burst of only one second at a Me 109F which promptly exploded in a gush of flames and dense black smoke; he flew through the fireball which showered a thousand bits of debris from 20,000 feet over the peaceful mid-afternoon French countryside north of Abbeville. As he put it in his combat report: 'Me 109 went to pieces.' He also convincingly demonstrated the long range efficiency of cannon in the hands of a skilled marksman on 26 March 1942, firing from 500 yards (twice the effective range of ·303 machine guns) and watched the Fw 190 go straight down into the Channel from 12,000ft north of Le Havre. It was a two-second burst, following one-second machine gun fire, admitted in his combat report with a touch of humour as fired 'more in hope than in anger'.

So, as can be seen, although Fighter Command had got itself sorted out with destroyed, probably destroyed and damaged, there were still anomalies which had Air Vice-Marshal Park (who knew a great deal about fighters) and Leigh-Mallory (who knew less) both been at the group commanders' conference might have been cleared up in the early days of 1940 and thus provided a better basis for the compilers of the command's operational instructions to the sweep pilots who followed in 1941 and 1942.

The charitable explanation of the section (d) remark on the effect of cannon is that gremlins got among the Waaf typists in the orderly room at Bentley Priory and were responsible for a clerical error. Cannon was used only experimentally in the Battle of Britain but it was standard armament on the Spitfire Vb, the sweep pilots' main mount, and after 18 months of circus operations in 1941 and 1942 there appears to be little excuse for the retention of such a misleading comment. In fact, cannon was the decisive fighter armament after 1940 despite the arguments of such machine gun protagonists as Douglas Bader.

Park might have had something to say about paragraph (iii) defining destroyed on 10 August. An engine fire in a fighter was doubly serious in that the pilot was sitting only a few feet away from it and may have only seconds to get out. The individual heroism of staying in the cockpit to fight it out (or reach base) from an aircraft blazing like a blowlamp was rare.

One useful piece of information which section (d) could have given – but didn't – would have eliminated some of the overclaiming. This was the ability to execute what was known in fighter circles as the 'ham manoeuvre', practised by both sides, which consisted in virtually crossing the controls to provide a skidding and erratic flight path to put a pursuing pilot off his aim. It was used when a pilot was on the wrong end of an astern attack, and it also simulated battle damage or that the pilot was wounded and his aircraft out of control.

It is interesting to note that during his early days with 65 Squadron in the Battle of Britain the squadron had, on 5 August, started using probable instead of destroyed unconfirmed on its combat reports, a full week before Air Ministry's ratification of the command conference decision. But on 12 August, the date of Finucane's first victory, the category destroyed unconfirmed was used for two of the squadron's other pilots flying from Manston on the same sortie at 11 30 am. Three other pilots also got 'probables': ie both categories meaning the same thing. This, and the fact that the two unconfirmed went on the squadron records as destroyed, indicates perhaps some confusion in the mind of the intelligence officer (or an argument with the two pilots concerned!). Paddy's combat report was the only one to have destroyed confirmed.

He continued to use the suffix (c) for confirmed against his victories from Manston, Tangmere and Kirton-in-Lindsey in his logbook entries up to his first one from Kenley on 3 August 1941. Thereafter he used (d) or destroyed.

An important consideration when assessing the results of combats from the combat reports and eyewitness accounts is the following information given to the author by General Adolf Galland:

The Me 109 could not pull out from a spin below 1000ft and from a dive could only pull out below 2000ft with reduced speed;

The Fw 190 could not pull out from below 3000ft in a dive at full speed and from a spin below 2000ft. The Fw 190 needed 20 to 25 per cent more height compared with the Me 109 F and G.

APPENDIX D

452 Squadron's scoreboard for August 1941

3 August   Finucane: Me 109 destroyed, Me 109 probably destroyed, circus to St Omer
Eccleton: Me 109 destroyed

9 August   Finucane: two Me 109s destroyed (including two shared), Circus 68 to Gosnay

16 August   Lewis: Me 109 destroyed (shared)
Thorold-Smith: Me 109 destroyed (shared)
Truscott: Me 109 destroyed
Chisholm: Me 109 destroyed (both shared)

19 August   Finucane: Me 109 destroyed, Circus 73 to St Omer, two Me 109s destroyed, Circus 75 to St Omer
Stuart: Me 109 destroyed, Circus 75
Tainton: Me 109 destroyed, Circus 75
Truscott: Me 109 destroyed, Circus 75
Chisholm: two Me 109s destroyed, Circus 75

26 August   Finucane: Me 109 destroyed, Me 109 probably destroyed, Circus 81 to Gosnay
Truscott: Me 109 probably destroyed
Stuart: Me 109 destroyed, Circus 87 to St Omer
Douglas: Me 109 destroyed

27 August   Finucane: two Me 109s destroyed, Circus 85 to St Omer
Thorold-Smith: Me 109 destroyed, Me 109 probably destroyed (this was shortly upgraded to destroyed)

APPENDIX E

11 (Fighter) Group list of pilots with twelve or more confirmed victories at 31 October 1941

F/Lt B E Finucane	452 Squadron	24½
W/Cdr D R S Bader	POW	22½
F/Lt G Allard	85 Squadron	19
W/Cdr J Rankin	Biggin Hill	18
S/Ldr A C Deere	602 Squadron	17¾
Polish pilot	303 Squadron	17
S/Ldr N Orton	54 Squadron	17
F/Lt Demozay	91 Squadron	15
S/Ldr H W Villa	65 Squadron	15
Polish pilot	303 Squadron	15
P/O Thorne	264 Squadron	13

APPENDIX F

Fighter Command list of pilots with twelve or more confirmed victories at 31 March 1942

W/Cdr A G Malan	61 OTU	32
S/Ldr B E Finucane	602 Squadron	29½
W/Cdr R R Stanford Tuck	POW	29
F/Lt J H Lacey	602 Squadron	25
F/Lt H S Lock	611 Squadron	24
W/Cdr D R S Bader	POW	22½
S/Ldr M N Crossley	–	22
W/Cdr R F Boyd	Kenley Wing	22
S/Ldr H M Stephen	234 Squadron	21
S/Ldr D A P McMullen	57 OTU	19
F/Lt G Allard	85 Squadron	19
S/Ldr R G Dutton	54 OTU	19
F/Lt H J L Hallowes	122 Squadron	18
S/Ldr F M R Carey	135 Squadron	18
W/Cdr J Rankin	–	18
French pilot	91 Squadron	18
S/Ldr A C Deere	–	17¾
W/Cdr M H Brown	–	17½
S/Ldr C F Gray	616 Squadron	17½
W/Cdr W D David	55 OTU	17
Sgt J Frantisek	303 Squadron	17
S/Ldr N Orton	54 Squadron	17
W/Cdr M L Robinson	–	17
S/Ldr R F D Morgan	–	16½
W/Cdr AH Boyd	–	16
F/O D E Kingaby	111 Squadron	16
S/Ldr JW Villa	61 OTU	15

W/Cdr J Cunningham	604 Squadron	15
Polish pilot	303 Squadron	15
F/Lt R F T Doe	57 OTU	14½
F/Lt D A S Mackay	130 Squadron	14½
F/Lt R P Stevens	151 Squadron	14½
S/Ldr J Ellis	1 Squadron	14
F/Lt J I Kilmartin	–	14
S/Ldr FJ Soper	257 Squadron	14
F/Lt J A A Gibson	457 Squadron	13½
S/Ldr C F Currant	501 Squadron	13
S/Ldr C R Edge	–	13
W/Cdr J W Simpson	–	13
F/Lt E R Thorne	264 Squadron	13
W/Cdr J A Kent	53 OTU	13
F/Lt J C Freeborn	57 OTU	12½
F/Lt F W Higginson	56 Squadron	12½

APPENDIX G

Fighter Command Offensive Operations

Casualties 1 March–12 April 1942

		German losses		RAF losses	
		Destroyed	Probable	Aircraft	pilots
3 March	Feint sweep	1	—	1	—
8	Circus	2	3	3	3
9	Circus	5	2	3	3
13	Circus	9	5	6	5
13	Roadstead	—	2	1	—
14	Roadstead	9	—	—	—
14	Ramrod	1	2	—	—
23	Sweep	1	—	—	—
24	Circus	2	1	7	7
25	Circus	2	—	—	—
25	Sweep	—	—	1	1
26	Ramrod	8	—	2	2
27	Ramrod	1	2	1	1
28	Rodeo	12	10	6	5
29	Rodeo	—	1	1	—
4 April	Circus	4	4	12	12
8	Rodeo	—	—	1	1
10	Rodeo	6	4	15	11
10	Rodeo	6	4	5	5
12	Circus	4	4	15	11
		67	**40**	**65**	**56**

Casualties 13 April-9 May 1942

		German losses		RAF losses	
13 April	Rodeo	1	1	—	—
14	Circus	3	1	2	2
14	Rodeo	1	1	2	2
15	Circus	3	4	3	3
16	Circus	—	1	—	—
16	Ramrod	4	1	2	2
16	Rodeo	—	1	3	2
17	Rodeo	—	1	1	1
17	Ramrod	—	—	1	—
17	Circus	3	—	—	—
24	Circus	1	1	10	9
24	Rodeo	3	1	—	—
25	Circus	3	2	14	14
25	Ramrod	5	—	1	—
26	Circus	2	1	—	—
26	Rodeo	2	1	4	3
27	Ramrod	—	—	1	1
27	Circus	10	8	13	12
27	Rodeo	—	—	2	2
28	Circus	3	5	6	6
29	Circus	2	2	2	2
30	Roadstead	1	—	—	—
30	Circus	5	4	7	5
30	Ramrod	—	1	—	—
1 May	Rodeo	1	1	2	1
1	Circus	—	4	6	6
3	Rodeo	3	2	—	—
3	Circus	1	1	—	—
3	Ramrod	—	—	3	2
4	Circus	6	—	3	3
4	Rodeo	1	2	4	3
5	Rodeo	2	3	2	1
5	Circus	2	4	6	5
6	Circus	1	1	1	1
9	Circus	1	—	8	8
		70	54	109	95
Totals 1 March-12 April		67	40	65	56
		137	**94**	**174**	**151**

Index

Enemy Coast Ahead – Uncensored
Leader of the Dambusters
Wing Commander Guy Gibson VC DSO DFC
One of the outstanding accounts of WWII
seen through the eyes of one of its most
respected and controversial personalities.
288 pages, soft cover
b&w photographs and illustrations
throughout
9 780859 791182 £10.95

Fist from the Sky
Peter C Smith
The story of Captain Takashige Egusa the
Imperial Japanese Navy's most illustrious
dive-bomber pilot of WWII
Over 75 B+W photographs
9 780859 79122 9 £10.95

The Luftwaffe Fighters' Battle of Britain
Chris Goss
An insight into the experiences of the
German fighter and bomber crews from the
attacker's viewpoint.
208 pages, soft cover
Over 140 photographs
9 780859 791519 £10.95

The Luftwaffe's Blitz
Chris Goss
The story of the Blitz from the German
aircrew's point of view and the opposing
forces of the RAF's embryonic night fighter
force.
208 pages, soft cover
Over 120 photographs
9 780859 791571 £10.95

Luftwaffe Fighter-Bombers over Britain
The Tip and Run Campaign 1942-1943
Chris Goss
As the Battle of Britain ended, the Luftwaffe
began the Tip-and-Run campaign of daylight
raids against English cities and towns
including, amongst others, London,
Eastbourne and Hastings. This is their story.
344 pages, soft cover
Over 250 photographs
9 780859 791762 £10.95

Pure Luck
Alan Bramson
An authorised biography of aviation pioneer
Sir Thomas Sopwith, 1888-1989
Foreword by HRH The Prince of Wales
288 pages, soft cover
Over 90 b&w photographs
9 780859 791069 £10.95

Thud Ridge
Jack Broughton
F-105 Thunderchief missions over the hostile
skies of North Vietnam
288 pages, soft cover
79 photographs plus maps and plans
9 780859 791168 £10.95

Sigh for a Merlin
Testing the Spitfire
Alex Henshaw
The enthralling account of Alex Henshaw's
life as a test pilot with the Spitfire.
240 pages, soft cover
b&w photographs throughout
9 780947 554835 £10.95

Spitfire
A Test Pilot's Story
Jeffrey Quill
The autobiography of an exceptional test pilot
and RAF and Fleet Air Arm fighter pilot.
336 pages, soft cover
b&w photographs throughout
9 780947 554729 £10.95

Stormbird
Hermann Buchner
Autobiography of one of the Luftwaffe's
highest scoring Me262 aces.
272 pages, soft cover
140 b&w photographs and 16 page colour
section
9 780859 791404 £10.95

We Landed By Moonlight
Hugh Verity
Secret RAF Landings in France 1940-1944
256 pages, soft cover
b&w photographs throughout
9 780947 554750 £10.95

Order online at
www.crecy.co.uk
or telephone +44 (0) 161 499 0024

Crécy Publishing 1a Ringway Trading Est,
Shadowmoss Rd, Manchester, M22 5LH
enquiries@crecy.co.uk